2010 SUPPLEMENT

FEDERAL COURTS AND THE LAW OF FEDERAL-STATE RELATIONS

SIXTH EDITION

by

PETER W. LOW
Hardy Cross Dillard Professor of Law
University of Virginia

JOHN C. JEFFRIES, JR.
David and Mary Harrison Distinguished Professor of Law
University of Virginia

CURTIS A. BRADLEY
Richard A. Horvitz Professor of Law
Duke University

FOUNDATION PRESS
2010

THOMSON REUTERS

© 2008, 2009 THOMSON REUTERS/FOUNDATION PRESS
© 2010 By THOMSON REUTERS/FOUNDATION PRESS

      1 New York Plaza, 34th Floor
      New York, NY 10004
      Phone Toll Free 1–877–888–1330
      Fax 646–424–5201
      foundation–press.com
Printed in the United States of America

ISBN 978–1–59941–806–3

Mat.# 40973437

PREFACE

Since publication of the Sixth Edition in 2008, Curtis A. Bradley, the Richard A. Horvitz Professor of Law at Duke University, has signed on as co-author of the annual Supplements and of future editions of the case-book. Professor Bradley is responsible for three new sections which appear in this Supplement and will be carried over to the next edition of the casebook. They include materials on International Tribunals (Ch. III, Sec. 4); Habeas Corpus and the War on Terror (Ch. VII, Sec. 5); and International Comity Abstention (Ch. VI, Sec. 5).

Additionally, three sections of the existing casebook have been revised to accommodate recent decisions. These include Federal Law in State Court (Ch. I, Sec. 2), which now features on *Haywood v. Drown* **(2009)**; Implied Rights of Action to Enforce Federal Statutes (Ch. II, Sec. 2), which is now built around *Stoneridge Investment Partners v. Scientific Atlanta* **(2008)**; and The Substance/Procedure Problem (Ch. V, Sec. 3), which has been revised in light of *Shady Grove Orthopedic Associates v. Allstate Ins. Co.* **(2010)**. The result is a Supplement of substantial length and, we hope, interest.

As always, other recent decisions are treated in notes, which also update references to the secondary literature.

PERMISSION TO DUPLICATE

There are many intersections between *Federal Courts and the law of Federal–State Relations* (6th ed. 2008) and Jeffries, Karlan, Low & Rutherglen, *Civil Rights Actions: Enforcing the Constitution* (2nd ed. 2007). Occasionally, a teacher using one book may wish to use material from the other book or its supplement. To facilitate such borrowings, we authorize teachers who have adopted either book to duplicate limited portions of the other or its annual supplement for distribution to their students. We are grateful to Foundation press for agreeing to make this option available.

PWL

JCJjr

CAB

Charlottesville and Durham

July 2010

TABLE OF CONTENTS

PART I.   FEDERALISM AND SEPARATION OF POWERS: THE BASIC STRUCTURE

CHAPTER I.   CHOICE OF LAW IN THE FEDERAL SYSTEM

CHAPTER III. CONGRESSIONAL CONTROL OF THE FEDERAL COURTS

CHAPTER IV. JUSTICIABILITY

PART II. THE JURISDICTION OF THE FEDERAL COURTS

CHAPTER V. SUBJECT MATTER JURISDICTION

PART III. FEDERAL COURT ENFORCEMENT OF FEDERAL RIGHTS

CHAPTER VII. HABEAS CORPUS

TABLE OF CASES

Principal cases are in bold type. Non-principal cases are in roman type. References are to Pages.

TABLE OF SECONDARY AUTHORITIES

2010 SUPPLEMENT

FEDERAL COURTS AND THE LAW OF FEDERAL–STATE RELATIONS

CHAPTER I

CHOICE OF LAW IN THE FEDERAL SYSTEM

Page 9, add after the first sentence of footnote a:

See also Tony A. Freyer, *Swift* and *Erie*: The Trials of an Ephemeral Landmark Case, 34 J. Sup. Ct. Hist. 261 (2009).

Page 14, add a footnote at the end of Note 6:

h. For a defense of the Mishkin position, see Bradford R. Clark, *Erie*'s Constitutional Source, 95 Cal. L. Rev. 1289 (2007). Clark concludes that "[t]he Supremacy Clause supplies specific textual, historical, and structural support for Mishkin's conclusions." One can infer from its structure that federal courts are precluded "from acting outside its terms to displace state law." For a sequel, see Bradford R. Clark, Federal Lawmaking and the Role of Structure in Constitutional Interpretation, 96 Cal. L. Rev. 699 (2008). There are two related articles in the same issue of the California Law Review: Craig Green, Repressing *Erie*'s Myth, 96 Cal. L. Rev. 595 (2008); Craig Green, *Erie* and Problems of Constitutional Structure, 96 Cal. L. Rev. 661 (2008).

Page 15, add at the end of the second paragraph of footnote h:

See also Richard A. Epstein, Federal Preemption, and Federal Common Law, in Nuisance Cases, 102 Nw. U. L. Rev. 551 (2008).

Page 18, add to the end of footnote k:

For consideration of the power of federal courts to make federal common law on "procedural" topics as a general matter, see Amy Coney Barrett, Procedural Common Law, 94 Va. L. Rev. 813 (2008).

Page 19, add to the citations in the last paragraph of footnote *l*:

Wendy B. Davis, De Facto Merger, Federal Common Law, and *Erie*: Constitutional Issues in Successor Liability, 2008 Colum. Bus. L. Rev. 529;

Page 23, add to the citations in footnote b:

Deborah J. Challener, Distinguishing Certification from Abstention in Diversity Cases: Postponement Versus Abdication of the Duty to Exercise Jurisdiction, 38 Rutgers L.J. 847 (2007).

Page 23, add at the end of footnote b:

See also Justin R. Long, Against Certification, 78 Geo. Wash. L. Rev. 114 (2009).

Page 35, delete *Howlett v. Rose*, pages 35–45 and substitute:

Haywood v. Drown

Supreme Court of the United States, 2009.
556 U.S. ___.

■ JUSTICE STEVENS delivered the opinion of the Court.

In our federal system of government, state as well as federal courts have jurisdiction over suits brought pursuant to 42 U.S.C. § 1983, the statute that creates a remedy for violations of federal rights committed by persons acting under color of state law. While that rule is generally applicable to New York's supreme courts—the State's trial courts of general jurisdiction—New York's Correction Law § 24 divests those courts of jurisdiction over § 1983 suits that seek money damages from correction officers. New York thus prohibits the trial courts that generally exercise jurisdiction over § 1983 suits brought against other state officials from hearing virtually all such suits brought against state correction officers. The question presented is whether that exceptional treatment of a limited category of § 1983 claims is consistent with the Supremacy Clause of the United States Constitution.

I

Petitioner, an inmate in New York's Attica Correctional Facility, commenced two § 1983 actions against several correction employees alleging that they violated his civil rights in connection with three prisoner disciplinary proceedings and an altercation. Proceeding pro se, petitioner filed his claims in State Supreme Court and sought punitive damages and attorney's fees. The trial court dismissed the actions on the ground that, under N. Y. Correct. Law Ann. § 24 (West 1987) (hereinafter Correction Law § 24), it lacked jurisdiction to entertain any suit arising under state or federal law seeking money damages from correction officers for actions taken in the scope of their employment. The intermediate appellate court summarily affirmed the trial court. The New York Court of Appeals, by a 4-to-3 vote, also affirmed.... [W]e granted certiorari [and] now reverse.

II

Motivated by the belief that damages suits filed by prisoners against state correction officers were by and large frivolous and vexatious, New York passed Correction Law § 24. The statute employs a two-step process to strip its courts of jurisdiction over such damages claims and to replace those claims with the State's preferred alternative. The provision states in full:

1. No civil action shall be brought in any court of the state, except by the attorney general on behalf of the state, against any

officer or employee of the department, in his personal capacity, for damages arising out of any act done or the failure to perform any act within the scope of employment and in the discharge of the duties by such officer or employee.

    2. Any claim for damages arising out of any act done or the failure to perform any act within the scope of employment and in the discharge of the duties of any officer or employee of the department shall be brought and maintained in the court of claims as a claim against the state.

Thus, under this scheme, a prisoner seeking damages from a correction officer will have his claim dismissed for want of jurisdiction and will be left, instead, to pursue a claim for damages against an entirely different party (the State) in the Court of Claims—a court of limited jurisdiction.[4]

    For prisoners seeking redress, pursuing the Court of Claims alternative comes with strict conditions. In addition to facing a different defendant, plaintiffs in that Court are not provided with the same relief, or the same procedural protections, made available in § 1983 actions brought in state courts of general jurisdiction. Specifically, under New York law, plaintiffs in the Court of Claims must comply with a 90–day notice requirement; are not entitled to a jury trial; have no right to attorney's fees; and may not seek punitive damages or injunctive relief.

    We must decide whether Correction Law § 24, as applied to § 1983 claims, violates the Supremacy Clause.

III

    This Court has long made clear that federal law is as much the law of the several States as are the laws passed by their legislatures. Federal and state law "together form one system of jurisprudence, which constitutes the law of the land for the State; and the courts of the two jurisdictions are not foreign to each other, nor to be treated by each other as such, but as courts of the same country, having jurisdiction partly different and partly concurrent." Claflin v. Houseman, 93 U.S. 130, 136–37 (1876). Although § 1983, a Reconstruction-era statute, was passed "to interpose the federal courts between the States and the people, as guardians of the people's federal rights," Mitchum v. Foster, 407 U.S. 225, 242 (1972), state courts as well as federal courts are entrusted with providing a forum for the vindication of federal rights violated by state or local officials acting under color of state law.

---

    4. Although the State has waived its sovereign immunity from liability by allowing itself to be sued in the Court of Claims, a plaintiff seeking damages against the State in that court cannot use § 1983 as a vehicle for redress because a State is not a "person" under § 1983. See Will v. Michigan Dept. of State Police, 491 U.S. 58, 66 (1989). [Thus, although state-law tort claims could be brought directly against the state, federal § 1983 damages actions (which include the availability of attorney's fees) could be brought only in federal court.—Addition to footnote by eds.]

So strong is the presumption of concurrency that it is defeated only in two narrowly defined circumstances: first, when Congress expressly ousts state courts of jurisdiction; and second, "[w]hen a state court refuses jurisdiction because of a neutral state rule regarding the administration of the courts," Howlett v. Rose, 496 U.S. 356, 372 (1990). Focusing on the latter circumstance, we have emphasized that only a neutral jurisdictional rule will be deemed a "valid excuse" for departing from the default assumption that "state courts have inherent authority, and are thus presumptively competent, to adjudicate claims arising under the laws of the United States." Tafflin v. Levitt, 493 U.S. 455, 458 (1990).

In determining whether a state law qualifies as a neutral rule of judicial administration, our cases have established that a State cannot employ a jurisdictional rule "to dissociate [itself] from federal law because of disagreement with its content or a refusal to recognize the superior authority of its source." Howlett, 496 U.S., at 371. In other words, although States retain substantial leeway to establish the contours of their judicial systems, they lack authority to nullify a federal right or cause of action they believe is inconsistent with their local policies. . . .

It is principally on this basis that Correction Law § 24 violates the Supremacy Clause. In passing Correction Law § 24, New York made the judgment that correction officers should not be burdened with suits for damages arising out of conduct performed in the scope of their employment. Because it regards these suits as too numerous or too frivolous (or both), the State's longstanding policy has been to shield this narrow class of defendants from liability when sued for damages.[5] The State's policy, whatever its merits, is contrary to Congress' judgment that _all_ persons who violate federal rights while acting under color of state law shall be held liable for damages. As we have unanimously recognized, "[a] State may not . . . relieve congestion in its courts by declaring a whole category of federal claims to be frivolous. Until it has been proved that the claim has no merit, that judgment is not up to the States to make." _Howlett_, 496 U.S., at 380. . . . That New York strongly favors a rule shielding correction officers from personal damages liability and substituting the State as the party responsible for compensating individual victims is irrelevant. The State cannot condition its enforcement of federal law on the demand that those individu-

---

5. In many respects, Correction Law § 24 operates more as an immunity-from-damages provision than as a jurisdictional rule. ... In Howlett v. Rose, 496 U.S. 356 (1990), we considered the question whether a Florida school board could assert a state-law immunity defense in a § 1983 action brought in state court when the defense would not have been available if the action had been brought in federal court. We unanimously held that the State's decision to extend immunity "over and above [that which is] already provided in § 1983 ... directly violates federal law," and explained that the "elements of, and the defenses to, a federal cause of action are defined by federal law." Thus, if Correction Law § 24 were understood as offering an immunity defense, _Howlett_ would compel the conclusion that it violates the Supremacy Clause.

als whose conduct federal law seeks to regulate must nevertheless escape liability.

IV

While our cases have uniformly applied the principle that a State cannot simply refuse to entertain a federal claim based on a policy disagreement, we have yet to confront a statute like New York's that registers its dissent by divesting its courts of jurisdiction over a disfavored federal claim in addition to an identical state claim. The New York Court of Appeals' holding was based on the misunderstanding that this equal treatment of federal and state claims rendered Correction Law § 24 constitutional. To the extent our cases have created this misperception, we now make clear that equality of treatment does not ensure that a state law will be deemed a neutral rule of judicial administration and therefore a valid excuse for refusing to entertain a federal cause of action.

Respondents correctly observe that, in the handful of cases in which this Court has found a valid excuse, the state rule at issue treated state and federal claims equally. In Douglas v. New York, N. H. & H. R. Co., 279 U.S. 377 (1929), we upheld a state law that granted state courts discretion to decline jurisdiction over state and federal claims alike when neither party was a resident of the State. Later, in Herb v. Pitcairn, 324 U.S. 117 (1945), a city court dismissed an action brought under the Federal Employers' Liability Act (FELA), 45 U.S.C. § 51 et seq., for want of jurisdiction because the cause of action arose outside the court's territorial jurisdiction. We upheld the dismissal on the ground that the State's venue laws were not being applied in a way that discriminated against the federal claim. In a third case, Missouri ex rel. Southern R. Co. v. Mayfield, 340 U.S. 1 (1950), we held that a State's application of the forum non conveniens doctrine to bar adjudication of a FELA case brought by nonresidents was constitutionally sound as long as the policy was enforced impartially. And our most recent decision finding a valid excuse, Johnson v. Fankell, 520 U.S. 911 (1997), rested largely on the fact that Idaho's rule limiting interlocutory jurisdiction did not discriminate against § 1983 actions.

Although the absence of discrimination is necessary to our finding a state law neutral, it is not sufficient. A jurisdictional rule cannot be used as a device to undermine federal law, no matter how evenhanded it may appear. As we made clear in *Howlett*, "[t]he fact that a rule is denominated jurisdictional does not provide a court an excuse to avoid the obligation to enforce federal law if the rule does not reflect the concerns of power over the person and competence over the subject matter that jurisdictional rules are designed to protect." Ensuring equality of treatment is thus the beginning, not the end, of the Supremacy Clause analysis.

In addition to giving too much weight to equality of treatment, respondents mistakenly treat this case as implicating the "great latitude [States enjoy] to establish the structure and jurisdiction of their own courts." *Howlett*, at 372. Although Correction Law § 24 denies state courts authority to entertain damages actions against correction officers, this case does not require us to decide whether Congress may compel a State to offer a forum, otherwise unavailable under state law, to hear suits brought pursuant to § 1983. The State of New York has made this inquiry unnecessary by creating courts of general jurisdiction that routinely sit to hear analogous § 1983 actions. ... For instance, if petitioner had attempted to sue a police officer for damages under § 1983, the suit would be properly adjudicated by a state supreme court. Similarly, if petitioner had sought declaratory or injunctive relief against a correction officer, that suit would be heard in a state supreme court. It is only a particular species of suits—those seeking damages relief against correction officers—that the State deems inappropriate for its trial courts.[6]

We therefore hold that, having made the decision to create courts of general jurisdiction that regularly sit to entertain analogous suits, New York is not at liberty to shut the courthouse door to federal claims that it considers at odds with its local policy.[7] A State's authority to organize its courts, while considerable, remains subject to the strictures of the Constitution. We have never treated a State's invocation of "jurisdiction" as a trump that ends the Supremacy Clause inquiry, and we decline to do so in this case. Because New York's supreme courts generally have personal jurisdiction over the parties in § 1983 suits brought by prisoners against correction officers and because they hear the lion's share of all other § 1983 actions, we find little concerning "power over the person and competence over the subject matter" in Correction Law § 24.[8]

6. While we have looked to a State's "common-law tort analogues" in deciding whether a state procedural rule is neutral, see Felder v. Casey, 487 U.S. 131, 146, n. 3 (1988), we have never equated "analogous claims" with "identical claims." Instead, we have searched for a similar claim under state law to determine whether a State has established courts of adequate and appropriate jurisdiction capable of hearing a § 1983 suit. See Testa v. Katt, 330 U.S. 386, 388, 394 (1947); Martinez v. California, 444 U.S. 277, 283–84, n.7 (1980) ("[W]here the same *type* of claim, if arising under state law, would be enforced in the state courts, the state courts are generally not free to refuse enforcement of the federal claim" (emphasis added)). Section 1983 damages claims against other state officials and equitable claims against correction officers are both sufficiently analogous to petitioner's § 1983 claims.

7. The dissent's contrary view is based on its belief that "States have unfettered authority to determine whether their local courts may entertain a federal cause of action." ... But this theory of the Supremacy Clause was raised and squarely rejected in *Howlett*. Respondents in that case "argued that a federal court has no power to compel a state court to entertain a claim over which the state court has no jurisdiction as a matter of state law." We declared that this argument had "no merit" and explained that it ignored other provisions of the Constitution, including the Full Faith and Credit Clause and the Privileges and Immunities Clause, which compel States to open their courts to causes of action over which they would normally lack jurisdiction. We saw no reason to treat the Supremacy Clause differently. Thus, to the extent the dissent resurrects this argument, we again reject it.

8. The dissent's proposed solution would create a blind spot in the Supremacy Clause. If New York had decided to employ a procedural rule to burden the enforcement of

Accordingly, the dissent's fear that "no state jurisdictional rule will be upheld as constitutional" is entirely unfounded. Our holding addresses only the unique scheme adopted by the State of New York—a law designed to shield a particular class of defendants (correction officers) from a particular type of liability (damages) brought by a particular class of plaintiffs (prisoners). Based on the belief that damages suits against correction officers are frivolous and vexatious, Correction Law § 24 is effectively an immunity statute cloaked in jurisdictional garb. Finding this scheme unconstitutional merely confirms that the Supremacy Clause cannot be evaded by formalism.

V

The judgment of the New York Court of Appeals is reversed, and the case is remanded to that court for further proceedings not inconsistent with this opinion. . . .

■ JUSTICE THOMAS, with whom THE CHIEF JUSTICE, JUSTICE SCALIA, and JUSTICE ALITO join as to Part III, dissenting.

The Court holds that New York Correction Law Annotated § 24, which divests New York's state courts of subject-matter jurisdiction over suits seeking money damages from correction officers, violates the Supremacy Clause of the Constitution because it requires the dismissal of federal actions brought in state court under 42 U.S.C. § 1983. I disagree. Because neither the Constitution nor our precedent requires New York to open its courts to § 1983 federal actions, I respectfully dissent.

I

Although the majority decides this case on the basis of the Supremacy Clause, the proper starting point is Article III of the Constitution. Article III, § 1, provides that "[t]he judicial Power of the United States, shall be vested in one supreme Court, and in such inferior Courts as the Congress may from time to time ordain and establish." The history of the drafting and ratification of this Article establishes that it leaves untouched the States' plenary authority to decide whether their local courts will have subject-matter jurisdiction over federal causes of action.

The text of Article III reflects the Framers' agreement that the National Government needed a Supreme Court. There was sharp disagree-

---

federal law, the dissent would find the scheme unconstitutional. Yet simply because New York has decided to impose an even greater burden on a federal cause of action by selectively withdrawing the jurisdiction of its courts, the dissent detects no constitutional violation. Thus, in the dissent's conception of the Supremacy Clause, a State could express its disagreement with (and even open hostility to) a federal cause of action, declare a desire to thwart its enforcement, and achieve that goal by removing the disfavored category of claims from its courts' jurisdiction. If this view were adopted, the lesson of our precedents would be that other States with unconstitutionally burdensome procedural rules did not go far enough "to avoid the obligation to enforce federal law." *Howlett*, 469 U.S., at 381.

ment at the Philadelphia Convention, however, over the need for lower federal courts. Several of the Framers, most notably James Madison, favored a strong central government that included lower federal tribunals. Under the Virginia Plan, the Constitution would have established a "National Judiciary ... to consist of one or more supreme tribunals, and of inferior tribunals to be chosen by the National Legislature." 1 Records of the Federal Convention of 1787, p. 21 (M. Farrand ed. 1911) (hereinafter Farrand). A revised version of the proposal, which stated that the National Judiciary would " 'consist of One supreme tribunal, and of one or more inferior tribunals,' " was approved on June 4, 1787.

The following day, however, John Rutledge raised an objection to "establishing any national tribunal except a single supreme one." He proposed striking the language providing for the creation of lower federal courts because state courts were "most proper" for deciding "all cases in the first instance." According to Rutledge, "the right of appeal to the supreme national tribunal [was] sufficient to secure the national rights [and] uniformity of Judgm[en]ts," and the lower federal courts were thus an "unnecessary encroachment" on the sovereign prerogative of the States to adjudicate federal claims. Madison nonetheless defended the Virginia Plan. He countered that "inferior [federal] tribunals ... dispersed throughout the Republic" were necessary to meet the needs of the newly formed government: "An effective Judiciary establishment commensurate to the legislative authority [is] essential. A Government without a proper Executive [and] Judiciary would be the mere trunk of a body without arms or legs to act or move." But despite Madison's objections, Rutledge's motion prevailed.

Madison and James Wilson soon thereafter proposed alternative language that " 'empowered [Congress] to institute inferior tribunals.' " This version moderated the original Virginia Plan because of the "distinction between establishing such tribunals absolutely, and giving a discretion to the Legislature to establish or not establish [inferior federal courts]." Over continued objections that such courts were an unnecessary expense and an affront to the States, the scaled-back version of the Virginia Plan passed.

On June 15, 1787, however, the New Jersey Plan was introduced. Although it did not directly challenge the decision to permit Congress to "institute" inferior federal courts, the plan, among other things, required state courts to adjudicate federal claims. ...

The introduction of the New Jersey Plan reignited the debate over the need for lower federal courts. ... At the conclusion of this debate, the New Jersey Plan, including its component requiring state-court consideration of federal claims, was defeated and the Madison–Wilson proposal was delivered to the Committee of Detail. The Committee amended the proposal's language to its current form in Article III, which gives Congress the power to "ordain and establish" inferior federal courts. The delegates to the

Constitutional Convention unanimously adopted this revised version and it was ultimately ratified by the States.

This so-called Madisonian Compromise bridged the divide "between those who thought that the establishment of lower federal courts should be constitutionally mandatory and those who thought there should be no federal courts at all except for a Supreme Court with, inter alia, appellate jurisdiction to review state court judgments." R. Fallon, D. Meltzer, & D. Shapiro, Hart and Wechsler's The Federal Courts and the Federal System 348 (4th ed. 1996). In so doing, the compromise left to the wisdom of Congress the creation of lower federal courts. . . .

The assumption that state courts would continue to exercise concurrent jurisdiction over federal claims was essential to this compromise. See The Federalist No. 82, pp. 130, 132 (E. Bourne ed. 1947) (A. Hamilton) ("[T]he inference seems to be conclusive, that the State courts would have a concurrent jurisdiction in all cases arising under the laws of the Union, where it was not expressly prohibited"). In light of that historical understanding, this Court has held that, absent an Act of Congress providing for exclusive jurisdiction in the lower federal courts, the "state courts have inherent authority, and are thus presumptively competent, to adjudicate claims arising under the laws of the United States." Tafflin v. Levitt, 493 U.S. 455, 458–59 (1990). As a result, "if exclusive jurisdiction [in the federal courts] be neither express nor implied, the State courts have concurrent jurisdiction whenever, by their own constitution, they are competent to take it." Claflin v. Houseman, 93 U.S. 130, 136 (1876).

The Constitution's implicit preservation of state authority to entertain federal claims, however, did not impose a duty on state courts to do so. As discussed above, there was at least one proposal to expressly require state courts to take original jurisdiction over federal claims (subject to appeal in federal court) that was introduced in an attempt to forestall the creation of lower federal courts. But in light of the failure of this proposal—which was offered before the adoption of the Madisonian Compromise—the assertions by its supporters that state courts would ordinarily entertain federal causes of action cannot reasonably be viewed as an assurance that the States would never alter the subject-matter jurisdiction of their courts. The Framers' decision to empower Congress to create federal courts that could either supplement or displace state-court review of federal claims, as well as the exclusion of any affirmative command requiring the States to consider federal claims in the text of Article III, confirm this understanding.[2]

2. See also Michael G. Collins, Article III Cases, State Court Duties, and the Madisonian Compromise, 1995 Wis. L. Rev. 39, 144 (1995) ("It is . . . extremely difficult to argue from the debatable assumption that state courts would be under an obligation to take all Article III judicial business in the first instance—as a quid pro quo for the Constitution's noninclusion of any reference to lower federal courts—to the conclusion that such a duty still existed when the second half of that bargain was decisively rejected

The earliest decisions addressing this question, written by then-serving and future Supreme Court Justices, confirm that state courts remain "tribunals over which the government of the Union has no adequate control, and which may be closed to any claim asserted under a law of the United States." Osborn v. Bank of United States, 9 Wheat. 738, 821 (1824). "The states, in providing their own judicial tribunals, have a right to limit, control, and restrict their judicial functions, and jurisdiction, according to their own mere pleasure." Mitchell v. Great Works Milling & Mfg. Co., 17 F. Cas. 496, 499 (No. 9,662) (CCD Me. 1843) (Story, J.). In short, there was "a very clear intimation given by the judges of the Supreme Court, that the state courts were not bound in consequence of any act of Congress, to assume and exercise jurisdiction in such cases. It was merely permitted to them to do so as far, as was compatible with their state obligations." 1 J. Kent, Commentaries on American Law 375 (1826).

Under our federal system, therefore, the States have unfettered authority to determine whether their local courts may entertain a federal cause of action. Once a State exercises its sovereign prerogative to deprive its courts of subject-matter jurisdiction over a federal cause of action, it is the end of the matter as far as the Constitution is concerned.

The present case can be resolved under this principle alone. New York Correction Law § 24 (NYCLA) provides that "[n]o civil action shall be brought in any court of the state, except by the attorney general on behalf of the state, against any officer or employee of the department, in his personal capacity, for damages arising out of any act done or the failure to perform any act within the scope of the employment and in the discharge of the duties by such officer or employee." The majority and petitioner agree that this statute erects a jurisdictional bar that prevents the state courts from entertaining petitioner's claim for damages under § 1983. Because New York's decision to withdraw jurisdiction over § 1983 damages actions—or indeed, over any claims—does not offend the Constitution, the judgment below should be affirmed.

II

The Court has evaded Article III's limitations by finding that the Supremacy Clause constrains the States' authority to define the subject-matter jurisdiction of their own courts. In particular, the Court has held that "the Federal Constitution prohibits state courts of general jurisdiction

(in the Madisonian Compromise, no less)"); James E. Pfander, Rethinking the Supreme Court's Original Jurisdiction in State–Party Cases, 82 Cal. L. Rev. 555, 596 (1994) ("The framers may well have assumed that the federal system would simply take the state courts as it found them; state courts could exercise a concurrent jurisdiction over any federal claims that fit comfortably within their pre-existing jurisdiction ... so long as the federal claims were not, by virtue of congressional decree, subject to the exclusive jurisdiction of the federal courts. It seems unlikely, however, that the framers would have chosen to compel the state courts to entertain federal claims against their will and in violation of their own jurisdictional limits").

from refusing" to entertain a federal claim "solely because the suit is brought under a federal law" as a "state may not discriminate against rights arising under federal laws." McKnett v. St. Louis & San Francisco R. Co., 292 U.S. 230, 233–34 (1934). There is no textual or historical support for the Court's incorporation of this antidiscrimination principle into the Supremacy Clause.

A

1

The Supremacy Clause provides that "[t]his Constitution, and the Laws of the United States which shall be made in Pursuance thereof . . . shall be the supreme Law of the Land; and the Judges in every State shall be bound thereby, any Thing in the Constitution or Laws of any State to the Contrary notwithstanding." Under this provision, "[t]he laws of the United States are laws in the several States, and just as much binding on the citizens and courts thereof as the State laws are. . . . The two together form one system of jurisprudence, which constitutes the law of the land for the State." Claflin, 93 U.S., at 136–37. Thus, a valid federal law is substantively superior to a state law; "if a state measure conflicts with a federal requirement, the state provision must give way." Swift & Co. v. Wickham, 382 U.S. 111, 120 (1965). As a textual matter, however, the Supremacy Clause does not address whether a state court must entertain a federal cause of action; it provides only a rule of decision that the state court must follow if it adjudicates the claim.

The Supremacy Clause's path to adoption at the Convention confirms this focus. Its precursor was introduced as part of the New Jersey Plan. But, as explained above, the New Jersey Plan also included an entirely separate provision that addressed state-court jurisdiction, which would have required all federal questions to "b[e] determined in the first instance in the courts of the respective states." 3 Farrand 287. These two provisions of the New Jersey Plan worked in tandem to require state courts to entertain federal claims and to decide the substantive dispute in favor of federal law if a conflict between the two arose.

After the adoption of the Madisonian Compromise and the defeat of the New Jersey Plan, the Framers returned to the question of federal supremacy. A proposal was introduced granting Congress the power to " 'negative all laws passed by the several States (contravening in the opinion of [Congress] the articles of Union, or any treaties subsisting under the authority of [Congress]).' " 2 id., at 27. James Madison believed the proposal "essential to the efficacy [and] security of the [federal] Gov[ern-men]t." But others at the Convention, including Roger Sherman, "thought it unnecessary, as the Courts of the States would not consider as valid any law contravening the Authority of the Union, and which the legislature would wish to be negatived." In the end, Madison's proposal was defeated. But as a substitute for that rejected proposal, Luther Martin resurrected the Supremacy Clause provision from the New Jersey Plan and it was unanimously approved.

This historical record makes clear that the Supremacy Clause's exclusive function is to disable state laws that are substantively inconsistent with federal law—not to require state courts to hear federal claims over which the courts lack jurisdiction. This was necessarily the case when the clause was first introduced as part of the New Jersey Plan, as it included a separate provision to confront the jurisdictional question. Had that plan prevailed and been ratified by the States, construing the Supremacy Clause to address state-court jurisdiction would have rendered the separate jurisdictional component of the New Jersey Plan mere surplusage.

The Supremacy Clause's exclusive focus on substantive state law is also evident from the context in which it was revived. First, the Clause was not adopted until after the New Jersey Plan's rejection, as part of the entirely separate debate over Madison's proposal to grant Congress the power to "negative" the laws of the States. By then, the Framers had already adopted Article III, thereby ending the fight over state-court jurisdiction. The question before the Convention thus was not which courts (state or federal) were best suited to adjudicate federal claims, but which branch of government (Congress or the courts) would be most effective in vindicating the substantive superiority of federal law. The Supremacy Clause was directly responsive to that question.

Second, the timing of the Clause's adoption suggests that the Framers viewed it as achieving the same end as Madison's congressional "negative" proposal. Although Madison believed that Congress could most effectively countermand inconsistent state laws, the Framers decided that the Judiciary could adequately perform that function. There is no evidence that the Framers envisioned the Supremacy Clause as having a substantively broader sweep than the proposal it replaced. And, there can be no question that Madison's congressional "negative" proposal was entirely unconcerned with the dispute over whether state courts should be required to exercise jurisdiction over federal claims. Indeed, Madison's proposal did not require the States to become enmeshed in any federal business at all; it merely provided that state laws could be directly nullified if Congress found them to be inconsistent with the Constitution or laws of the United States. The role of the Supremacy Clause is no different. It does not require state courts to entertain federal causes of action. Rather, it only requires that in

---

4. Madison did not believe that federal courts were up to the task. ... He had even less faith in state courts. See 2 Ferrand, at 27–28 ("Confidence can (not) be put in the State Tribunals as guardians of the National authority and interests"). In light of Madison's mistrust of state courts, any suggestion that he drafted Article III to require state courts to entertain federal claims, or that he advocated for the inclusion in the Constitution of a provision guaranteeing the supremacy of federal law as a means of accomplishing that same goal, would be doubtful. Madison appears to have preferred that the state courts hear as little federal business as possible.

reaching the merits of such claims, state courts must decide the legal question in favor of the "law of the Land." . . .[5]

The supremacy of federal law, therefore, is not impugned by a State's decision to strip its local courts of subject-matter jurisdiction to hear certain federal claims. Subject-matter jurisdiction determines only whether a court has the power to entertain a particular claim—a condition precedent to reaching the merits of a legal dispute. Although the line between subject-matter jurisdiction over a claim and the merits of that claim can at times prove difficult to draw, the distinction is crucial in the Supremacy Clause context. If the state court does not reach the merits of the dispute for lack of statutory or constitutional jurisdiction, the preeminence of federal law remains undiminished. . . .

2

The Court was originally faithful to this conception of federal supremacy. In *Claflin*, the Court concluded that because the federal statute under consideration did not deprive the state court of jurisdiction, the state court was competent to resolve the claim. But the Court was careful to also explain that the Constitution did not impose an obligation on the States to accept jurisdiction over such claims. See 93 U.S., at 137 (explaining that there "is no reason why the State courts should not be open for the prosecution of rights growing out of the laws of the United States, to which their jurisdiction is competent, and not denied"). The Constitution instead left the States with the choice—but not the obligation—to entertain federal actions.

Then in Second Employers' Liability Cases, 223 U.S. 1 (1912), the Court applied the rule set forth in *Claflin* and correctly rejected a Connecticut court's refusal to enforce the 1908 Federal Employers' Liability Act (FELA), 45 U.S.C. § 51 et seq. FELA neither provided for exclusive federal

---

5. The majority contends that the Full Faith and Credit Clause and the Privileges and Immunities Clause support its view of the Supremacy Clause because each "compel[s] States to open their courts to causes of action over which they would normally lack jurisdiction"(citing Howlett v. Rose, 496 U.S. 356, 381–82 (1990)). But the majority has it backwards. The Full Faith and Credit Clause and the Privileges and Immunities Clause include a textual prohibition on discrimination that the Supremacy Clause lacks. See Art. IV, § 1 ("Full Faith and Credit shall be given in each State to the public Acts, Records, and judicial Proceedings of every other State"); Art. IV, § 2 ("The Citizens of each State shall be entitled to all Privileges and Immunities of Citizens in the several States"). The Framers' decision to address state-to-state discrimination in these two clauses without taking similar steps with respect to federal-state relations governed by the Supremacy Clause aligns with reasons given for abandoning the Articles of Confederation, see The Federalist No. 42, p. 292 (E. Bourne ed. 1947) (J. Madison) (describing the Full Faith and Credit Clause as "an evident and valuable improvement on the clause relating to this subject in the articles of Confederation"), and the principle of dual sovereignty that the Constitution preserves, see Texas v. White, 7 Wall. 700, 725 (1869). Accordingly, contrary to the majority's supposition, there are in fact strong "reason[s] to treat the Supremacy Clause differently" from the Full Faith and Credit and Privileges and Immunities Clauses.

jurisdiction nor attempted to require state courts to entertain claims brought under it. Therefore, the statute was enforceable "as of right, in the courts of the States *when their jurisdiction, as prescribed by local laws, is adequate to the occasion*." 223 U.S., at 55 (emphasis added). Connecticut had not deprived its courts of subject-matter jurisdiction over FELA claims; thus, the state court's refusal to hear the claim was "not because the ordinary jurisdiction of the Superior Courts, as defined by the constitution and laws of the State, was deemed inadequate or not adapted to the adjudication of such a case." Rather, the state court took the position that "it would be inconvenient and confusing for the same court, in dealing with cases of the same general class, to apply in some the standards of right established by the congressional act and in others the different standards recognized by the laws of the State."

The Court's reversal of such a decision is compatible with the original understanding of Article III and the Supremacy Clause. Because there was no question that the state court had subject-matter jurisdiction under state law to adjudicate the federal claim, the Court correctly observed that the state court's refusal to decide the case amounted to a policy dispute with federal law: "When Congress, in the exertion of the power confided to it by the Constitution, adopted that [federal] act, it spoke for all the people and all the States, and thereby established a policy for all. That policy is as much the policy of Connecticut as if the act had emanated from its own legislature, and should be respected accordingly in the courts of the State." It was for this specific reason, then, that the Court rejected Connecticut's refusal to adjudicate the federal claim. As the Court correctly noted, the "existence of the jurisdiction creates an implication of duty to exercise it, and that its exercise may be onerous does not militate against that implication."

But nothing in *Second Employers'* suggested that the Supremacy Clause could pre-empt a state law that deprived the local court of subject-matter jurisdiction over the federal claim. Instead, the *Second Employers'* Court took exactly the opposite position on this question: "[W]e deem it well to observe that there is not here involved any attempt by Congress to enlarge or regulate the jurisdiction of state courts ... but only a question of the duty of such a court, when its ordinary jurisdiction as prescribed by local laws is appropriate to the occasion."

The Court again confronted this issue in *Douglas v. New York, N. H. & H. R. Co.*, 279 U.S. 377 (1929). There, the Court considered whether a New York court was required to hear a claim brought under FELA. Unlike the Connecticut court in *Second Employers'*, however, the New York court did not have jurisdiction under state law to entertain the federal cause of action. As a result, this Court upheld the state-court ruling that dismissed the claim. ... [B]ecause the New York court lacked subject-matter jurisdiction under state law, it was not "otherwise competent" to adjudicate the federal claim.

In sum, *Claflin*, *Second Employers'*, and *Douglas* together establish that a state courts inability to entertain a federal claim because of a lack of state-law jurisdiction is an "otherwise valid excuse" that in no way denies the superiority of federal substantive law. It simply disables the state court from adjudicating a claim brought under that federal law.

3

It was not until five years after *Douglas* that the Court used the Supremacy Clause to strike down a state jurisdictional statute for its failure to permit state-court adjudication of federal claims. See *McKnett v. St. Louis & San Francisco R. Co.*, 292 U.S. 230 (1934). The Court started by correctly noting that it "was settled" in *Second Employers'* "that a state court whose ordinary jurisdiction as prescribed by local laws is appropriate to the occasion, may not refuse to entertain suits under [FELA]." Yet, even though the Alabama court *lacked* such jurisdiction over the relevant federal claim pursuant to a state statute, the *McKnett* Court held that the state court had improperly dismissed the federal claim.

According to the Court, "[w]hile Congress has not attempted to compel states to provide courts for the enforcement of [FELA], the Federal Constitution prohibits state courts of general jurisdiction from refusing to do so solely because the suit is brought under a federal law. The denial of jurisdiction by the Alabama court is based solely upon the source of law sought to be enforced. The plaintiff is cast out because he is suing to enforce a federal act. A state may not discriminate against rights arising under federal laws."

For all the reasons identified above, *McKnett* cannot be reconciled with the decisions of this Court that preceded it. Unlike the Connecticut court in *Second Employers'*, the Alabama Supreme Court did not indulge its own bias against adjudication of federal claims in state court by refusing to hear a federal claim over which it had subject-matter jurisdiction. Rather, like the New York court decision affirmed in *Douglas*, the Alabama court's dismissal merely respected a jurisdictional barrier to adjudication of the federal claim imposed by state law. The fact that Alabama courts were competent to hear similar state-law claims should have been immaterial. Alabama had exercised its sovereign right to establish the subject-matter jurisdiction of its courts. Under *Claflin* and its progeny, that legislative judgment should have been upheld.

Despite *McKnett*'s infidelity to the Constitution and more than a century of Supreme Court jurisprudence, the Court's later decisions have repeated *McKnett*'s declaration that state jurisdictional statutes must be policed for antifederal discrimination. See, e.g., Testa v. Katt, 330 U.S. 386, 394 (1947) ("It is conceded that this same type of claim arising under Rhode Island law would be enforced by that State's courts. . . . Under these circumstances the State courts are not free to refuse enforcement of petitioners' claim"); Howlett v. Rose, 496 U.S. 356, 375 (1990) ("[W]hether the question is framed in pre-emption terms, as petitioner would have it, or in the obligation to assume jurisdiction over a 'federal' cause of action, ... the Florida court's refusal to entertain one discrete category of § 1983 claims, when the court entertains similar state-law actions against state defendants, violates the Supremacy Clause"). The outcome in these cases, however, can be reconciled with first principles notwithstanding the Court's stated reliance on *McKnett*'s flawed interpretation of the Supremacy Clause.[6]

In *Testa*, the Court struck down the Rhode Island Supreme Court's refusal to entertain a claim under the federal Emergency Price Control Act. There was no dispute that "the Rhode Island courts [had] jurisdiction adequate and appropriate under established local law to adjudicate this action." The Rhode Island court nevertheless declined to exercise that jurisdiction under its decision in Robinson v. Norato, 71 R. I. 256, 258, 43 A.2d 467, 468 (1945), which had relied on a "universally acknowledged" doctrine "of private international law" as a basis for refusing to adjudicate federal "penal" claims. Because the Rhode Island Supreme Court had invoked this common-law doctrine despite the existence of state-law statutory jurisdiction over the federal claims, this Court correctly ruled that the state court's "policy against enforcement ... of statutes of other states and the United States which it deems penal, [could not] be accepted as a 'valid excuse.'"

Testa thus represents a routine application of the rule of law set forth in *Second Employers'*: As long as jurisdiction over a federal claim exists as a matter of state law, state-court judges cannot sua sponte refuse to enforce federal law because they disagree with Congress' decision to allow for adjudication of certain federal claims in state court.

In *Howlett*, the Court likewise correctly struck down a Florida Supreme Court decision affirming the dismissal of a § 1983 suit on state-law sovereign immunity grounds. The Florida court had interpreted the State's statutory "waiver of sovereign immunity" not to extend to federal claims brought in state court. According to the state court, absent a statutory waiver, Florida's pre-existing common-law sovereign immunity rule provid-

---

6. Other decisions also have articulated this antidiscrimination principle. See, e.g., Johnson v. Fankell, 520 U.S. 911 (1997); Missouri ex rel. Southern R. Co. v. Mayfield, 340 U.S. 1 (1950); Herb v. Pitcairn, 324 U.S. 117 (1945); Miles v. Illinois Central R. Co., 315 U.S. 698 (1942). The outcomes in these cases nonetheless preserved state-court jurisdictional autonomy. In *Johnson* and *Herb*, the Court sustained the state-court dismissals of the federal claims as nondiscriminatory. In *Mayfield*, the Court never decided whether the state court had jurisdiction over the rele-

vant federal claim; rather, it remanded the case to the Missouri Supreme Court based on the state court's possibly erroneous interpretation of federal law at issue in that case. Finally, in *Miles*, the Court struck down a Tennessee decision that enjoined a citizen of that State from pursuing a FELA action in Missouri state court "on grounds of inequity." The Court correctly held that, so long as jurisdiction existed under Missouri law, the Tennessee court could not rely on its own notions of "inequity" to thwart the vindication of a federal right in state court.

ed a "blanket immunity on [state] governmental entities from federal civil rights actions under § 1983" brought in Florida courts. Based on this rule, the Florida Supreme Court affirmed the dismissal with prejudice of the § 1983 suit against the state officials.

No antidiscrimination rule was required to strike down the Florida Supreme Court's decision. Even though several Florida courts had concluded that the defense of sovereign immunity was jurisdictional, "[t]he force of the Supremacy Clause is not so weak that it can be evaded by mere mention of the word 'jurisdiction.' " That is, state courts cannot evade their obligation to enforce federal law by simply characterizing a statute or common-law rule as "jurisdictional"; the state law must in fact operate in a jurisdictional manner. No matter where the line between subject-matter jurisdiction and the merits is drawn, Florida's "common law immunity" rule crossed it.

First, because the Florida Supreme Court had dismissed the § 1983 lawsuit with prejudice, its decision was on the merits. Second, Florida's sovereign immunity rule violated the Supremacy Clause by operating as a state-law defense to a federal law. Resolving a federal claim with preclusive effect based on a state-law defense is far different from simply closing the door of the state courthouse to that federal claim. The first changes federal law by denying relief on the merits; the second merely dictates the forum in which the federal claim will be heard.

In the end, of course, "the ultimate touchstone of constitutionality is the Constitution itself and not what we have said about it." Graves v. New York ex rel. O'Keefe, 306 U.S. 466, 491–92 (1939) (Frankfurter, J., concurring). And contrary to *McKnett*, the Constitution does not require state courts to give equal billing to state and federal claims. To read the Supremacy Clause to include an anti-discrimination principle undermines the compromise that shaped Article III and contradicts the original understanding of Constitution. There is no justification for preserving such a principle. But even if the Court chooses to adhere to the antidiscrimination rule as part of the Supremacy Clause inquiry, the rule's infidelity to the text, structure, and history of the Constitution counsels against extending the principle any further than our precedent requires.

B

Although the Supremacy Clause does not, on its own force, pre-empt state jurisdictional statutes of any kind, it may still pre-empt state law once Congress has acted. Federal law must prevail when Congress validly enacts a statute that expressly supersedes state law, or when the state law conflicts with a federal statute. NYCLA § 24 does not fall prey to either category of pre-emption.[8]

---

8. Because 42 U.S.C. § 1983 does not pre-empt NYCLA § 24, there is no need to reach the more difficult question of whether Congress has the delegated authority under

First, federal law does not expressly require New York courts to accept jurisdiction over § 1983 suits. Under § 1983, any state official who denies "any citizen of the United States or other person within the jurisdiction thereof ... any rights, privileges, or immunities secured by the Constitution and laws, shall be liable to the party injured in an action at law, suit in equity, or other proper proceeding for redress." The statute addresses who may sue and be sued for violations of federal law. But it includes no substantive command requiring New York to provide a state judicial forum to a § 1983 plaintiff. ...

Second, NYCLA § 24 does not conflict with § 1983. As explained above, Congress did not grant § 1983 plaintiffs a "right" to bring their claims in state court or "guarantee" that the state forum would remain open to their suits. Moreover, Congress has created inferior federal courts that have the power to adjudicate all § 1983 actions. And this Court has expressly determined that § 1983 plaintiffs do not have to exhaust state-court remedies before proceeding in federal court. See Patsy v. Board of Regents of State of Fla., 457 U.S. 496, 516 (1982).

Therefore, even if every state court closed its doors to § 1983 plaintiffs, the plaintiffs could proceed with their claims in the federal forum. And because the dismissal of § 1983 claims from state court pursuant to NYCLA § 24 is for lack of subject-matter jurisdiction, it has no preclusive effect on claims refiled in federal court, see Allen v. McCurry, 449 U.S. 90, 94, 105 (1980) (requiring "a final judgment on the merits" before a § 1983 would be barred in federal court under the doctrine of claim preclusion), and thus does not alter the substance of the federal claim. Any contention that NYCLA § 24 conflicts with § 1983 therefore would be misplaced.

The Court nevertheless has relied on an expansive brand of "conflict" pre-emption to strike down state-court procedural rules that are perceived to "burde[n] the exercise of the federal right" in state court. Felder v. Casey, 487 U.S. 131, 141 (1988). In such cases, the Court has asked if the state-law rule, when applied "to § 1983 actions brought in state courts [is] consistent with the goals of the federal civil rights laws, or does the enforcement of such a requirement instead 'stand as an obstacle to the accomplishment and execution of the full purposes and objectives of Congress'?" See id., at 138 (quoting Hines v. Davidowitz, 312 U.S. 52, 67 (1941)). There has been no suggestion in this case, however, that NYCLA § 24 is a procedural rule that must be satisfied in order to bring the § 1983 action in state court. As explained above, petitioner's claim was not

the Constitution to require state courts to entertain a federal cause of action. Compare Printz v. United States, 521 U.S. 898, 907 (1997) (suggesting that Congress' authority in this regard was "perhaps implicit in one of the provisions of the Constitution [Article III, § 1], and was explicit in another [Article VI, cl. 2]"); Saikrishna Bangalore Prakash, Field Office Federalism, 79 Va. L. Rev. 1957, 2032 (1993) ("As a matter of original understanding, the Founding Generation understood that state courts could be commandeered to enforce federal law"), with Prigg v. Pennsylvania, 16 Pet. 539, 615 (1842) (concluding that state courts could not "be compelled to enforce" the 1793 Fugitive Slave Act).

procedurally deficient; the state court simply lacked the power to adjudicate the claim. Thus, the *Felder* line of cases is inapplicable to this case.

But even if there were such a claim made in this case, the Supremacy Clause supplies this Court with no authority to pre-empt a state procedural law merely because it "burdens the exercise" of a federal right in state court. "Under the Supremacy Clause, state law is pre-empted only by federal law 'made in Pursuance' of the Constitution—not by extratextual considerations of the purposes underlying congressional inaction," such as a desire to ensure that federal law is not burdened by state-law procedural obligations. Wyeth v. Levine, 555 U.S. ___, ___ (2009) (THOMAS, J., concurring in judgment). A sweeping approach to pre-emption based on perceived congressional purposes "leads to the illegitimate—and thus, unconstitutional—invalidation of state laws." Id., at ___. I cannot agree with the approach employed in *Felder* "that pre-empts state laws merely because they 'stand as an obstacle to the accomplishment and execution of the full purposes and objectives' of federal law . . . as perceived by this Court." 555 U.S., at ___.

[handwritten margin note: The purposes of a law cannot pre-empt, only the text can.]

III

Even accepting the entirety of the Court's precedent in this area of the law, however, I still could not join the majority's resolution of this case as it mischaracterizes and broadens this Court's decisions. The majority concedes not only that NYCLA § 24 is jurisdictional, but that the statute is neutral with respect to federal and state claims. Nevertheless, it concludes that the statute violates the Supremacy Clause because it finds that "equality of treatment does not ensure that a state law will be deemed a neutral rule of judicial administration and therefore a valid excuse for refusing to entertain a federal cause of action." This conclusion is incorrect in light of Court precedent for several reasons.

A

The majority mischaracterizes this Court's precedent when it asserts that jurisdictional neutrality is "the beginning, not the end, of the Supremacy Clause analysis." As explained above, "subject to only one limitation, each State of the Union may establish its own judicature, distribute judicial power among the courts of its choice, [and] define the conditions for the exercise of their jurisdiction and the modes of their proceeding, to the same extent as Congress is empowered to establish a system of inferior federal courts within the limits of federal judicial power." Brown v. Gerdes, 321 U.S. 178, 188 (1944) (Frankfurter, J., concurring). That "one limitation" is the neutrality principle that the Court has found in the Supremacy Clause. Here, it is conceded that New York has deprived its courts of subject-matter jurisdiction over a particular class of claims on terms that treat federal and state actions equally. That is all this Court's precedent requires.

The majority's assertion that jurisdictional neutrality is not the touchstone because "[a] jurisdictional rule cannot be used as a device to undermine federal law, no matter how even-handed it may appear," reflects a misunderstanding of the law. A jurisdictional statute simply deprives the relevant court of the power to decide the case altogether. Such a statute necessarily operates without prejudice to the adjudication of the matter in a competent forum. Jurisdictional statutes therefore by definition are incapable of undermining federal law. NYCLA § 24 no more undermines § 1983 than the amount-in-controversy requirement for federal diversity jurisdiction undermines state law. The relevant law (state or federal) remains fully operative in both circumstances. The sole consequence of the jurisdictional barrier is that the law cannot be enforced in one particular judicial forum.[10]

As a result, the majority's focus on New York's reasons for enacting this jurisdictional statute is entirely misplaced. The States "remain independent and autonomous within their proper sphere of authority." *Printz v. United States*, 521 U.S. 898, 928 (1997). New York has the organic authority, therefore, to tailor the jurisdiction of state courts to meet its policy goals.

It may be true that it was "Congress' judgment that *all* persons who violate federal rights while acting under color of state law shall be held liable for damages." But Congress has not enforced that judgment by statutorily requiring the States to open their courts to *all* § 1983 claims. And this Court has "never held that state courts must entertain § 1983 suits." *National Private Truck Council, Inc. v. Oklahoma Tax Comm'n*, 515 U.S. 582, 587, n.4 (1995). Our decisions have held only that the States cannot use jurisdictional statutes to discriminate against federal claims. Because NYCLA § 24 does not violate this command, any policy-driven reasons for depriving jurisdiction over a "federal claim in addition to an identical state claim" are irrelevant for purposes of the Supremacy Clause.

---

10. If by asserting that state law is not permitted to "undermine federal law," the majority instead is arguing that NYCLA § 24 is a procedural rule that too heavily "burdens the exercise of the federal right" in state court, see *Felder*, 487 U.S., at 141, its argument is equally misplaced. First, the majority concedes that NYCLA § 24 is not a state procedural rule. Second, applying the reasoning of *Felder* to a jurisdictional statute like NYCLA § 24 would overrule all of the Court s decisions upholding state laws that decline jurisdiction over federal claims, and would virtually ensure that in future cases, no state jurisdictional rule will be upheld as constitutional. By simply rendering a federal claim noncognizable in state court, a statute depriving a state court of subject-matter jurisdiction (even under the terms and conditions permitted by this Court's precedent) will always violate *Felder*'s command that a state rule must not undermine the "remedial objectives" of a federal claim. The jurisdictional statute also will unavoidably implicate *Felder*'s concern that a state rule should not inevitably produce a different outcome depending on whether a claim is asserted in state or federal court. A state jurisdictional statute necessarily will result in a different outcome in state court, where it will cause dismissal of the federal claim, than in federal court, where that claim will be heard. It is for this reason that the Court has been careful to keep its examination of state jurisdictional statutes and state procedural rules in different categories.

This Court's decision in *Howlett* is not to the contrary. Despite the majority's assertion, *Howlett* does not stand for the proposition "that a State cannot employ a jurisdictional rule 'to dissociate itself from federal law because of disagreement with its content or a refusal to recognize the superior authority of its source.'" As an initial matter, the majority lifts the above quotation—which was merely part of a passage explaining that a "State may not discriminate against federal causes of action"—entirely out of context. *Howlett*'s reiteration of *McKnett*'s neutrality command, which is all the selected quotation reflects, offers no refuge to the majority in light of its concession that NYCLA § 24 affords "equal treatment" to "federal and state claims."

Howlett instead stands for the unremarkable proposition that States may not add immunity defenses to § 1983. A state law is not jurisdictional just because the legislature has "denominated" it as such. As the majority observes, the State's "invocation of 'jurisdiction'" cannot "trump" the "Supremacy Clause inquiry." The majority, therefore, is correct that a state court's decision "to nullify a federal right or cause of action [that it] believe[s] is inconsistent with [its] local policies" cannot evade the Supremacy Clause by hiding behind a jurisdictional label, because "the Supremacy Clause cannot be evaded by formalism." Rather, a state statute must in fact *operate* jurisdictionally: It must deprive the court of the power to hear the claim and it must not preclude relitigation of the action in a proper forum. *Howlett* proved the point by striking down a state-law immunity rule that bore the jurisdictional label but operated as a defense on the merits and provided for the dismissal of the state court action with prejudice.

. . . Unlike the Florida immunity rule in *Howlett*, NYCLA § 24 is not a defense to a federal claim and the dismissal it authorizes is without prejudice. For this reason, NYCLA § 24 is not merely "denominated" as jurisdictional—it actually is jurisdictional. The New York courts, therefore, have not declared a "category" of § 1983 claims to be "'frivolous'" or to have "'no merit'" in order to "'relieve congestion'" in the state-court system (quoting *Howlett*, at 380). These courts have simply recognized that they lack the power to adjudicate this category of claims regardless of their merit.

The majority's failure to grapple with the clear differences between the immunity rule at issue in *Howlett* and NYCLA § 24 proves that its decision is untethered from precedent. And more broadly, the majority's failure to account for the important role of claim preclusion in evaluating whether a statute is jurisdictional undermines the important line drawn by this Court's decisions between subject-matter jurisdiction and the merits. See Marrese v. American Academy of Orthopaedic Surgeons, 470 U.S. 373, 382 (1985) ("With respect to matters that were not decided in the state proceedings . . . claim preclusion generally does not apply where 'the plaintiff was unable to . . . seek a remedy because of the limitations on the subject matter jurisdiction of the courts' " (quoting Restatement (Second) of Judgments § 26(1)(c)(1982))).

The majority's principal response is that NYCLA § 24 "is effectively an immunity statute cloaked in jurisdictional garb." But this curious rejoinder resurrects an argument that the majority abandons earlier in its own opinion. The majority needs to choose. Either it should definitively commit to making the impossible case that a statute denying state courts the power to entertain a claim without prejudice to its reassertion in federal court is an immunity defense in disguise, or it should clearly explain why some other aspect of *Howlett* controls the outcome of this case. This Court has required Congress to speak clearly when it intends to "upset the usual constitutional balance of federal and state powers." Gregory v. Ashcroft, 501 U.S. 452, 460 (1991). It should require no less of itself.

At bottom, the majority's warning that upholding New York's law "would permit a State to withhold a forum for the adjudication of any federal cause of action with which it disagreed as long as the policy took the form of a jurisdictional rule" is without any basis in fact. This Court's jurisdictional neutrality command already guards against antifederal discrimination. A decision upholding NYCLA § 24, which fully adheres to that rule, would not "circumvent our prior decisions." It simply would adhere to them.[11]

B

The majority also incorrectly concludes that NYCLA § 24 is not a neutral jurisdictional statute because it applies to a "narrow class of defendants" and because New York courts "hear the lion's share of all other § 1983 actions." A statute's jurisdictional status does not turn on its

---

11. The majority also suggests that allowing jurisdictional neutrality to be the test "would create a blind spot in the Supremacy Clause" because a procedural rule that too heavily burdens a federal cause of action would be struck down as unconstitutional while "a State could express its disagreement with (and even open hostility to) a federal cause of action, declare a desire to thwart its enforcement, and achieve that goal by removing the disfavored category of claims from its courts' jurisdiction." This is incorrect for at least two reasons. First, as explained above, a State may permissibly register its hostility to federal law only by subjecting analogous state-law claims to equally disfavored treatment. Hostility to federal law is thus irrelevant under this Court's precedent—the Supremacy Clause is concerned only with whether there is antifederal discrimination. Second, the majority obscures important dif-ferences between procedural rules, like the notice-of-claim rule at issue in *Felder*, and neutral jurisdictional statutes like NYCLA § 24. Unlike a neutral jurisdictional statute, which merely prevents a state court from entertaining a federal claim, failure to comply with a state procedural rule will result in dismissal of a federal claim with prejudice. Contrary to the majority's assertion, there-fore, it is not that state courts with "unconstitutionally burdensome procedural rules did not go far enough"—it is instead that they went too far by placing an insurmountable procedural hurdle in the plaintiff's path that led to a judgment against him on the merits. As a result, the Court's assessment of whether a state procedural rule too heavily burdens a federal right does not have any bearing on the Court's continued adherence to the neutrality principle as the sole determinant in evaluating state-law jurisdictional statutes.

narrowness or on its breadth. Rather, as explained above, a statute's jurisdictional status turns on the grounds on which the state-law dismissal rests and the consequences that follow from such rulings. No matter how narrow the majority perceives NYCLA § 24 to be, it easily qualifies as jurisdictional under this established standard. Accordingly, it is immaterial that New York has chosen to allow its courts of general jurisdiction to entertain § 1983 actions against certain categories of defendants but not others (such as correction officers), or to entertain § 1983 actions against particular defendants for only certain types of relief.

Building on its assumption that a statute's jurisdictional status turns on its scope, the majority further holds that "having made the decision to create courts of general jurisdiction that regularly sit to entertain analogous suits, New York is not at liberty to shut the courthouse door to federal claims that it considers at odds with its local policy." But whether two claims are "analogous" is relevant only for purposes of determining whether a state jurisdictional statute discriminates against federal law. This inquiry necessarily requires an evaluation of the similarities between *federal* and *state* law claims to assess whether state-court jurisdiction is being denied to a federal claim simply because of its federal character.

In contrast, the majority limits its analysis to state-law claims, finding discrimination based solely on the fact that state law provides jurisdiction in state court for claims against state officials who serve in "analogous" roles to the correction officers. The majority's inquiry is not probative of antifederal discrimination, which is the concern that first led this Court in *McKnett* to find a Supremacy Clause limitation on state-court jurisdictional autonomy. Consequently, there is no support for the majority's assertion that New York's decision to treat police officers differently from correction officers for purposes of civil litigation somehow violates the Constitution.

Worse still, the majority concludes that § 1983 claims for damages against "other state officials" are "sufficiently analogous to petitioner's § 1983 claims" to trigger a Supremacy Clause violation. Under this reasoning, if a State grants its trial courts jurisdiction to hear § 1983 claims for damages against *any* state official, the State's decision to deny those courts the power to entertain some narrower species of § 1983 claims—even on jurisdictionally neutral terms—a fortiori violates the Supremacy Clause. The majority's assurance that its holding is applicable only to New York's "unique scheme" thus rings hollow. The majority is forcing States into an all-or-nothing choice that neither the Constitution nor this Court's decisions require.

Indeed, the majority's novel approach breaks the promise that the States still enjoy " 'great latitude … to establish the structure and jurisdiction of their own courts' " (quoting *Howlett*, 496 U.S., at 372). It cannot be that New York has forsaken the right to withdraw a particular class of claims from its courts' purview simply because it has created courts of general jurisdiction that would otherwise have the power to hear suits for damages against correction officers. The Supremacy Clause does not fossilize the jurisdiction of state courts in their original form. Under this Court's precedent, States remain free to alter the structure of their judicial system even if that means certain federal causes of action will no longer be heard in state court, so long as States do so on nondiscriminatory terms. Today's decision thus represents a dramatic and unwarranted expansion of this Court's precedent.

IV

"[I]n order to protect the delicate balance of power mandated by the Constitution, the Supremacy Clause must operate only in accordance with its terms." *Wyeth*, 555 U.S., at ___. (THOMAS, J., concurring in judgment). By imposing on state courts a duty to accept subject-matter jurisdiction over federal § 1983 actions, the Court has stretched the Supremacy Clause beyond all reasonable bounds and upended a compromise struck by the Framers in Article III of the Constitution. Furthermore, by declaring unconstitutional even those laws that divest state courts of jurisdiction over federal claims on a non-discriminatory basis, the majority has silently overturned this Court's unbroken line of decisions upholding state statutes that are materially indistinguishable from the New York law under review. And it has transformed a single exception to the rule of state judicial autonomy into a virtually ironclad obligation to entertain federal business. I respectfully dissent.

Page 48, delete Note 4, pages 48–50, renumber Note 5 on page 50 as Note 8, and add:

4. *Howlett v. Rose*. Before *Haywood*, the most prominent recent decision was Howlett v. Rose, 496 U.S. 356 (1990). Like *Haywood*, *Howlett* involved a civil rights plaintiff who (unusually) chose to bring his federal claims in state court and who there encountered state-court limitations on 42 U.S.C. § 1983. The plaintiff in *Howlett* was a former high school student who sued the school board (and three officials) for an allegedly illegal search of his car and the resulting suspension. School boards and other local governments are proper defendants under § 1983, Monell v. Department of Social Services, 436 U.S. 658 (1978), though states and state agencies are not. Will v. Michigan Dept. of State Police, 491 U.S. 58 (1989). Thus, so far as federal law was concerned, Howell was entitled to bring a § 1983 action (as well as related state-law claims) against the school board in either state or federal court. The Florida courts, however, concluded that Florida's statutory waiver of sovereign immunity applied only to state-law claims and thus barred suit against the school board in state court.

So phrased, the ruling of the Florida courts that the school board enjoyed an immunity not recognized by federal law seems a straightforward violation of the Supremacy Clause, and perhaps that is all that need have been said. The Supreme Court, however, wrote more elaborately to review the principles applicable in the area. The Court concluded: (1) that federal claims ordinarily are enforceable in state court; (2) that a "valid excuse" for declining to hear federal claims cannot violate or be inconsistent with federal law; but (3) that a state court ordinarily can refuse jurisdiction under "a neutral state rule regarding the administration of the courts." The attempt to characterize Florida's position as a neutral jurisdictional rule of this sort was unanimously rejected:

> The state of Florida has constituted the Circuit Court for Pinellas County as a court of general jurisdiction. It exercises jurisdiction over tort claims by private citizens against state entities (including school boards), of the size and type of petitioner's claim here, and it can enter judgment against them. That court also exercises jurisdiction over § 1983 actions against individual officers and is fully competent to provide the remedies the federal statute requires. Petitioner has complied with all the state law procedures for invoking the jurisdiction of that court.

The fact that the state called its immunity rule "jurisdictional" was of no consequence: "The force of the Supremacy Clause is not so weak that it can be evaded by mere mention of the word 'jurisdiction.'"

5. Questions and Comments on *Haywood*. As the *Haywood* opinions reveal, the propositions for which these cases stand may be formulated in at least three ways. Most broadly, *Testa, Howlett,* and *Haywood* may be taken to stand for the proposition that state courts with general jurisdiction cannot decline to adjudicate federal claims for reasons reflecting disagreement with federal policy. Under this reading, *Haywood* was correctly decided, because New York's reasons for redirecting damages actions against corrections officers were contrary to the federal policy embodied in § 1983.

A second reading is slightly narrower. It would take the true principle to be only that state courts with jurisdiction to hear "analogous" state claims cannot discriminate against federal claims by excluding them from state-court jurisdiction. This formulation explains *Testa* and *Howlett* but arguably not *Haywood*. As Justice Thomas pointed out in Part III of his dissent (joined by Roberts, Scalia, and Alito), New York's law treated damage actions against corrections officers exactly the same, whether they were state or federal. Thus, if discrimination against federal claims were the only issue, *Haywood* arguably should have gone the other way.

The most narrow reading is apparently endorsed only by Justice Thomas. He argued in Parts I and II of his dissent that states should be free to discriminate against federal claims so long as the approach is genuinely jurisdictional. Put differently, Thomas believes that states should be free to exclude federal claims from state court so long as (1) Congress has not commanded otherwise (in a valid exercise of its constitutional authority) and (2) the resulting judgments are jurisdictional only, do not resolve the merits, and therefore do not preclude vindication of federal claims in federal court. Even this narrowest statement of the governing principles is sufficient to explain *Howlett*, which is perhaps why the decision was unanimous. It may also be sufficient to explain *Testa* if, like Justice Thomas, one takes the fact that there was no generally applicable, legislative policy denying state-court jurisdiction as decisive. At the least, Thomas's dissent suggests that the broad proposition for which *Testa* is typically cited was not necessarily essential to its disposition.

6. Questions and Comments on the Supremacy Clause. What is the source of the obligation of state courts to hear federal claims?[b] Justice Black in *Testa* and Justice Stevens in both *Howlett* and *Haywood* say that the requirement comes from the Supremacy Clause. An opposing view was expressed in Terrence Sandalow, *Henry v. Mississippi* and the Adequate State Ground: Proposals for a Revised Doctrine, 1965 Sup.Ct.Rev. 187, 206–07:*

> [*Testa* may] be taken to mean that the Constitution, presumably through the Supremacy Clause, directly imposes upon the states an obligation to enforce federal claims that Congress has not committed to the exclusive jurisdiction of the federal courts. Yet it is difficult to perceive the federal interest that justifies so substantial an intrusion upon the power of the states to determine the purposes to be served by agencies of state government. [In] *Testa* a federal court was open to the plaintiff, so that a decision sustaining the refusal to adjudicate would in no way have interfered with the vindication of federal rights. Conceding, therefore, that a state may not pursue a policy inconsistent with that established by federal law, it is by no means apparent that the state [court] in *Testa* . . . had done so. Federal policy was substantive, that recovery should be permitted under specified circumstances. State policy, on the other hand, was concerned only with the use to be made of state courts, a matter not touched by the federal policy.

> The Court's reliance on the Supremacy Clause appears to come to no more than it would be unseemly for the state to refuse recognition of rights conferred by federal law—particularly if similar rights under state law are adjudicated in state courts. [T]hat does not seem an adequate justification. [T]he allocation of burdens between state and federal judiciaries seems peculiarly a matter for determination by Congress. Recognition of congressional power to require the exercise of jurisdiction by state courts would permit ample protection of any federal interests. In the

b. Since questions of state sovereign immunity are often implicated, the issue of whether state courts are obligated to provide remedies for federal constitutional claims has been postponed to Chapter VIII.

absence of a declaration by Congress that state courts must enforce state rights that Congress has created, there appears to be no substantial reason why the Supreme Court should enforce such an obligation.

Sandalow suggests that if the state courts are to have an obligation to hear federal statutory claims, it should come from Congress, not the Supreme Court.[c] What happens when Congress *permits*, but does not *command*, the states to exercise concurrent jurisdiction? At least three solutions seem possible. First, state courts could be required to hear a federal claim only when Congress explicitly says so. Second, the Supreme Court could direct state courts to hear a federal claim only when the purposes of the particular federal statute would be materially advanced by state-court enforcement. Third, the Court could create a general obligation, with appropriate exceptions, that state courts hear all federal claims over which state jurisdiction is permitted. The Court seems to have chosen the third option. Is this the best choice?

7. Questions and Comments on "Valid Excuse." These cases can also be questioned from a different direction. If, as *Haywood*, *Howlett* and *Testa* suggest, state courts are required to hear federal claims, why should they be permitted to decline jurisdiction when they have a "valid excuse"? Consider again the views of Terrence Sandalow:

> If the duty of the state courts to accept jurisdiction flows from the obligation to respect federal policy, there is no apparent reason why the state should not be required to accept jurisdiction even though it would not entertain an analogous forum-created right. Federal policy is the same whatever lines the state has drawn in defining the jurisdiction of its courts over local claims. If the state may not assert a policy at variance with that expressed by the federal law, adjudication of the claim would seem to be required even in the absence of discrimination since, insofar as the local jurisdictional rule prevents adjudication, it is to that extent, under the reasoning of *Mondou*, inconsistent with the policy underlying

---

c. Of course, this assumes that Congress has the power to require states to hear federal claims. That is certainly the conventional understanding, but Justice Thomas evidently has his doubts. See footnote 8 of his dissent in *Haywood*, and his remark, speaking for the Court, in National Private Truck Council, Inc. v. Oklahoma Tax Commission, 515 U.S. 582 (1995), that "[f]or purposes of this case, we will assume without deciding that state courts generally must hear § 1983 suits." He then added the following footnote:

We have never held that state courts must entertain § 1983 suits. See Martinez v. California, 444 U.S. 277, 283 n.7 (1980) ("We have never considered . . . the question whether a state *must* entertain a claim under § 1983"). Cf. Arkansas Writers' Project, Inc. v. Ragland, 481 U.S. 221, 234 n.7 (1987) (observing that whether state courts must assume jurisdiction over § 1983 claims involving state taxes "is not entirely clear").

the federal claim. Some support for this view may be found in *Testa*.[d]

Page 66, omit the first paragraph of Note 3 and substitute:

3. Questions and Comments on *Tarble's Case*. In a sense, *Tarble's Case* is the converse of *Haywood v. Drown*. Both cases concern whether the Supreme Court is justified, in the absence of Congressional command, in restricting state control over the cases to be heard in its own court system. In *Haywood* the question was whether a reluctant state court should be required to hear a federal claim; in *Tarble* the question was whether an eager state court should be foreclosed from hearing a federal claim.

Page 100, add a footnote at the end of Note 1:

a. For a recent application of the rule of *Michigan v. Long*, see Florida v. Powell, 559 U.S. ___ (2010). In ruling in the defendant's favor on a *Miranda* issue, the Florida Supreme Court invoked both that decision and a provision of the Florida constitution. Finding that the Florida Supreme Court had "treated state and federal law as interchangeable and interwoven," the Supreme Court of the United States granted certiorari, reversed the *Miranda* ruling, and remanded to the state court. Only Justice Stevens dissented on reviewability.

d. Compare Nicole A. Gordon and Douglas Gross, Justiciability of Federal Claims in State Court, 59 Notre Dame L.Rev. 1145 (1984) (arguing that "the supremacy clause ... requires state courts to vindicate federal rights, even when similar rights under state law are held to be non-justiciable"). For a very different perspective on the jurisdictional autonomy of state courts, see Michael G. Collins, Article III Cases, State Court Duties, and the Madisonian Compromise, 1995 Wis. L. Rev. 39 (attacking the historical foundation of *Testa v. Katt* and calling for "curbs on Congress's ability further to conscript state courts in the administration of federal law"). See also Anthony J. Bellia, Jr., Congressional Power and State Court Jurisdiction, 94 Geo. L.J. 949 (2006).— [Footnote by eds.]

CHAPTER II

THE POWER OF FEDERAL COURTS TO CREATE FEDERAL LAW

Page 133, add at the end of footnote a:

For careful consideration of the implications of *Clearfield*, see Ernest A. Young, Preemption and Federal Common Law, 83 Notre Dame L. Rev. 1639 (2008).

Page 133, add at the end of footnote b:

See also Richard A. Epstein, Federal Preemption, and Federal Common Law, in Nuisance Cases, 102 Nw. U. L. Rev. 551 (2008).

Page 175, delete *Gebser v. Lago Independent School District* and accompanying note at pages 175–84, and substitute the following:

[handwritten: DC → dismissed affirmed AFFIRMED]

Stoneridge Investment Partners, LLC v. Scientific–Atlanta, Inc.

Supreme Court of the United States, 2008.
552 U.S. 148.

■ JUSTICE KENNEDY delivered the opinion of the Court.

We consider the reach of the private right of action the Court has found implied in § 10(b) of the Securities Exchange Act of 1934, as amended, 15 U.S.C. § 78j(b), and SEC Rule 10b–5, 17 CFR § 240.10b–5 (2007). *[handwritten: Statute + rule]* In this suit investors alleged losses after purchasing common stock. They sought to impose liability on entities who, acting both as customers and suppliers, agreed to arrangements that allowed the investors' company to mislead its auditor and issue a misleading financial statement affecting the stock price. We conclude the implied right of action does not reach the customer/supplier companies because the investors did not rely upon their statements or representations. *[handwritten: Ruling]* We affirm the judgment of the Court of Appeals.

I

This class-action suit by investors was filed against Charter Communications, Inc., in the United States District Court for the Eastern District of Missouri. *[handwritten: Fed. Court.]* Stoneridge Investment Partners, LLC, a limited liability company organized under the laws of Delaware, was the lead plaintiff and is petitioner here.

Charter issued the financial statements and the securities in question. It was a named defendant along with some of its executives and Arthur Andersen LLP, Charter's independent auditor during the period in question. We are concerned, though, with two other defendants, respondents here. Respondents are Scientific–Atlanta, Inc., and Motorola, Inc. They were suppliers, and later customers, of Charter.

For purposes of this proceeding, we take these facts, alleged by petitioner, to be true. Charter, a cable operator, engaged in a variety of fraudulent practices so its quarterly reports would meet Wall Street expectations for cable subscriber growth and operating cash flow. The fraud included misclassification of its customer base; delayed reporting of terminated customers; improper capitalization of costs that should have been shown as expenses; and manipulation of the company's billing cutoff dates to inflate reported revenues. In late 2000, Charter executives realized that, despite these efforts, the company would miss projected operating cash flow numbers by $15 to $20 million. To help meet the shortfall, Charter decided to alter its existing arrangements with respondents, Scientific–Atlanta and Motorola. . . .

Respondents supplied Charter with the digital cable converter (set top) boxes that Charter furnished to its customers. Charter arranged to overpay respondents $20 for each set top box it purchased until the end of the year, with the understanding that respondents would return the overpayment by purchasing advertising from Charter. The transactions, it is alleged, had no economic substance; but, because Charter would then record the advertising purchases as revenue and capitalize its purchase of the set top boxes, in violation of generally accepted accounting principles, the transactions would enable Charter to fool its auditor into approving a financial statement showing it met projected revenue and operating cash flow numbers. Respondents agreed to the arrangement.

So that Arthur Andersen would not discover the link between Charter's increased payments for the boxes and the advertising purchases, the companies drafted documents to make it appear the transactions were unrelated and conducted in the ordinary course of business. Following a request from Charter, Scientific–Atlanta sent documents to Charter stating—falsely—that it had increased production costs. It raised the price for set top boxes for the rest of 2000 by $20 per box. As for Motorola, in a written contract Charter agreed to purchase from Motorola a specific number of set top boxes and pay liquidated damages of $20 for each unit it did not take. The contract was made with the expectation Charter would fail to purchase all the units and pay Motorola the liquidated damages.

To return the additional money from the set top box sales, Scientific–Atlanta and Motorola signed contracts with Charter to purchase advertising time for a price higher than fair value. The new set top box agreements were backdated to make it appear that they were negotiated a month before the advertising agreements. The backdating was important to convey the impression that the negotiations were unconnected, a point Arthur Andersen considered necessary for separate treatment of the transactions. Charter recorded the advertising payments to inflate revenue and operating cash flow by approximately $17 million. The inflated number was shown on financial statements filed with the Securities and Exchange Commission (SEC) and reported to the public.

Respondents had no role in preparing or disseminating Charter's financial statements. And their own financial statements booked the transactions as a wash, under generally accepted accounting principles. It is alleged respondents knew or were in reckless disregard of Charter's intention to use the transactions to inflate its revenues and knew the resulting financial statements issued by Charter would be relied upon by research analysts and investors. Petitioner filed a securities fraud class action on behalf of purchasers of Charter stock alleging that, by participating in the transactions, respondents violated § 10(b) of the Securities Exchange Act of 1934 and SEC Rule 10b–5.

The District Court granted respondents' motion to dismiss for failure to state a claim on which relief can be granted. The United States Court of Appeals for the Eighth Circuit affirmed. In its view the allegations did not show that respondents made misstatements relied upon by the public or that they violated a duty to disclose; and on this premise it found no violation of § 10(b) by respondents. At most, the court observed, respondents had aided and abetted Charter's misstatement of its financial results; but, it noted, there is no private right of action for aiding and abetting a § 10(b) violation. See Central Bank of Denver, N.A. v. First Interstate Bank of Denver, N.A., 511 U.S. 164, 191 (1994). . . .

II

Section 10(b) of the Securities Exchange Act makes it

unlawful for any person, directly or indirectly, by the use of any means or instrumentality of interstate commerce or of the mails, or of any facility of any national securities exchange . . . [t]o use or employ, in connection with the purchase or sale of any security . . . any manipulative or deceptive device or contrivance in contravention of such rules and regulations as the Commission may prescribe as necessary or appropriate in the public interest or for the protection of investors.

The SEC, pursuant to this section, promulgated Rule 10b–5, which makes it unlawful

(a) To employ any device, scheme, or artifice to defraud,

(b) To make any untrue statement of a material fact or to omit to state a material fact necessary in order to make the statements made, in the light of the circumstances under which they were made, not misleading, or

    (c) To engage in any act, practice, or course of business which operates or would operate as a fraud or deceit upon any person,

in connection with the purchase or sale of any security.

Rule 10b–5 encompasses only conduct already prohibited by § 10(b). Though the text of the Securities Exchange Act does not provide for a private cause of action for § 10(b) violations, the Court has found a right of action implied in the words of the statute and its implementing regulation. Superintendent of Ins. of N.Y. v. Bankers Life & Casualty Co., 404 U.S. 6, 13, n.9 (1971). In a typical § 10(b) private action a plaintiff must prove (1) a material misrepresentation or omission by the defendant; (2) scienter; (3) a connection between the misrepresentation or omission and the purchase or sale of a security; (4) reliance upon the misrepresentation or omission; (5) economic loss; and (6) loss causation. See Dura Pharmaceuticals, Inc. v. Broudo, 544 U.S. 336, 341–42 (2005).

In *Central Bank,* supra, the Court determined that § 10(b) liability did not extend to aiders and abettors. The Court found the scope of § 10(b) to be delimited by the text, which makes no mention of aiding and abetting liability. The Court doubted the implied § 10(b) action should extend to aiders and abettors when none of the express causes of action in the securities Acts included that liability. It added the following:

> Were we to allow the aiding and abetting action proposed in this case, the defendant could be liable without any showing that the plaintiff relied upon the aider and abettor's statements or actions. Allowing plaintiffs to circumvent the reliance requirement would disregard the careful limits on 10b–5 recovery mandated by our earlier cases,

The decision in *Central Bank* led to calls for Congress to create an express [private] cause of action for aiding and abetting within the Securities Exchange Act. ... Congress did not follow this course. Instead, in § 104 of the Private Securities Litigation Reform Act of 1995 (PSLRA), it directed prosecution of aiders and abettors by the SEC. 15 U.S.C. § 78t(e).

The § 10(b) implied private right of action does not extend to aiders and abettors. The conduct of a secondary actor must satisfy each of the elements or preconditions for liability; and we consider whether the allegations here are sufficient to do so.

III

[Our] interpretation of the holding from the Court of Appeals opinion is that the court was stating only that any deceptive statement or act respondents made was not actionable because it did not have the requisite proximate relation to the investors' harm. That conclusion is consistent with our own determination that respondents' acts or statements were not relied upon by the investors and that, as a result, liability cannot be imposed upon respondents.

A

Reliance by the plaintiff upon the defendant's deceptive acts is an essential element of the § 10(b) private cause of action. Basic, Inc. v. Levinson, 485 U.S. 224 (1988). . . . We have found a rebuttable presumption of reliance in two different circumstances. First, if there is an omission of a material fact by one with a duty to disclose, the investor to whom the duty was owed need not provide specific proof of reliance. Second, under the fraud-on-the-market doctrine, reliance is presumed when the statements at issue become public. The public information is reflected in the market price of the security. Then it can be assumed that an investor who buys or sells stock at the market price relies upon the statement.

Neither presumption applies here. Respondents had no duty to disclose; and their deceptive acts were not communicated to the public. No member of the investing public had knowledge, either actual or presumed, of respondents' deceptive acts during the relevant times. Petitioner, as a result, cannot show reliance upon any of respondents' actions except in an indirect chain that we find too remote for liability. . . .

B

Invoking what some courts call "scheme liability," petitioner nonetheless seeks to impose liability on respondents even absent a public statement. In our view this approach does not answer the objection that petitioner did not in fact rely upon respondents' own deceptive conduct.

Liability is appropriate, petitioner contends, because respondents engaged in conduct with the purpose and effect of creating a false appearance of material fact to further a scheme to misrepresent Charter's revenue. The argument is that the financial statement Charter released to the public was a natural and expected consequence of respondents' deceptive acts; had respondents not assisted Charter, Charter's auditor would not have been fooled, and the financial statement would have been a more accurate reflection of Charter's financial condition. That causal link is sufficient, petitioner argues, to apply Basic's presumption of reliance to respondents' acts.

In effect petitioner contends that in an efficient market investors rely not only upon the public statements relating to a security but also upon the transactions those statements reflect. Were this concept of reliance to be adopted, the implied cause of action would reach the whole marketplace in which the issuing company does business; and there is no authority for this rule.

As stated above, reliance is tied to causation, leading to the inquiry whether respondents' acts were immediate or remote to the injury. . . . [W]e conclude respondents' deceptive acts, which were not disclosed to the investing public, are too remote to satisfy the requirement of reliance. It was Charter, not respondents, that misled its auditor and filed fraudulent financial statements; nothing respondents did made it necessary or inevitable for Charter to record the transactions as it did.

The petitioner invokes the private cause of action under § 10(b) and seeks to apply it beyond the securities markets—the realm of financing business—to purchase and supply contracts—the realm of ordinary business operations. The latter realm is governed, for the most part, by state law. It is true that if business operations are used, as alleged here, to affect securities markets, the SEC enforcement power may reach the culpable actors. It is true as well that a dynamic, free economy presupposes a high degree of integrity in all of its parts, an integrity that must be underwritten by rules enforceable in fair, independent, accessible courts. Were the implied cause of action to be extended to the practices described here, however, there would be a risk that the federal power would be used to invite litigation beyond the immediate sphere of securities litigation and in areas already governed by functioning and effective state-law guarantees. . . .

Petitioner's theory, moreover, would put an unsupportable interpretation on Congress' specific response to *Central Bank* in § 104 of the PSLRA. Congress amended the securities laws to provide for limited coverage of aiders and abettors. Aiding and abetting liability is authorized in actions brought by the SEC but not by private parties. See 15 U.S.C. § 78t(e). Petitioner's view of primary liability makes any aider and abettor liable under § 10(b) if he or she committed a deceptive act in the process of providing assistance. Were we to adopt this construction of § 10(b), it would revive in substance the implied cause of action against all aiders and abettors except those who committed no deceptive act in the process of facilitating the fraud; and we would undermine Congress' determination that this class of defendants should be pursued by the SEC and not by private litigants. See Alexander v. Sandoval, 532 U.S. 275, 290 (2001) ("The express provision of one method of enforcing a substantive rule suggests that Congress intended to preclude others.").

This is not a case in which Congress has enacted a regulatory statute and then has accepted, over a long period of time, broad judicial authority to define substantive standards of conduct and liability. And in accord with the nature of the cause of action at issue here, we give weight to Congress' amendment to the Act restoring aiding and abetting liability in certain cases but not others. The amendment, in our view, supports the conclusion that there is no liability. . . .

C

The history of the § 10(b) private right and the careful approach the Court has taken before proceeding without congressional direction provide further reasons to find no liability here. The § 10(b) private cause of action is a judicial construct that Congress did not enact in the text of the relevant statutes. Though the rule once may have been otherwise, see J.I. Case Co. v. Borak, 377 U.S. 426, 432–33 (1964), it is settled that there is an implied cause of action only if the underlying statute can be interpreted to disclose the intent to create one, see, e.g., *Alexander*, supra, at 286–87. This is for good reason. In the absence of congressional intent the Judiciary's recognition of an implied private right of action

> necessarily extends its authority to embrace a dispute Congress has not assigned it to resolve. This runs contrary to the established principle that "[t]he jurisdiction of the federal courts is carefully guarded against expansion by judicial interpretation . . .," American Fire & Casualty Co. v. Finn, 341 U.S. 6, 17 (1951), and conflicts with the authority of Congress under Art. III to set the limits of federal jurisdiction.

Cannon v. University of Chicago, 441 U.S. 677, 746 (1979) (Powell, J., dissenting). . . . The determination of who can seek a remedy has significant consequences for the reach of federal power. See Wilder v. Virginia Hospital Assn., 496 U.S. 498, 509, n.9 (1990) (requirement of congressional intent reflects a concern, grounded in separation of powers, that Congress rather than the courts controls the availability of remedies for violations of statutes).

Concerns with the judicial creation of a private cause of action caution against its expansion. The decision to extend the cause of action is for Congress, not for us. Though it remains the law, the § 10(b) private right should not be extended beyond its present boundaries.

This restraint is appropriate in light of the PSLRA, which imposed heightened pleading requirements and a loss causation requirement upon any private action arising from the Securities Exchange Act. See 15 U.S.C. § 78u–4(b). It is clear these requirements touch upon the implied right of action, which is now a prominent feature of federal securities regulation. See Merrill Lynch, Pierce, Fenner & Smith Inc. v. Dabit, 547 U.S. 71, 81–82 (2006); see also S.Rep. No. 104–98, p. 4–5 (1995), U.S.Code Cong. & Admin.News 1995, pp. 679, 684 (recognizing the § 10(b) implied cause of action, and indicating the PSLRA was intended to have Congress . . . reassert its authority in this area). Congress thus ratified the implied right of action after the Court moved away from a broad willingness to imply private rights of action. See Merrill Lynch, Pierce, Fenner & Smith, Inc. v. Curran, 456 U.S. 353, 381–82 and n. 66 (1982). It is appropriate for us to assume that when § 78u–4 was enacted, Congress accepted the § 10(b) private cause of action as then defined but chose to extend it no further. . . .

The judgment of the Court of Appeals is affirmed, and the case is remanded for further proceedings consistent with this opinion.

■ JUSTICE BREYER took no part in the consideration or decision of this case.

■ JUSTICE STEVENS, with whom JUSTICE SOUTER and JUSTICE GINSBURG join, dissenting.

Charter Communications, Inc., inflated its revenues by $17 million in order to cover up a $15 to $20 million expected cash flow shortfall. It could not have done so absent the knowingly fraudulent actions of Scientific–Atlanta, Inc., and Motorola, Inc. Investors relied on Charter's revenue statements in deciding whether to invest in Charter and in doing so relied on respondents' fraud, which was itself a deceptive device prohibited by § 10(b) of the Securities Exchange Act of 1934. 15 U.S.C. § 78j(b). This is enough to satisfy the requirements of § 10(b) and enough to distinguish this case from Central Bank of Denver, N.A. v. First Interstate Bank of Denver, N.A., 511 U.S. 164 (1994).

The Court seems to assume that respondents' alleged conduct could subject them to liability in an enforcement proceeding initiated by the Government, but nevertheless concludes that they are not subject to liability in a private action brought by injured investors because they are, at most, guilty of aiding and abetting a violation of § 10(b), rather than an actual violation of the statute. . . . The Court's conclusion that no violation of § 10(b) giving rise to a private right of action has been alleged in this case rests on two faulty premises: (1) the Court's overly broad reading of Central Bank and (2) the view that reliance requires a kind of super-causation—a view contrary to our holding in Basic Inc. v. Levinson, 485 U.S. 224 (1988). These two points merit separate discussion.

I

. . . What the Court fails to recognize is that this case is critically different from Central Bank because the bank in that case did not engage in any deceptive act and, therefore, did not itself violate § 10(b). The Court sweeps aside any distinction, remarking that holding respondents liable would reviv[e] the implied cause of action against all aiders and abettors except those who committed no deceptive act in the process of facilitating the fraud. But the fact that Central Bank engaged in no deceptive conduct whatsoever—in other words, that it was at most an aider and abettor—sharply distinguishes Central Bank from cases that do involve allegations of such conduct. . . .

II

The Court's next faulty premise is that petitioner is required to allege that Scientific–Atlanta and Motorola made it necessary or inevitable for Charter to record the transactions in the way it did, in order to demonstrate reliance. . . . Lower courts have correctly stated that the causation necessary to demonstrate reliance is not a difficult hurdle to clear in a private right of action under § 10(b). Reliance is often equated with transaction causation. Dura Pharmaceuticals, Inc. v. Broudo, 544 U.S. 336, 341, 342 (2005). Transaction causation, in turn, is often defined as requiring an allegation that but for the deceptive act, the plaintiff would not have entered into the securities transaction. See, e.g., Lentell v. Merrill Lynch & Co., 396 F.3d 161, 172 (2d Cir. 2005); Binder v. Gillespie, 184 F.3d 1059, 1065–66 (9th Cir. 1999).

Even if but-for causation, standing alone, is too weak to establish reliance, petitioner has also alleged that respondents proximately caused Charter's misstatement of income; petitioner has alleged that respondents knew their deceptive acts would be the basis for statements that would influence the market price of Charter stock on which shareholders would rely. Thus, respondents' acts had the foreseeable effect of causing petitioner to engage in the relevant securities transactions. The Restatement (Second) of Torts § 533, pp. 72–73 (1977), provides that [t]he maker of a fraudulent misrepresentation is subject to liability . . . if the misrepresentation, although not made directly to the other, is made to a third person and the maker intends or has reason to expect that its terms will be repeated or its substance communicated to the other. The sham transactions described in the complaint in this case had the same effect on Charter's profit and loss statement as a false entry directly on its books that included $17 million of gross revenues that had not been received. And respondents are alleged to have known that the outcome of their fraudulent transactions would be communicated to investors. . . .

Finally, the Court relies on the course of action Congress adopted after our decision in *Central Bank* to argue that siding with petitioner on reliance would run contrary to congressional intent. Senate hearings on *Central Bank* were held within one month of our decision. Less than one year later, Senators Dodd and Domenici introduced S. 240, which became the Private Securities Litigation Reform Act of 1995 (PSLRA). Congress stopped short of undoing *Central Bank* entirely, instead adopting a compromise which restored the authority of the SEC to enforce aiding and abetting liability. A private right of action based on aiding and abetting violations of § 10(b) was not, however, included in the PSLRA, despite support from Senator Dodd and members of the Senate Subcommittee on Securities. This compromise surely provides no support for extending *Central Bank* in order to immunize an undefined class of actual violators of § 10(b) from liability in private litigation. . . . That Congress chose not to restore the aiding and abetting liability removed by *Central Bank* does not mean that Congress wanted to exempt from liability the broader range of conduct that today's opinion excludes.

. . . I respectfully dissent from the Court's continuing campaign to render the private cause of action under § 10(b) toothless. I would reverse the decision of the Court of Appeals.

III

While I would reverse for the reasons stated above, I must also comment on the importance of the private cause of action that Congress implicitly authorized when it enacted the Securities Exchange Act of 1934. A theme that underlies the Court's analysis is its mistaken hostility towards the § 10(b) private cause of action. The Court's current view of implied causes of action is that they are merely a relic of our prior heady days. Correctional Services Corp. v. Malesko, 534 U.S. 61, 75 (2001) (Scalia, J., concurring). Those heady days persisted for two hundred years.

During the first two centuries of this Nation's history much of our law was developed by judges in the common-law tradition. A basic principle animating our jurisprudence was enshrined in state constitution provisions guaranteeing, in substance, that every wrong shall have a remedy.[12] Fashioning appropriate remedies for the violation of rules of law designed to protect a class of citizens was the routine business of judges. See Marbury v. Madison, 5 U.S. (1 Cranch) 137, 166 (1803). While it is true that in the early days state law was the source of most of those rules, throughout our history—until 1975—the same practice prevailed in federal courts with regard to federal statutes that left questions of remedy open for judges to answer. In Texas & Pacific R. Co. v. Rigsby, 241 U.S. 33, 39 (1916), this Court stated the following:

> A disregard of the command of the statute is a wrongful act, and where it results in damage to one of the class for whose especial benefit the statute was enacted, the right to recover the damages from the party in default is implied, according to a doctrine of the common law expressed in ... these words: "So, in every case, where a statute enacts, or prohibits a thing for the benefit of a person, he shall have a remedy upon the same statute for the thing enacted for his advantage, or for the recompense of a wrong done to him contrary to the said law." (Per Holt, C. J., Anon., 6 Mod. 26, 27.)

Judge Friendly succinctly described the post-*Rigsby,* pre–1975 practice in his opinion in Leist v. Simplot, 638 F.2d 283, 298–99 (2d Cir. 1980):

> Following *Rigsby* the Supreme Court recognized implied causes of action on numerous occasions, see, e.g., Wyandotte Transportation Co. v. United States, 389 U.S. 191 (1967) (sustaining implied cause of action by United States for damages under Rivers and Harbors Act for removing negligently sunk vessel despite express remedies of in rem action and criminal penalties); United States v. Republic Steel Corp., 362 U.S. 482 (1960) (sustaining implied cause of action by United States for an injunction under the Rivers and Harbors Act); Tunstall v. Locomotive Firemen & Enginemen, 323 U.S. 210 (1944) (sustaining implied cause of action by union member against union for discrimination among

12. Today, the guarantee of a remedy for every injury appears in nearly three-quar-   ters of state constitutions. ...

members despite existence of Board of Mediation); Sullivan v. Little Hunting Park, Inc., 396 U.S. 229 (1969) (sustaining implied private cause of action under 42 U.S.C. § 1982); Allen v. State Board of Elections, 393 U.S. 544 (1969) (sustaining implied private cause of action under § 5 of the Voting Rights Act despite the existence of a complex regulatory scheme and explicit rights of action in the Attorney General); and, of course, [previously cited] decisions under the securities laws. As the Supreme Court itself has recognized, the period of the 1960's and early 1970's was one in which the "Court had consistently found implied remedies." Cannon v. University of Chicago, 441 U.S. 677, 698 (1979).

In a law-changing opinion written by Justice Brennan in 1975, the Court decided to modify its approach to private causes of action. Cort v. Ash, 422 U.S. 66 (constraining courts to use a strict four-factor test to determine whether Congress intended a private cause of action). A few years later, in Cannon v. University of Chicago, 441 U.S. 677 (1979), we adhered to the strict approach mandated by *Cort v. Ash* in 1975, but made it clear that our evaluation of congressional action in 1972 must take into account its contemporary legal context. That context persuaded the majority that Congress had intended the courts to authorize a private remedy for members of the protected class.

Until *Central Bank,* the federal courts continued to enforce a broad implied cause of action for the violation of statutes enacted in 1933 and 1934 for the protection of investors. As Judge Friendly explained:

During the late 1940's, the 1950's, the 1960's and the early 1970's there was widespread, indeed almost general, recognition of implied causes of action for damages under many provisions of the Securities Exchange Act, including not only the antifraud provisions, §§ 10 and 15(c)(1), but many others. These included the provision, § 6(a)(1), requiring securities exchanges to enforce compliance with the Act and any rule or regulation made thereunder and provisions governing the solicitation of proxies [*J.I. Case v. Borak*]. Writing in 1961, Professor Loss remarked with respect to violations of the antifraud provisions that with one exception "not a single judge has expressed himself to the contrary." 3 Securities Regulation 1763–64. When damage actions for violation of § 10(b) and Rule 10b–5 reached the Supreme Court, the existence of an implied cause of action was not deemed worthy of extended discussion. Superintendent of Insurance v. Bankers Life & Casualty Co., 404 U.S. 6 (1971).

In light of the history of court-created remedies and specifically the history of implied causes of action under § 10(b), the Court is simply wrong when it states that Congress did not impliedly authorize this private cause of action when it first enacted the statute. Courts near in time to the enactment of the securities laws recognized that the principle in *Rigsby* applied to the securities laws. Congress enacted § 10(b) with the understanding that federal courts respected the principle that every wrong would have a remedy. Today's decision simply cuts back further on Congress' intended remedy. I respectfully dissent.

ADDITIONAL NOTES ON IMPLIED RIGHTS OF ACTION

1. Questions and Comments on *Stoneridge Investment Partners*. There are at least three dimensions to controversies over judicial creation of private rights of action to enforce federal statutes. The first is simply whether, in the circumstances, private enforcement is a good idea. This aspect of the dispute was not front-and-center in *Stoneridge*, but the majority's comments about the risks of extending 10b–5 to ordinary business operations that would normally be controlled by state law suggests hesitation on the merits. Evaluation of the costs and benefits of private enforcement in a particular context may often be important background for disputes over the scope of judicial authority. Such concerns, which are inherently contextual, are more clearly evident in Gebser v. Lago Vista Independent School District, 524 U.S. 274 (1998), which is noted below.

A second dimension to these controversies is the degree to which Congress's provision of one remedy impliedly excludes others. That was the inference that the *Stoneridge* majority drew from the fact that Congress had explicitly authorized SEC (but not private) actions against aiders and abettors in the Private Securities Litigation Reform Act of 1995 (PSLRA). It was also the point of the Court's parenthetical after citation of Alexander v. Sandoval, 532 U.S. 275, 290 (2001): "The express provision of one method of enforcing a substantive rule suggests that Congress intended to preclude others." Potentially, that inference casts a long shadow. Presumably, every federal statute provides some means of enforcement. If the explicit provision of one remedy precludes judicial recognition of others, then the inquiry is more or less at an end. Of course, the Court said only that the express provision of one remedy "suggests" an intent to preclude others, and that the plausibility of that suggestion will depend heavily on context. A note below on *Alexander v. Sandoval* illustrates the point.

For present purposes, the most interesting analysis of *Stoneridge* is the most general. *Stoneridge* demonstrates that the Court has come a long way from the days of *J.I. Case*, when private rights of action were more or less routinely created, especially in the area of securities law. More than anything else, *Stoneridge* reflects a complete reversal in judicial attitude toward such creativity. While *J.I. Case* suggested that a private right of action would be recognized unless the defendant demonstrated a very good reason not to do so, *Stoneridge* seems at least to have reversed the presumption. Today, the plaintiff who seeks to establish an "implied" right of action bears a heavy burden of grounding that argument in legislative design and intent.

   2. ***Gebser v. Lago Vista Independent School District.*** The significance of the "merits"—that is, the soundness in policy of allowing private damage actions in specific contexts—surfaced in Gebser v. Lago Vista Independent School District, 524 U.S. 274 (1998). In Cannon v. University of Chicago, 441 U.S. 677 (1979), the Court, over the often-quoted dissent of Justice Powell, recognized an implied private right to injunctive enforcement of Title IX of the Education Amendments of 1972, which prohibits sex discrimination in any education program receiving federal funds. Subsequently, Franklin v. Gwinnett County Public Schools, 503 U.S. 60 (1992), extended the implied right to actions for money damages. *Gebser* involved a damages action against a school district for sexual harassment by a teacher. The teacher had sexual relations with an eighth-grade middle-school student, but neither the student nor anyone else reported the misconduct to the teacher's superiors. The matter came to light only when a policeman caught them in the act, after which the teacher was immediately fired. When the student and the student's parents subsequently sued the school district, the question was whether liability could rest on respondeat superior.

   The dissenters in *Gebser* took the view that *Cannon* and *Franklin* had established a private right to enforce Title IX through actions for money damages and that no judicial restrictions were appropriate. Speaking for himself and for Justices Souter, Ginsburg, and Breyer, Justice Stevens referenced *Cannon*'s conclusion that Congress intended Title IX to be enforceable in the same way as Title VI of the 1964 Civil Rights Act, which had been judicially interpreted to authorize money damages. "As long as the intent of Congress is clear," said Stevens, "an implicit command has the same legal force as one that is explicit." He also noted the presumption asserted by Justice White, writing for the Court in *Franklin*, that "Congress intends to authorize 'all appropriate remedies' unless it expressly indicates otherwise":

>   Because these constructions of the statute have been accepted by Congress and are unchallenged here, they have the same legal effect as if the private cause of action seeking damages had been explicitly, rather than implicitly, authorized by Congress. We should therefore seek guidance from the text of the statute and settled legal principles rather than from our views about sound policy.

   The majority disagreed. Writing for the Court, Justice O'Connor said that, "[b]ecause the private right of action under Title IX is judicially implied, we have a measure of latitude to shape a sensible remedial scheme that best comports with the statute." Specifically, the Court concluded that it would be unwise to permit damages actions against a school district without actual notice of the misconduct:

> [I]n cases like this one that do not involve official policy of the recipient [of federal funds] entity, we hold that a damages remedy will not lie under Title IX unless an official who at a minimum has authority to address the alleged discrimination and to institute correction measures on the recipient's behalf has actual knowledge of the discrimination in the recipient's programs and fails adequately to respond.

As no responsible official had knowledge of the teacher's misconduct in *Gebser*, the school district was not liable.

In a sense, *Gebser* involves an unusual role reversal. Liberal Justices, who typically support judicial authority to recognize private rights of action, argued that the Court lacked authority to limit a right of action so recognized. Conservative Justices, who typically decry judicial creativity, argued that the fact that the damages action under Title IX was "implied" in the first place provided ample authority for limiting constructions to serve sound policy. Are both positions internally inconsistent? If not, who has the better side of the argument?

3. *Alexander v. Sandoval.* Although the contexts were different, the issues of judicial authority that divided the Court in *Stoneridge* also surfaced in Alexander v. Sandoval, 532 U.S. 275 (2001). The case concerned private enforcement of Title VI of the Civil Rights Act of 1964, a provision prohibiting recipients of federal funds from discriminating on grounds of "race, color or national origin."

The dispute arose when Alabama amended its Constitution to declare English its official language. The Alabama Department of Public Safety then decided to administer driver's license examinations only in English. Sandoval brought a class action, claiming that this decision had the effect of subjecting non-English speakers to discrimination based on national origin. This discriminatory effect was said to violate a regulation promulgated by the Department of Justice under § 602 of Title VI, which prohibited funding recipients from using "criteria or methods of administration which have the effect of subjecting individuals to discrimination because of their race, color, or national origin. . . ." 28 CFR § 42.104(b)(2) (1999).

Cannon v. University of Chicago, 441 U.S. 677 (1979), had found a private right of action to enforce § 601 of Title VI, and that provision had subsequently been ratified by Congress. Of its own force, however, Title VI—specifically § 601—reaches only *intentional* discrimination. Alexander v. Choate, 469 U.S. 287, 293 (1985). The attack on actions having only a discriminatory *effect*—known in the field as "disparate impact"—rested entirely on the DOJ regulation promulgated under § 602, and the Court, speaking through Justice Scalia, found no congressional intent to authorize private enforcement of § 602:

We therefore begin (and find that we can end) our search for Congress's intent with the text and structure of Title VI. Section 602 authorizes federal agencies "to effectuate the provisions of [§ 601] ... by issuing rules, regulations, or orders of general applicability." 42 U.S.C. § 2000d–1. It is immediately clear that the "rights-creating" language so critical to the Court's analysis in *Cannon* of § 601, see 441 U.S. at 690 n.13, is completely absent from § 602. Whereas § 601 decrees that "no person ... shall ... be subjected to discrimination," 42 U.S.C. § 2000d, the text of § 602 provides that "each Federal department and agency ... is authorized and directed to effectuate the provisions of [§ 601]," 42 U.S.C. § 2000d–1. Far from displaying congressional intent to create new rights, § 602 limits agencies to "effectuating" rights already created by § 601. ... So far as we can tell, this authorizing portion of § 602 reveals no congressional intent to create a private right of action.

Nor do the methods that § 602 goes on to provide for enforcing its authorized regulations manifest an intent to create a private remedy; if anything, they suggest the opposite. Section 602 empowers agencies to enforce their regulations either by terminating funding to the "particular program, or part thereof," that has violated the regulation or "by any other means authorized by law," 42 U.S.C. § 2000d–1. No enforcement action may be taken, however, "until the department or agency concerned has advised the appropriate person or persons of the failure to comply with the requirement and has determined that compliance cannot be secured by voluntary means." Ibid. And every agency enforcement action is subject to judicial review. § 2000d–2. If an agency attempts to terminate program funding, still more restrictions apply. The agency head must "file with the committees of the House and Senate having legislative jurisdiction over the program or activity involved a full written report of the circumstances and the grounds for such action." § 2000d–1. And the termination of funding does not "become effective until thirty days have elapsed after the filing of such report." Ibid. Whatever these elaborate restrictions on agency enforcement may imply for the private enforcement of rights created *outside* of § 602, they tend to contradict a congressional intent to create privately enforceable rights through § 602 itself. The express provision of one method of enforcing a substantive rule suggests that Congress intended to preclude others. ...

Neither as originally enacted nor as later amended does Title VI display an intent to create a freestanding private right of action to enforce regulations promulgated under § 602. We therefore hold that no such right of action exists.

Dissent

Justices Stevens, Souter, Ginsburg, and Breyer dissented. Speaking for the dissenters, Justice Stevens said that the decision was "the unconscious product of the majority's profound distaste for implied causes of action rather than an attempt to discern the intent of the Congress that enacted Title VI of the Civil Rights Act of 1964." One evidence of this distaste was the majority's willingness to infer from specifically provided remedies (agency enforcement through cut-off of funds, etc.) an intent to preclude others. This reasoning has broad potential reach, as presumably every federal statute will explicitly provide some means of enforcement. If that suggests an intent to preclude others, the argument would apply to most of the implied right of action cases ever considered by the Supreme Court.

Finally, *Sandoval* is interesting for another reason. Title 42 U.S.C. § 1983 authorizes a private right of action against anyone who violates a federal statute while acting "under color of" state law. Obviously, the defendants in *Sandoval* were state officers and so could have been sued under § 1983 without resort to an "implied" cause of action directly under Title VI. It was this possibility that led Justice Stevens to remark, in dissent:

> [T]o the extent that the majority denies relief to the respondents merely because they neglected to mention 42 U.S.C. § 1983 in framing their Title VI claim, this case is something of a sport. Litigants who in the future wish to enforce the Title VI regulations against state actors in all likelihood must only reference § 1983 to obtain relief; indeed, the plaintiffs in this case (or other similarly situated individuals) presumably retain the option of re-challenging Alabama's English-only policy in a complaint that invokes § 1983 even after today's decision.

Is it conceivable that *Sandoval* actually involved only a pleading error in the plaintiffs' failure to invoke § 1983? Some lower courts so concluded. Analytically, this position is tenable, as 42 U.S.C. § 1983 purports to provide a private right of action to enforce rights secured by the "Constitution *and laws*" of the United States (emphasis added). Under the broad reading of that language in Maine v. Thiboutot, 448 U.S. 1 (1980), § 1983 would provide an independent damages remedy any time that the person who violated a federal statute acted under color of state law. The Supreme Court, however, has been in retreat from this proposition almost since the day it was announced. In recent years, in particular, the Court has moved to align the use of § 1983 to enforce federal statutes with its more restrictive approach to inferring private rights of action directly from federal statutes. See generally Chapter IX, Section 4, which deals at length with the enforcement of non-constitutional rights under § 1983.

Page 220, add a new Note 2(iii):

(iii) ***Hui v. Castaneda.*** When Francisco Castaneda was detained by the U.S. Immigration and Customs Enforcement, he brought to the attention of Public Health Service officers an irregular lesion on his penis. Despite frequent complaints, the lesion was not biopsyed for nearly a year, by which time the cancer was too far advanced for effective treatment. Three months before his death, Castaneda sued Dr. Ester Hui, the responsible physician, and others for deliberate indifference to serious medical needs in violation of his Fifth and Eighth Amendment rights. On the authority of Carlson v. Green, 446 U.S. 14 (1980), the Ninth Circuit approved a *Bivens* action, despite an alternative remedy against the United States under the Federal Tort Claims Act. Speaking through Justice Sotomayor, the Supreme Court unanimously reversed:

> Our inquiry in this case begins and ends with the text of 42 U.S.C. § 233(a). That statute provides in pertinent part:
>
>> [t]he remedy *against the United States* . . . for damage for personal injury, including death, resulting from the performance of medical, surgical, dental, or related functions . . . by any commissioned officer or employee of the Public Health Service while acting within the scope of his office or employment, *shall be exclusive of any other action or proceeding by reason of the same subject-matter against the officer or employee* (or his estate) whose act or omission gave rise to the claim (emphasis added).

Carlson was inapposite. It and subsequent cases had asked whether an implied right of action was available to remedy certain injuries. The question here was one of immunity from suit:

[handwritten margin note: Immunity question.]

> Even in circumstances in which a *Bivens* remedy is generally available, an action under *Bivens* will be defeated if the defendant is immune from suit. . . . As noted, the text of § 233(a) plainly indicates that it precludes a *Bivens* action against petitioners for the harm alleged in this case.

The Court did not otherwise call *Carlson* into question or suggest that it had been overruled.

Page 221, add at the end of Note 5:

For an article criticizing the case-by-case approach of current law and arguing for the presumptive availability of *Bivens* remedies, see James E. Pfander and David Baltimanis, Rethinking *Bivens*: Legitimacy and Constitutional Adjudication, 98 Geo. L.J. 117 (2009). Pfander and Baltimanis pay particular attention to post-*Bivens* legislation, which they interpret as reflecting Congress's desire to preserve and ratify the general availability of *Bivens* actions. For article on *Bivens* actions after 9/11, see Stephen I. Vladeck, National Security and *Bivens* after *Iqbal*, 14 Lewis & Clark L. Rev. 255 (2010). Vladeck argues that, contrary to the trend in recent decisions, "*Bivens* remedies are particularly appropriate in national security litigation, both because *other* defenses will preclude legal relief in appropriate cases and because the political process is less likely to provide its own remedies." And in the same symposium issue, Sheldon Nahmod argues that Ashcroft v. Iqbal, 556 U.S. ___ (2009), was correct in limiting supervisory liability to constitutional violations committed by the supervisors themselves (with whatever mens rea such violations require), as distinct from supervisory actions that permit or cause constitutional violations by others. See Sheldon Nahmod, Constitutional Torts, Over–Deterrence and Supervisory Liability After *Iqbal*, 14 Lewis & Clark L. Rev. 279 (2009).

Page 229, add new Notes 2 and 3 and renumber the remaining Notes:

2. The Alien Tort Statute. The Alien Tort Statute (ATS), also sometimes called the Alien Tort Claims Act, was first enacted in 1789 as part of the First Judiciary Act. Before *Filartiga*, the ATS successfully served as the basis for jurisdiction in only two reported cases—an admiralty case in the 1790s, and an international child custody case in the 1960s. There is almost no legislative history for the ATS, and its original purposes are uncertain. In 1975, Judge Henry Friendly, an expert on the jurisdiction of the federal courts, described the statute as "a kind of legal Lohengrin; although it has been with us since the first Judiciary Act ... no one seems to know whence it came." IIT v. Vencap, Ltd., 519 F.2d 1001, 1015 (2d Cir. 1975).

A variety of theories have been proposed about why the First Congress enacted the ATS. One common theory is that the ATS was designed to ensure the availability of a federal forum in certain tort cases in which the United States would have had an obligation under international law to provide an adequate means of redress. Commentators cite to an incident in 1784 involving an assault on a French ambassador in Philadelphia, in which the Continental Congress was concerned that state authorities might not adequately prosecute the case. If this theory accurately describes the original purpose of the ATS, is the assertion of jurisdiction in *Filartiga* consistent with this purpose? Was the United States responsible for providing redress for the tort in that case? As long as the text of the ATS fits the circumstances of that case, does the original purpose matter?

For discussion of this and other theories about the original meaning of the ATS, see Curtis A. Bradley, The Alien Tort Statute and Article III, 42 Va. J. Int'l L. 587 (2002); Anne–Marie Burley (Slaughter), The Alien Tort Statute and the Judiciary Act of 1789: A Badge of Honor, 83 Am. J. Int'l L. 461 (1989); William R. Casto, The Federal Courts' Protective Jurisdiction over Torts Committed in Violation of the Law of Nations, 18 Conn. L. Rev. 467 (1986); William S. Dodge, The Historical Origins of the Alien Tort Statute: A Response to the "Originalists," 19 Hastings Int'l & Comp. L. Rev. 221 (1996); Thomas H. Lee, The Safe Conduct Theory of the Alien Tort Statute, 106 Colum. L. Rev. 830 (2006); John M. Rogers, The Alien Tort Statute and How Individuals "Violate" International Law, 21 Vand. J. Transnat'l L. 47 (1988); Joseph Modeste Sweeney, A Tort Only in Violation of the Law of Nations, 18 Hastings Int'l & Comp. L. Rev. 445 (1995).

3. The Article III Issue in *Filartiga*. In order for a federal district court to exercise subject matter jurisdiction, the case must fall within both a federal statutory grant of jurisdiction and one of the "cases or controversies" listed in Article III. The statutory basis for jurisdiction in *Filartiga* was the ATS. What was the Article III basis? The Supreme Court has long held that suits between aliens, even aliens from different countries, do not satisfy even the minimal diversity of citizenship required for purposes of Article III diversity jurisdiction. See Mossman v. Higginson, 4 U.S. (4 Dall.) 12, 14 (1800). In *Filartiga*, both the plaintiffs and the defendant were citizens of Paraguay, so Article III diversity jurisdiction was not available. The Court in *Filartiga* concluded, however, that the case properly fell within Article III federal question jurisdiction because the law of nations had the status of federal common law. Is the court's treatment of the law of nations as federal common law consistent with the materials on federal common law in Section 1 of this Chapter?

Page 232, add a footnote at the end of Note 4:

g. For an argument that *Erie* has little relevance to the modern development of federal common law, including federal common law relating to CIL, see Craig Green, Repressing *Erie*'s Myth, 96 Cal. L. Rev. 595 (2008). For a response, see Bradford R. Clark, Federal Lawmaking and the Role of Structure in Constitutional Interpretation, 96 Cal. L. Rev. 699 (2008).

Page 235, delete Note 7 and replace with the following:

7. CIL as Post-*Erie* General Common Law? Most commentators now agree that, before *Erie*, customary international law (CIL)[k] was treated by the courts as part of the general common law. That is, CIL was viewed by both federal and state courts as a potential rule of decision in cases in which the courts otherwise had jurisdiction and there was no controlling contrary authority, but federal court interpretations of this law did not bind state courts and cases arising under this law did not on that basis arise under the laws of the United States for purposes of Article III. It was against this backdrop that the Supreme Court stated in The Paquete Habana, 175 U.S. 677, 700 (1900) (a decision relied upon by the court in *Filartiga*) that "international law is part of our law" and should be resorted to "where there is no treaty, and no controlling executive or legislative act or judicial decision."

Some commentators have argued that, despite *Erie*'s announcement that "[t]here is no federal general common law," CIL should continue to be treated by courts today as general common law. Ernest Young argues, for example, that CIL "should be viewed as 'general' law, just as it was in the nineteenth century under *Swift v. Tyson*," and that federal courts should apply it like they apply foreign law, based on conflict of laws principles. See

k. On pages 229–35 of the casebook, the abbreviation for customary international law was incorrectly written as "CIR" rather than "CIL." This error will be corrected in subsequent printings of the book.

Ernest A. Young, Sorting Out the Debate Over Customary International Law, 42 Va. J. Int'l L. 365, 467–68 (2002). Similarly, Alex Aleinikoff contends that CIL should be considered "nonpreemptive, nonfederal law," such that "[a] federal court decision on CIL would not bind states; it would simply announce the rule for the federal branches." T. Alexander Aleinikoff, International Law, Sovereignty, and American Constitutionalism: Reflections on the Customary International Law Debate, 98 Am. J. Int'l L. 91, 97 (2004). See also A. M. Weisburd, State Courts, Federal Courts, and International Cases, 20 Yale J. Int'l L. 1, 48–49 (1995).

What are the implications of adopting this conception of the domestic status of CIL? Under this conception, would the federal courts have the constitutional authority to exercise jurisdiction over a case, like the one in *Filartiga*, involving a suit between foreign citizens for a violation of CIL?

8. Supreme Court Citation of Foreign and International Materials. There has been significant debate in recent years, both among the Supreme Court Justices and among academic commentators, about the Court's citation of foreign and international materials in decisions interpreting the U.S. Constitution. In addition to death penalty decisions such as *Roper*, the Court cited such materials in a decision concerning gay rights, see Lawrence v. Texas, 539 U.S. 558 (2003), and Justice Ginsburg referred to such materials in a concurrence in a decision concerning affirmative action, see Grutter v. Bollinger, 539 U.S. 306, 344 (2003). In a sense, these decisions allow for a more significant role for international custom in the U.S. legal system than the "modern position" described in the prior notes, since, unlike a federal common law decision, a decision interpreting the Constitution cannot be overridden by Congress. On the other hand, the Court has so far looked to foreign and international materials only for non-binding guidance when interpreting the Constitution and has not suggested that courts are obligated to apply these materials to displace U.S. law.

After several years of relative silence on this issue, the Court returned to it in Graham v. Florida, 560 U.S. ___ (2010). In an opinion by Justice Kennedy, the Court held that it violates the Eighth Amendment's ban on cruel and unusual punishments to impose life imprisonment without parole on a juvenile for a non-homicide offense. Near the end of the opinion, the Court included a section that drew support from the fact that, "in continuing to impose life without parole sentences on juveniles who did not commit homicide, the United States adheres to a sentencing practice rejected the world over." The Court made clear that "[t]his observation does not control our decision." But it noted that in past cases it had "looked beyond our Nation's borders for support for its independent conclusion that a particular punishment is cruel and unusual" and said that "[t]oday we continue that longstanding practice in noting the global consensus against the sentencing practice in question." Justice Thomas, joined by Justices Scalia and Alito, dissented, stating in a footnote that foreign laws and sentencing practices are "irrelevant to the meaning of our Constitution or the Court's discernment of any longstanding tradition in *this* Nation."

Critics of the Court's reliance on these materials contend that although the materials might be relevant to the *design* of a constitution, they are not relevant to the *interpretation* of a constitution, especially a longstanding written constitution like the one in the United States. They also contend that the Court is haphazard and selective in its reliance on foreign and international materials—ignoring them, for example, in cases concerning abortion rights and freedom of speech, where foreign law tends to be more restrictive. Supporters of the Court's reliance on such materials respond that such reliance is not a new phenomenon and that the Court has in fact looked to foreign and international materials in constitutional interpretation since early in the Court's history. They also note that constitutional interpretation often involves pragmatic judgments, and they argue that, in making such judgments, the Court can benefit from the views and experiences of other countries that have addressed similar issues.

Justice Scalia has been a particularly vigorous opponent of the citation of foreign and international materials in constitutional interpretation, while at the same time acknowledging that such materials might be relevant in other contexts, such as when interpreting a treaty. During their confirmation hearings, both Chief Justice Roberts and Justice Alito were asked about the Court's citation of foreign and international materials in constitutional interpretation, and both were critical of the practice. There have been a number of proposals in Congress to prohibit the Court from relying on such materials, but no such legislation has yet been enacted. Would such legislation be constitutional? Can Congress regulate what the Court looks to and cites in its constitutional decisions?

Numerous articles have been written about this controversy. For articles critical of the Court's reliance on foreign and international materials, see, for example, Roger P. Alford, Misusing International Sources to Interpret the Constitution, 98 Am. J. Int'l L. 57 (2004); Kenneth Anderson, Foreign Law and the U.S. Constitution, Pol'y Rev., June & July 2005, at 33; Robert J. Delahunty & John Yoo, Against Foreign Law, 29 Harv. J.L. & Pub. Pol'y 291 (2005); John O. McGinnis, Foreign to Our Constitution, 100 Nw. U.L. Rev. 303 (2006); and Ernest A. Young, Foreign Law and the Denominator Problem, 119 Harv. L. Rev. 148 (2005). For articles that are more supportive, see, for example, Sarah H. Cleveland, Our International Constitution, 31 Yale J. Int'l 1 (2006); Daniel A. Farber, The Supreme Court, the Law of Nations, and Citations of Foreign Law: The Lessons of History, 95 Cal. L. Rev. 1335 (2007); Gerald L. Neuman, The Uses of International Law in Constitutional Interpretation, 98 Am. J. Int'l L. 82 (2004); Austen L. Parrish, Storm in a Teacup: The U.S. Supreme Court's Use of Foreign Law, 2007 U. Ill. L. Rev. 637 (2007); and Mark Tushnet, When is Knowing Less Better than Knowing More? Unpacking the Controversy over Supreme Court Reference to Non–U.S. Law, 90 Minn. L. Rev.

1275 (2006); Stephen Yeazell, When and How U.S. Courts Should Cite Foreign Law, 26 Const. Comm. 59 (2009).

Page 236, renumber Note 8 as Note 9, and insert at the end:

For yet another perspective on the debate over the domestic status of CIL, see Anthony J. Bellia Jr. & Bradford R. Clark, The Federal Common Law of Nations, 109 Colum. L. Rev. 1 (2009). Bellia and Clark posit an "allocation of powers approach" to the status of CIL in the U.S. legal system. They explain that, throughout much of U.S. history, the Supreme Court enforced other nations' "perfect rights" under CIL (and close analogues to those rights), which involved rights relating to territorial sovereignty, the conduct of diplomatic relations, treaty obligations, and freedom on the seas. They further explain that the breach of such rights was historically a just cause for war, and they argue that the Court enforced them in order to ensure that the decision to commit the United States to war would rest exclusively with the federal political branches, not the judiciary or the states. By their account, the Court applied CIL not because it was viewed as inherently part of federal law, but rather because its application in these contexts was thought to be required by the Constitution's allocation of powers to Congress and the executive branch. When viewed in historical context, they contend, "the best reading of Supreme Court precedent . . . is that the law of nations does not apply as preemptive federal law by virtue of any general Article III power to fashion federal common law, but only when necessary to preserve and implement distinct Article I and Article II powers to recognize foreign nations, conduct foreign relations, and decide momentous questions of war and peace."

Page 255, delete footnote a and add the following:

NOTES ON *SOSA v. ALVAREZ–MACHAIN*

1. Questions and Comments on Sosa. All nine Justices in *Sosa* agreed that the Alien Tort Statute (ATS) is a "strictly jurisdictional" statute that does not by itself confer a cause of action. On what basis, therefore, did the majority find that the ATS authorizes a cause of action for a "relatively modest set" of claims involving violations of the law of nations? The majority concluded that, when the ATS was first enacted in 1789, Congress would have assumed that some law of nations claims could have been brought without the need for a statutory cause of action. In applying the ATS today, should the Court be attempting to give effect to a congressional assumption about, in the Court's words, the "interaction between the ATS at the time of its enactment and the ambient law of the era"? Or do the arguments for judicial caution, also recited by the majority, suggest that Congress should be required to update the ATS before it is used as a vehicle for redressing modern violations of the law of nations?

Does the fact that Congress had not acted to disapprove the *Filartiga* line of cases suggest that it had acquiesced in the modern uses of the ATS?

After *Sosa*, when should courts recognize a cause of action in an ATS case? The Court stated that a cause of action should not be recognized under the ATS "for violations of any international law norm with less definite content and acceptance among civilized nations than the historical paradigms familiar when [the ATS] was enacted." Does this test provide enough guidance to the lower courts? Will the test ensure, as the Court claims, that the use of the ATS will be limited to a "narrow class" of causes of action?

2. Implications of *Sosa* for the Domestic Status of CIL. What, if anything, does *Sosa* suggest about the domestic status of the law of nations, or customary international law (CIL), outside the context of ATS litigation? Some commentators have argued that *Sosa* provides support for the "modern position" that all of CIL has the status of post-*Erie* federal common law. See, e.g., Ralph G. Steinhardt, Laying One Bankrupt Critique to Rest: *Sosa v. Alvarez–Machain* and the Future of International Human Rights Litigation in U.S. Courts, 57 Vand. L. Rev. 2241, 2255 (2004). Professors Bradley, Goldsmith, and Moore argue, by contrast, that "the decision in *Sosa* cannot reasonably be read as embracing the modern position and, indeed, is best read as rejecting it." Curtis A. Bradley, Jack L. Goldsmith & David H. Moore, *Sosa*, Customary International Law, and the Continuing Relevance of *Erie*, 120 Harv. L. Rev. 869, 873 (2007). Among other things, these authors contend that "[c]ommentators who construe *Sosa* as embracing the modern position have confounded the automatic incorporation of CIL as domestic federal law in the absence of congressional authorization (that is, the modern position) with the entirely different issue of whether and to what extent a particular statute, the Alien Tort Statute (ATS), authorizes courts to apply CIL as domestic federal law." These authors make clear that they do not call for a rejection of all judicial incorporation of CIL into federal common law, but they believe that "courts can domesticate CIL only in accordance with the requirements and limitations of post-*Erie* federal common law," limitations that the authors maintain were reaffirmed by the Court in *Sosa*. For commentary on the Bradley/Goldsmith/Moore article, see William S. Dodge, Customary International Law and the Question of Legitimacy, 120 Harv. L. Rev. F. 19 (2007), and Ernest A. Young, *Sosa* and the Retail Incorporation of International Law, 120 Harv. L. Rev. F. 28 (2007).

3. Suits Against Corporations Under the ATS. In recent years, a number of ATS suits have been brought against private corporations, on the theory that they either violated one of the few international human rights norms that apply to private actors (such as the prohibition on slavery) or that they "aided and abetted" violations of international human rights law committed by foreign governments. The allegations in these cases vary from case to case and range from merely doing business with an oppressive regime to knowingly participating in abuses. Should these corporate ATS cases be allowed under *Sosa*? Or should courts insist on more express authorization from Congress before allowing such suits?

The aiding and abetting basis for liability has the potential to substantially expand the scope of ATS litigation, since corporations often have business and investment projects in countries with less than stellar human rights practices. To date, most courts have been receptive to this theory of liability, although they have struggled with articulating the proper standard. A prominent example is Khulumani v. Barclay National Bank Ltd., 504 F.3d 254 (2d Cir. 2007). That case involved class action lawsuits brought under the ATS against a variety of corporations that did business in South Africa during that country's racist apartheid regime. The plaintiffs sought to hold the corporations liable for having aided and abetted the regime's human rights violations. The Supreme Court referred specifically to the proceedings in this case in footnote 21 of its decision in *Sosa*.

After *Sosa*, the District Court in the South Africa case dismissed the aiding and abetting claims, reasoning that the allowance of such claims would not be consistent with the cautious approach to ATS liability mandated by the Supreme Court. On appeal, however, the Second Circuit reversed, in a 2–1 decision. The two judges in the majority wrote separate opinions because, while they agreed that the aiding and abetting claims should be allowed to go forward, they disagreed over the standard that should be applied in determining aiding and abetting liability. One judge argued that the aiding and abetting standard should be derived from international law, in particular the standard for criminal aiding and abetting liability that is set forth in the treaty establishing the International Criminal Court. The other argued that the standard for aiding and abetting liability should be derived from domestic federal common law principles as reflected most notably in the Restatement (Second) of Torts. The dissenting judge contended that the aiding and abetting claims did not meet the test for ATS liability established in *Sosa* because there was no settled principle of international law holding corporations (as opposed to natural persons) liable for aiding and abetting, and also that the claims should be dismissed out of deference to the Executive Branch and the government of South Africa, both of which expressed opposition to the lawsuit.

The defendants in this case sought Supreme Court review of the Second Circuit's decision, and they were supported in their effort by an amicus curiae brief filed by the U.S. government. The Court nevertheless denied review, noting that it lacked a quorum to hear the case, apparently because four Justices had a conflict of interest as a result of ownership of stock in companies involved in the lawsuit. On remand, the District Court rejected the defendants' contention that the case should be dismissed based either on international comity towards South Africa or out of deference to the views of the Executive. See In re South African Apartheid Litigation, 617 F. Supp. 2d 228 (S.D.N.Y. 2009).

The Second Circuit subsequently clarified the aiding and abetting standard in Presbyterian Church of Sudan v. Talisman Energy, Inc., 582 F.3d 244 (2d Cir. 2009). In that case, a group of current and former residents of Sudan sued Talisman Energy, Inc., a Canadian corporation, under the ATS. The plaintiffs alleged that, in order to facilitate the development of oil concessions in Sudan by its affiliates, Talisman had either aided and abetted or conspired with the Sudanese government in actions that constituted genocide, war crimes, and crimes against humanity. The Second Circuit concluded that it should look to international law to determine the standard for accessorial liability under the ATS, and it found that international law supported this type of liability only when there is a showing that the defendant acted with the purpose of facilitating the underlying violations of international law. There was insufficient international consensus, the court reasoned, to support the imposition of broader liability based on mere knowledge of the underlying wrongdoing, and the court also expressed concern that a knowledge-based standard of liability would convert the ATS into "a vehicle for private parties to impose embargos or international sanctions through civil actions in United States courts." The court reviewed the plaintiffs' evidence and determined that it did not satisfy the "purpose" test, and, as a result, it affirmed a grant of summary judgment in favor of Talisman.

If followed by other courts (or approved by the Supreme Court), what effect is the approach in *Presbyterian Church* likely to have on ATS suits brought against corporations? How easy will it be for plaintiffs to satisfy the "purpose" test applied by the court?

For articles discussing the issue of corporate liability under the ATS, see, for example, Doug Cassel, Corporate Aiding and Abetting of Human Rights Violations: Confusion in the Courts, 6 Nw. U.J. Int'l Hum. Rts. 304 (2008), Chimene Keitner, Conceptualizing Complicity in Alien Tort Cases, 60 Hastings L.J. 61 (2008), and Michael D. Ramsey, International Law Limits on Investor Liability in Human Rights Litigation, 50 Harv. Int'l L.J. 271 (2009).

4. Foreign Official Immunity. In most situations involving alleged human rights abuses committed by foreign governments, the governments will have immunity from suit in U.S. courts pursuant to the Foreign Sovereign Immunities Act (FSIA), which provides that, subject to certain specified exceptions, "a foreign state shall be immune from the jurisdiction of the courts of the United States." Although tort cases are excepted, the exception applies only if the damage or injury from the tort occurs in the United States. As a result, instead of suing foreign governments directly, plaintiffs in ATS cases often sue the individual foreign officials who were allegedly involved in or responsible for the abuses. This is what happened in the seminal *Filartiga* case, for example, in which the plaintiffs sued a former Paraguayan police inspector. Until recently, courts had not given much consideration to the possibility that suits against foreign officials might be barred by principles of immunity. In part this was due to the fact that the FSIA makes no specific mention of suits against individual officials, and, in defining "foreign state," merely states that this term "includes a political subdivision of a foreign state or an agency or instrumentality of a foreign state."

Despite the lack of clear support in the text of the FSIA, a number of circuit courts in non-ATS cases came to the conclusion that a suit against a foreign official for conduct that was carried out in his or her official capacity is a suit against an "agency or instrumentality" of a foreign state and thus is covered by the FSIA's immunity provisions. The leading decision was Chuidian v. Philippine National Bank, 912 F.2d 1095 (9th Cir. 1990). In that case, a Philippine citizen brought suit against a member of a Philippine governmental commission, after the defendant had instructed a bank to dishonor a letter of credit that had been issued by a prior government of the Philippines. In concluding that the suit was governed by the FSIA, the Ninth Circuit noted that foreign officials had been entitled to immunity under the common law prior to the enactment of the FSIA, and the court reasoned that it would be "illogical" to think that Congress in the FSIA eliminated this immunity "implicitly and without comment." The court added that "to allow unrestricted suits against individual foreign officials acting in their official capacities [would allow] litigants to accomplish indirectly what the [FSIA] barred them from doing directly," and "would defeat the purposes of the Act." Several other circuit courts subsequently reached the same conclusion.

Eventually, some courts began applying this reasoning to ATS suits. For example, in a case brought under the ATS against a retired Israeli general for war crimes allegedly committed in Lebanon, the D.C. Circuit reasoned that "[a]n individual qualifies for [FISA] immunity when he acts in his official capacity for the state." Belhas v. Ya'alon, 515 F.3d 1279, 1283 (D.C. Cir. 2008). The court noted that in that case the plaintiffs had "only alleged acts done in [the general's] official capacity and have in no instance alleged acts that were either personal or private in nature." It also noted that Israel's ambassador had transmitted a letter to the court stating that the general's actions were carried out in the course of his official duties. The court concluded: "In light of the absence of any indication in the complaint that [the general] acted outside his scope of authority and the Israeli ambassador's statement that his actions were within the authority given to him by the State of Israel, [the general] qualifies for the immunity provided by the FSIA."

In Samantar v. Yousuf, 560 U.S. ___ (2010), however, the Supreme Court unanimously held that suits against individual foreign officials are not covered by the FSIA. In that case, a group of Somalis sued a former high-ranking Somali official under the ATS, alleging that during the 1980s the official exercised control over Somalia's military forces, and that these forces engaged in acts of torture, murder, and arbitrary detention. The defendant official argued that the suit was barred by the FSIA, either because the suit in effect was against the "foreign state" under the terms of the FSIA, or because the defendant qualified as an "agency or instrumentality" of the foreign state. In an opinion by Justice Stevens, the Court rejected these arguments. The Court found that there was insufficient evidence in the text of the FSIA to indicate that Congress intended to address suits against individual officials. While acknowledging that foreign officials had some immunity under the pre-FSIA common law, and that "in some circumstances the immunity of the foreign state extends to an individual for acts taken in his official capacity," the Court reasoned that "it does not follow from this premise that Congress intended to codify that immunity in the FSIA."

The Court described the pre-FSIA common law regime as involving a "two-step procedure":

> Under that procedure, the diplomatic representative of the sovereign could request a "suggestion of immunity" from the State Department. If the request was granted, the district court surrendered its jurisdiction. But "in the absence of recognition of the immunity by the Department of State," a district court "had authority to decide for itself whether all the requisites for such immunity existed." Ex parte Peru, 318 U.S. 578, 587 (1943).

The Court acknowledged that one of the purposes of the FSIA was "to transfer primary responsibility for deciding 'claims of foreign states to immunity' from the State Department to the courts," but it said that it had "been given no reason to believe that Congress saw as a problem, or wanted to eliminate, the State Department's role in determinations regarding individual official immunity."

The Court denied that its holding would allow plaintiffs to circumvent the FSIA through artful pleading:

> Even if a suit is not governed by the Act, it may still be barred by foreign sovereign immunity under the common law. And not every suit can successfully be pleaded against an individual official alone. Even when a plaintiff names only a foreign official, it may be the case that the foreign state itself, its political subdivision, or an agency or instrumentality is a required party, because that party has "an interest relating to the subject of the action" and "disposing of the action in the person's absence may ... as a practical matter impair or impede the person's ability to protect the interest." Fed. Rule Civ. Proc. 19(a)(1)(B). If this is the case, and the entity is immune from suit under the FSIA, the district court may have to dismiss the suit, regardless of whether the official is immune or not under the common law. See Republic of Philippines v. Pimentel, 553 U.S. 851, 867 (2008) ("[W]here sovereign immunity is asserted, and the claims of the sovereign are not frivolous, dismissal of the action must be ordered where there is a potential for injury to the interests of the absent

sovereign"). Or it may be the case that some actions against an official in his official capacity should be treated as actions against the foreign state itself, as the state is the real party in interest. Cf. Kentucky v. Graham, 473 U.S. 159, 166 (1985) ("[A]n official-capacity suit is, in all respects other than name, to be treated as a suit against the entity. It is *not* a suit against the official personally, for the real party in interest is the entity.").

Emphasizing the "narrowness" of its ruling, the Court remanded the case to the district court so that it could consider "[w]hether [the defendant] may be entitled to immunity under the common law, and whether he may have other valid defenses to the grave charges against him."

This decision leaves open a number of questions that the lower courts will now need to address. In particular, they will need to determine the scope of the common law immunity that the Court says was not superseded by the FSIA. In making that determination, one issue will be the extent to which principles of CIL should inform the common law of immunity. In *Samantar*, the Court said very little about international law, simply noting that "[b]ecause we are not deciding that the FSIA bars petitioner's immunity but rather that the Act does not address the question, we need not determine whether declining to afford immunity to petitioner would be consistent with international law."

Another issue will be how to distinguish between actions taken by foreign officials in their personal capacity from actions taken in their official capacity. On that issue, it may be relevant that the Court in *Samantar* cites as a "Cf." to Kentucky v. Graham, 473 U.S. 159 (1985). *Graham* was a domestic civil rights case in which the Court held that an attorney's fee award could not be imposed on a state based on the success of a suit brought against one of the state's officials in their personal capacity. The sentence from *Graham* that the Court quotes in *Samantar* came in the context of an effort to "unravel once again the distinctions between personal-and official-capacity suits," a distinction that the Court said "apparently continues to confuse lawyers and confound lower courts":

> Personal-capacity suits seek to impose personal liability upon a government official for actions he takes under color of state law. Official-capacity suits, in contrast, "generally represent only another way of pleading an action against an entity of which an officer is an agent." Monell v. New York City Dept. of Social Services, 436 U.S. 658, 690, n. 55 (1978). As long as the government entity receives notice and an opportunity to respond, an official-capacity suit is, in all respects other than name, to be treated as a suit against the entity. It is *not* a suit against the official personally, for the real party in interest is the entity. Thus, while an award of damages against an official in his personal capacity can be executed only against the official's personal assets, a plaintiff seeking to recover on a damages judgment in an official-capacity suit must look to the government entity itself.

Does this discussion in *Graham* clarify the distinction between personal-capacity and official-capacity suits? In any event, is it relevant to suits against foreign officials?

As the citation to *Graham* indicates, and as discussed in Chapter 8 of the casebook, potentially analogous issues of immunity arise in domestic civil rights litigation. State governments have broad immunity from private lawsuits under the Eleventh Amendment and related doctrines, but the Supreme Court has held that this immunity is not generally triggered by a lawsuit that is brought against a state official and seeks a damages award that will be enforceable only against the official's personal assets. This is true even if it is the state's policy to indemnify the official. If this jurisprudence were applied to suits against foreign officials, including international human rights suits brought under the ATS, it might suggest that there should be no immunity as long as the suit seeks only damages from the official. Domestic civil rights suits, however, do not present the same foreign relations and international law issues presented by suits against foreign officials. For consideration of these and other differences between domestic civil rights litigation and human rights litigation brought against foreign officials, see Curtis A. Bradley & Jack L. Goldsmith, Foreign Sovereign Immunity and Domestic Officer Suits, 13 Green Bag 2d 137 (2010).

5. Exhaustion of Remedies. Some defendants in ATS cases have argued that international law requires that a plaintiff exhaust local remedies before pursuing an action in a foreign court, and have sought to have U.S. courts apply this requirement. The Ninth Circuit considered this issue in Sarei v. Rio Tinto, PLC, 550 F.3d 822 (9th Cir. 2008) (en banc). In that case, former residents of Bougainville, Papua New Guinea, sued the Rio Tinto company under the ATS, alleging that, in connection with its mining operations in Bougainville, Rio Tinto was involved in or facilitated war crimes, crimes against humanity, racial discrimination, and environmental torts. In an en banc decision, the Ninth Circuit remanded the case to the district court for consideration of whether to dismiss the claims as a result of a failure to exhaust local remedies. The lead plurality opinion found that "certain ATS claims are appropriately considered for exhaustion under both domestic prudential standards and core principles of international law," but it declined to impose an absolute requirement of exhaustion in ATS cases. Instead, it reasoned that an exhaustion requirement should be applied as a "prudential" matter in cases that have little connection to the United States, "particularly—but not exclusively—with respect to claims that do not involve matters of 'universal concern.'"

For additional discussion of the issue of exhaustion in ATS cases, see Note, The Alien Tort Statute, Forum Shopping, and the Exhaustion of Local Remedies Norm, 121 Harv. L. Rev. 2110 (2008). For an extension of the idea outside the ATS context to a case involving an alleged expropriation of property, see Cassirer v. Kingdom of Spain, 580 F.3d 1048 (9th Cir. 2009).

6. Bibliography. For additional commentary on *Sosa* and its implications, see William R. Casto, The New Federal Common Law of Tort Remedies for Violations of International Law, 37 Rutgers L. J. 635 (2006); William S. Dodge, Bridging *Erie*: Customary International Law in the U.S. Legal System After *Sosa v. Alvarez–Machain*, 12 Tulsa J. Comp. & Int'l L. 87 (2004); William A. Fletcher, International Human Rights Law in American Courts, 93 Va. L. Rev. 653 (2007); Julian Ku & John Yoo, Beyond Formalism in Foreign Affairs: A Functional Approach to the Alien Tort Statute, 2004 Sup. Ct. Rev. 153; David H. Moore, An Emerging Uniformity for International Law, 75 Geo. Wash. L. Rev. 1 (2006); Pamela J. Stephens, Spinning *Sosa*: Federal Common Law, the Alien Tort Statute, and Judicial Restraint, 25 B.U. Int. L.J. 1 (2007); G. Edward White, A Customary International Law of Torts, 41 Val. U.L. Rev. 755 (2006); Note, An Objection to *Sosa*—And to the New Federal Common Law, 119 Harv. L. Rev. 2077 (2006).

CHAPTER III

CONGRESSIONAL CONTROL OF THE FEDERAL COURTS

Page 262, add at the end of footnote g:

And of course if Congress has exercised its lawful authority to narrow the scope of the rights being asserted, the jurisdiction-stripping issue is not difficult. For an elaboration of this proposition, see Howard M. Wasserman, Jurisdiction, Merits, and Non–Extant Rights, 56 U. Kan. L. Rev. 227 (2008).

Page 267, delete footnote c and replace with the following:

c. The only Supreme Court decision that arguably held unconstitutional an effort by Congress to make an "exception" to the Supreme Court's jurisdiction is United States v. Klein, 80 U.S. (13 Wall.) 128 (1871). *Klein* is exceedingly complex, and the Court's opinion is far from clear. The meaning of *Klein* is considered in the Notes following coverage of Plaut v. Spendthrift Farm, Inc., 514 U.S. 211 (1995), and Miller v. French, 530 U.S. 327 (2000), in Section 5 of this Chapter. Two of the articles cited there (by Lawrence Sager and Daniel J. Meltzer) appear in a symposium. Other articles in the symposium address issues covered in the materials currently under consideration. See Vicki C. Jackson, Introduction: Congressional Control of Jurisdiction and the Future of the Federal Courts— Opposition, Agreement, and Hierarchy, 86 Geo. L.J. 2445 (1998); David Cole, Jurisdiction and Liberty: Habeas Corpus and Due Process as Limits on Congress's Control of Federal Jurisdiction, 86 Geo. L.J. 2481 (1998); John Harrison, Jurisdiction, Congressional Power, and Constitutional Remedies, 86 Geo. L.J. 2513 (1998); Judith Resnick, The Federal Courts and Congress: Additional Sources, Alternative Texts, and Altered Aspirations, 86 Geo. L.J. 2589 (1998).

Page 276, add a footnote at the end of Note 5:

l. Using *Hamdan* as an illustration, Peter Smith argues that "the [Supreme] Court's self-professed textualists advance strict, textually based interpretations of jurisdictional statutes that eliminate or limit federal court jurisdiction; at the same time they remain willing to offer wholly atextual interpretations of jurisdictional statutes that appear to grant more expansive jurisdiction to reach the same conclusion." Peter J. Smith, Textualism and Jurisdiction, 108 Colum. L. Rev. 1883, 1911 (2008).

Page 277, add to the citations in the second sentence of footnote e:

William A. Fletcher, Congressional Power over the Jurisdiction of Federal Courts: The Meaning of the Word "All" in Article III, 59 Duke L.J. 929 (2010);

Page 282, add at the end of footnote r:

For an argument that the First Amendment limits the ability of Congress to exclude federal court jurisdiction over issues associated with public prayer, see Joseph Blocher, Amending the Exceptions Clause, 92 Minn. L. Rev. 971 (2008).

Page 284, add a new first paragraph at the end of Note 7:

For an elaborate discussion of many of the issues raised by Neuborne, see Gil Seinfeld, The Federal Courts as a Franchise: Rethinking the Justifications for Federal Question Jurisdiction, 97 Cal. L. Rev. 95 (2009). Seinfeld critiques what he calls the traditional "bias-uniformity-expertise" mantra and offers a "Federal Franchise" model as an explanation for the uniqueness of federal courts. Federal courts are best seen as a "chain of dispute resolution forums with a set of basic characteristics held in common across branches, regardless of the location in which any particular branch sits." This way of looking at it, he says, "shifts attention away from what federal judges might do *to federal law*, and directs it, instead, to the experience of the lawyer and litigant *in federal court*. . . . It carries the promise . . . of inverting the dynamics of insider and outsider status that might otherwise be in play."

Page 288, add a footnote at the end of Note 3:

d. For historical examination of the original meaning of "arising under" jurisdiction, see Anthony J. Bellia, Jr., The Origins of Article III "Arising Under" Jurisdiction, 57 Duke L.J. 263 (2007). Bellia pays particular attention to *Osborn v. Bank of United States* and concludes, contrary to the modern understanding, that the Marshall Court's decisions do not support extending "arising under" jurisdiction beyond cases where "federal law would be determinative of the right or title asserted in the federal proceeding."

Page 299, add to footnote b:

James E. Pfander, Protective Jurisdiction, Aggregate Litigation, and the Limits of Article III, 95 Cal. L. Rev. 1423 (2007); Carlos M. Vazquez, The Federal "Claim" in the District Courts: *Osborn*, *Verlinden*, and Protective Jurisdiction, 95 Cal. L. Rev. 1731 (2007); Ernest A. Young, Stalking the Yeti: Protective Jurisdiction, Foreign Affairs Removal, and Complete Preemption, 95 Cal. L. Rev. 1775 (2007).

Page 341, add at the end of Note 3:

Finally, for an ambitious article relating Article I courts to other constitutional issues, including standing, the doctrine of the political question, and the requirements of procedural due process, see John Harrison, The Relation Between Limitations on and Requirements of Article III Adjudication, 95 Cal. L. Rev. 1367 (2007).

Page 345, add the following Note:

6. Military Courts. As noted in Justice Brennan's plurality opinion in *Northern Pipeline*, the U.S. military has long used non-Article III courts to adjudicate criminal offenses committed by service personnel and others connected to the military. The jurisdiction and procedures of these "courts-martial" have historically been regulated by Congress, pursuant to its authority "to make Rules for the Government and Regulation of the land and naval Forces." U.S. Const., art. I, § 8, cl. 14. Since 1950, these regulations have been set forth in the Uniform Code of Military Justice, 10 U.S.C. § 801 et seq. Court-martial decisions are made by a panel of military officers. These decisions can be appealed first through the chain of command and then to the U.S. Court of Appeals for the Armed Forces, a non-Article III court composed of five civilian judges who serve fifteen-year terms. Decisions of that court can be reviewed by the Supreme Court on a petition for a writ of certiorari.

The Supreme Court has upheld the constitutionality of military courts-martial, reasoning that

> Congress has the power to provide for the trial and punishment of military and naval offences in the manner then and now practiced by civilized nations; and that the power to do so is given without any connection between it and the 3d article of the Constitution defining the judicial power of the United States; indeed, that the two powers are entirely independent of each other.

Dynes v. Hoover, 61 U.S. (20 How.) 65, 79 (1858). The Court has also held, however, that civilian U.S. citizens not employed by the military cannot be tried by courts-martial, even if they are dependents of a service member living with them on a military base abroad. See Reid v. Covert, 354 U.S. 1 (1957); Kinsella v. United States ex rel. Singleton, 361 U.S. 234 (1960). The Court has explained that "[t]he test for jurisdiction . . . is one of status, namely, whether the accused in the court-martial proceeding is a person who can be regarded as falling within the term 'land and naval Forces.' " *Kinsella*, 361 U.S. at 240–41.

A different type of military court is a "military commission." Unlike courts-martial, military commissions have not traditionally been regulated by Congress but rather have been established pursuant to the President's commander-in-chief authority. "Throughout U.S. history, military commissions have been used for three basic purposes: to administer justice in territories occupied by the United States; to replace civilian courts in parts of the United States where martial law has been declared; and to try enemy belligerents for violations of the laws of war." Curtis A. Bradley, The Story of Ex parte Milligan: Military Trials, Enemy Combatants, and Congressional Authorization, in Presidential Power Stories 95–96 (Christopher H. Schroeder & Curtis A. Bradley eds., 2009). These commissions were used extensively by the Union military during the Civil War and also in the occupied South during the Reconstruction period following the War. The Supreme Court held in 1866, however, that a civilian who is not connected to the military cannot be tried by a military commission in the absence of a valid declaration of martial law, reasoning that such a trial would violate both Article III and the jury trial rights of the accused. See Ex parte Milligan, 71 U.S. 2 (1866). During World War II, the Court upheld President Roosevelt's use of a military commission to try eight Nazi agents (including at least one U.S. citizen) for violations of the laws of war, after they had surreptitiously entered the United States with plans to commit sabotage. See Ex parte Quirin, 317 U.S. 1 (1942).

After the September 11, 2001 terrorist attacks in the United States, President George Bush authorized the use of military commissions to try certain non-U.S. citizens connected with terrorism. In 2006, however, the Supreme Court held that the military commission system that the Bush administration had established violated requirements that Congress had imposed on the use of military commissions—in particular, a requirement that "the rules applied to military commissions must be the same as those applied to courts-martial unless such uniformity proves impracticable." Hamdan v. Rumsfeld, 548 U.S. 557, 619 (2006). Congress responded to this decision by enacting the Military Commissions Act of 2006, which authorized the use of military commissions for certain terrorist detainees, detailed the procedures for these commissions, and defined the crimes that could be prosecuted before them. The new military commission system has been used in only a few cases, however, and when President Obama took office in January 2009 he suspended the use of the commissions. In 2009, after President Obama had taken office, Congress enacted a revised Military Commissions Act, which, among other things, increased the procedural protections for defendants.

For a description of the court-martial system, see Estela I. Valez Pollack, Military Courts Martial: An Overview, CRS Report for Congress (May 26, 2004), at http://www.fas.org/man/crs/RS21850.pdf. For discussion of the history of the use of military commissions, see David J. Bederman, Article II Courts, 44 Mercer L. Rev. 825 (1993); David W. Glazier, Note, Kangaroo Court or Competent Tribunal?: Judging the 21st Century Military Commission, 89 Va. L. Rev. 2005 (2003); Detlev F. Vagts, Military Commissions: The Forgotten Reconstruction Chapter, 23 Am. U. Int'l L. Rev. 231 (2008). For discussion of the use of military commissions in the war on terror, see Curtis A. Bradley & Jack L. Goldsmith, The Constitutional Validity of Military Commissions, 5 Green Bag 2d 249 (2002); Neal K. Katyal & Laurence H. Tribe, Waging War, Deciding Guilt: Trying the Military Tribunals, 111 Yale L.J. 1259 (2002); Detlev F. Vagts, Military Commissions: Constitutional Limits on Their Role in the War on Terror, 102 Am. J. Int'l L. 573 (2008).

Page 349, add a new Note 8 and renumber the remaining Notes:

8. Consent to Jury Selection by Magistrates. In Peretz v. United States, 501 U.S. 923 (1991), the Court, in a five-four decision, held that the Federal Magistrates Act permits magistrate judges to preside over jury selection in felony criminal trials if the parties consent. The Court reasoned that, to the extent defendants have a constitutional right to have an Article III judge preside over jury selection, they can waive that right, just as they can waive many other constitutional rights. Even if a litigant may not waive the structural protections provided by Article III, the Court was "convinced that no such structural protections are implicated by the procedure followed in this case." Noting that magistrates are appointed and subject to removal by Article III judges, and that the district court decides whether to invoke the magistrate's assistance and whether to empanel the jury selected by the magistrate, the Court concluded that "there is no danger that the use of the magistrate involves a 'congressional attempt "to transfer jurisdiction [to non-Article III tribunals] for the purpose of emasculating" constitutional courts. . . .' "

In Gonzalez v. United States, 553 U.S. 242 (2008), the Court held that the defendant's consent for this use of magistrates may be provided by the defendant's counsel, without any express consent by the defendant personally. The Court reasoned that "acceptance of a magistrate judge at the jury selection phase is a tactical decision that is well suited for the attorney's own decision. . . . Requiring the defendant to consent to a magistrate judge only by way of an on-the-record personal statement . . . would burden the trial process, with little added protection for the defendant." The only dissent came from Justice Thomas, who argued that *Peretz* should be overruled.

Page 350, add a new Section 4 and renumber the current Section 4 to Section 5:

SECTION 4: INTERNATIONAL TRIBUNALS

Medellin v. Texas

Supreme Court of the United States, 2008.
552 U.S. 491.

■ CHIEF JUSTICE ROBERTS delivered the opinion of the Court.

The International Court of Justice (ICJ), located in the Hague, is a tribunal established pursuant to the United Nations Charter to adjudicate disputes between member states. In the Case Concerning Avena and Other Mexican Nationals (Mex. v. U.S.), 2004 I.C.J. 12 (Judgment of Mar. 31) (*Avena*), that tribunal considered a claim brought by Mexico against the United States. The ICJ held that, based on violations of the Vienna Convention [on Consular Relations], 51 named Mexican nationals were entitled to review and reconsideration of their state-court convictions and sentences in the United States. This was so regardless of any forfeiture of the right to raise Vienna Convention claims because of a failure to comply with generally applicable state rules governing challenges to criminal convictions.

In Sanchez–Llamas v. Oregon, 548 U.S. 331 (2006)—issued after *Avena* but involving individuals who were not named in the *Avena* judgment—we held that, contrary to the ICJ's determination, the Vienna Convention did not preclude the application of state default rules. After the *Avena* decision, President George W. Bush determined, through a Memorandum to the Attorney General (Feb. 28, 2005), that the United States would "discharge its international obligations" under *Avena* "by having State courts give effect to the decision."

Petitioner José Ernesto Medellín, who had been convicted and sentenced in Texas state court for murder, is one of the 51 Mexican nationals named in the *Avena* decision. Relying on the ICJ's decision and the President's Memorandum, Medellín filed an application for a writ of habeas corpus in state court. The Texas Court of Criminal Appeals dismissed Medellín's application as an abuse of the writ under state law, given Medellín's failure to raise his Vienna Convention claim in a timely manner under state law. We granted certiorari to decide two questions. *First*, is the ICJ's judgment in *Avena* directly enforceable as domestic law in a state court in the United States? *Second*, does the President's Memorandum independently require the States to provide review and reconsideration of the claims of the 51 Mexican nationals named in *Avena* without regard to state procedural default rules? We conclude that neither *Avena* nor the President's Memorandum constitutes directly enforceable federal law that pre-empts state limitations on the filing of successive habeas petitions. We therefore affirm the decision below.

I

A

In 1969, the United States, upon the advice and consent of the Senate, ratified the Vienna Convention, and the Optional Protocol Concerning the Compulsory Settlement of Disputes to the Vienna Convention (Optional Protocol or Protocol). Article 36 of the Convention ... provides that if a person detained by a foreign country "so requests, the competent authorities of the receiving State shall, without delay, inform the consular post of the sending State" of such detention, and "inform the [detainee] of his righ[t]" to request assistance from the consul of his own state.

The Optional Protocol provides a venue for the resolution of disputes arising out of the interpretation or application of the Vienna Convention. Under the Protocol, such disputes "shall lie within the compulsory jurisdiction of the International Court of Justice" and "may accordingly be brought before the [ICJ] ... by any party to the dispute being a Party to the present Protocol."

The ICJ is "the principal judicial organ of the United Nations." United Nations Charter, Art. 92. It was established in 1945 pursuant to the United Nations Charter. The ICJ Statute—annexed to the U.N. Charter—provides the organizational framework and governing procedures for cases brought before the ICJ.

Under Article 94(1) of the U.N. Charter, "[e]ach Member of the United Nations undertakes to comply with the decision of the [ICJ] in any case to which it is a party." The ICJ's jurisdiction in any particular case, however, is dependent upon the consent of the parties. The ICJ Statute delineates two ways in which a nation may consent to ICJ jurisdiction: It may consent generally to jurisdiction on any question arising under a treaty or general international law, or it may consent specifically to jurisdiction over a particular category of cases or disputes pursuant to a separate treaty. The United States originally consented to the general jurisdiction of the ICJ ... in 1946. The United States withdrew from general ICJ jurisdiction in 1985. By ratifying the Optional Protocol to the Vienna Convention, the United States consented to the specific jurisdiction of the ICJ with respect to claims arising out of the Vienna Convention. On March 7, 2005, subsequent to the ICJ's judgment in *Avena*, the United States gave notice of withdrawal from the Optional Protocol to the Vienna Convention. ...

II

Medellin first contends that the ICJ's judgment in *Avena* constitutes a "binding" obligation on the state and federal courts of the United States. He argues that "by virtue of the Supremacy Clause, the treaties requiring compliance with the *Avena* judgment are *already* the 'Law of the Land' by which all state and federal courts in this country are 'bound.' " Accordingly, Medellin argues, *Avena* is a binding federal rule of decision that pre-empts contrary state limitations on successive habeas petitions.

No one disputes that the *Avena* decision—a decision that flows from the treaties through which the United States submitted to ICJ jurisdiction with respect to Vienna Convention disputes—constitutes an *international* law obligation on the part of the United States. But not all international law obligations automatically constitute binding federal law enforceable in United States courts. The question we confront here is whether the *Avena* judgment has automatic *domestic* legal effect such that the judgment of its own force applies in state and federal courts.

This Court has long recognized the distinction between treaties that automatically have effect as domestic law, and those that—while they constitute international law commitments—do not by themselves function as binding federal law. The distinction was well explained by Chief Justice Marshall's opinion in Foster v. Neilson, 27 U.S. 253 (1829), overruled on other grounds, United States v. Percheman, 32 U.S. 51 (1833), which held that a treaty is "equivalent to an act of the legislature," and hence self-executing, when it "operates of itself without the aid of any legislative provision." When, in contrast, "[treaty] stipulations are not self-executing they can only be enforced pursuant to legislation to carry them into effect." Whitney v. Robertson, 124 U.S. 190, 194 (1888). In sum, while treaties "may comprise international commitments ... they are not domestic law unless Congress has either enacted implementing statutes or the treaty itself conveys an intention that it be 'self-executing' and is ratified on these terms." Igartua–De La Rosa v. United States, 417 F.3d 145, 150 (1st Cir. 2005) (en banc) (Boudin, C. J.).[2]

---

2. The label "self-executing" has on occasion been used to convey different meanings. What we mean by "self-executing" is that the treaty has automatic domestic effect as federal law upon ratification. Conversely, a "non-self-executing" treaty does not by itself give rise to domestically enforceable federal law. Whether such a treaty has domestic effect depends upon implementing legislation passed by Congress.

A treaty is, of course, "primarily a compact between independent nations." Head Money Cases, 112 U.S. 580, 598 (1884). It ordinarily "depends for the enforcement of its provisions on the interest and the honor of the governments which are parties to it." ... Only "[i]f the treaty contains stipulations which are self-executing, that is, require no legislation to make them operative, [will] they have the force and effect of a legislative enactment." Whitney v. Robertson, 124 U.S. 190, 194 (1888).

Medellin and his amici nonetheless contend that the Optional Protocol, United Nations Charter, and ICJ Statute supply the "relevant obligation" to give the *Avena* judgment binding effect in the domestic courts of the United States. Because none of these treaty sources creates binding federal law in the absence of implementing legislation, and because it is uncontested that no such legislation exists, we conclude that the *Avena* judgment is not automatically binding domestic law.

A

The interpretation of a treaty, like the interpretation of a statute, begins with its text. Air France v. Saks, 470 U.S. 392, 396–97 (1985). Because a treaty ratified by the United States is "an agreement among sovereign powers," we have also considered as "aids to its interpretation" the negotiation and drafting history of the treaty as well as "the postratification understanding" of signatory nations. Zicherman v. Korean Air Lines Co., 516 U.S. 217, 226 (1996).

As a signatory to the Optional Protocol, the United States agreed to submit disputes arising out of the Vienna Convention to the ICJ. The Protocol provides: "Disputes arising out of the interpretation or application of the [Vienna] Convention shall lie within the compulsory jurisdiction of the International Court of Justice." Of course, submitting to jurisdiction and agreeing to be bound are two different things. A party could, for example, agree to compulsory nonbinding arbitration. Such an agreement would require the party to appear before the arbitral tribunal without obligating the party to treat the tribunal's decision as binding.

The most natural reading of the Optional Protocol is as a bare grant of jurisdiction. It provides only that "[d]isputes arising out of the interpretation or application of the [Vienna] Convention shall lie within the compulsory jurisdiction of the International Court of Justice" and "may accordingly be brought before the [ICJ] ... by any party to the dispute being a Party to the present Protocol." The Protocol says nothing about the effect of an ICJ decision and does not itself commit signatories to comply with an ICJ judgment. The Protocol is similarly silent as to any enforcement mechanism.

The obligation on the part of signatory nations to comply with ICJ judgments derives not from the Optional Protocol, but rather from Article

94 of the United Nations Charter—the provision that specifically addresses the effect of ICJ decisions. Article 94(1) provides that "[e]ach Member of the United Nations *undertakes to comply* with the decision of the [ICJ] in any case to which it is a party." (Emphasis added.) The Executive Branch contends that the phrase "undertakes to comply" is not "an acknowledgement that an ICJ decision will have immediate legal effect in the courts of U.N. members," but rather "a *commitment* on the part of U.N. Members to take *future* action through their political branches to comply with an ICJ decision."

We agree with this construction of Article 94. The Article is not a directive to domestic courts. It does not provide that the United States "shall" or "must" comply with an ICJ decision, nor indicate that the Senate that ratified the U.N. Charter intended to vest ICJ decisions with immediate legal effect in domestic courts. Instead, "[t]he words of Article 94 ... call upon governments to take certain action." Committee of United States Citizens Living in Nicaragua v. Reagan, 859 F.2d 929, 938 (CADC 1988). In other words, the U.N. Charter reads like "a compact between independent nations" that "depends for the enforcement of its provisions on the interest and the honor of the governments which are parties to it." *Head Money Cases*, 112 U.S., at 598.

The remainder of Article 94 confirms that the U.N. Charter does not contemplate the automatic enforceability of ICJ decisions in domestic courts. Article 94(2)—the enforcement provision—provides the sole remedy for noncompliance: referral to the United Nations Security Council by an aggrieved state.

The U.N. Charter's provision of an express diplomatic—that is, nonjudicial—remedy is itself evidence that ICJ judgments were not meant to be enforceable in domestic courts. See *Sanchez–Llamas*, 548 U.S., at 347. And even this "quintessentially *international* remed[y]," id., at 355, is not absolute. First, the Security Council must "dee[m] necessary" the issuance of a recommendation or measure to effectuate the judgment. Second, as the President and Senate were undoubtedly aware in subscribing to the U.N. Charter and Optional Protocol, the United States retained the unqualified right to exercise its veto of any Security Council resolution. . . .

If ICJ judgments were instead regarded as automatically enforceable domestic law, they would be immediately and directly binding on state and federal courts pursuant to the Supremacy Clause. Mexico or the ICJ would have no need to proceed to the Security Council to enforce the judgment in this case. Noncompliance with an ICJ judgment through exercise of the Security Council veto—always regarded as an option by the Executive and ratifying Senate during and after consideration of the U.N. Charter, Optional Protocol, and ICJ Statute—would no longer be a viable alternative. There would be nothing to veto. In light of the U.N. Charter's remedial scheme, there is no reason to believe that the President and Senate signed up for such a result.

In sum, Medellin's view that ICJ decisions are automatically enforceable as domestic law is fatally undermined by the enforcement structure established by Article 94. His construction would eliminate the option of noncompliance contemplated by Article 94(2), undermining the ability of the political branches to determine whether and how to comply with an ICJ judgment. Those sensitive foreign policy decisions would instead be transferred to state and federal courts charged with applying an ICJ judgment directly as domestic law. And those courts would not be empowered to decide whether to comply with the judgment—again, always regarded as an option by the political branches—any more than courts may consider whether to comply with any other species of domestic law. This result would be particularly anomalous in light of the principle that "[t]he conduct of the foreign relations of our Government is committed by the Constitution to the Executive and Legislative—'the political'—Departments." Oetjen v. Central Leather Co., 246 U.S. 297, 302 (1918).

The ICJ Statute, incorporated into the U.N. Charter, provides further evidence that the ICJ's judgment in *Avena* does not automatically constitute federal law judicially enforceable in United States courts. To begin with, the ICJ's "principal purpose" is said to be to "arbitrate particular disputes between national governments." *Sanchez–Llamas*, supra, at 355. Accordingly, the ICJ can hear disputes only between nations, not individuals. More important, Article 59 of the statute provides that "[t]he decision of the [ICJ] has *no binding force* except between the parties and in respect of that particular case." (Emphasis added.) The dissent does not explain how Medellin, an individual, can be a party to the ICJ proceeding.

Medellin argues that because the *Avena* case involves him, it is clear that he—and the 50 other Mexican nationals named in the *Avena* decision—should be regarded as parties to the *Avena* judgment. But cases before the ICJ are often precipitated by disputes involving particular persons or entities, disputes that a nation elects to take up as its own. That has never been understood to alter the express and established rules that only nation-states may be parties before the ICJ, and—contrary to the position of the dissent—that ICJ judgments are binding only between those parties. . . .

It is, moreover, well settled that the United States' interpretation of a treaty "is entitled to great weight." Sumitomo Shoji America, Inc. v. Avagliano, 457 U.S. 176, 184–85 (1982); see also El Al Israel Airlines, Ltd. v. Tsui Yuan Tseng, 525 U.S. 155, 168 (1999). The Executive Branch has unfailingly adhered to its view that the relevant treaties do not create domestically enforceable federal law. . . .

C

Our conclusion that *Avena* does not by itself constitute binding federal law is confirmed by the "postratification understanding" of signatory nations. There are currently 47 nations that are parties to the Optional

Protocol and 171 nations that are parties to the Vienna Convention. Yet neither Medellin nor his amici have identified a single nation that treats ICJ judgments as binding in domestic courts. In determining that the Vienna Convention did not require certain relief in United States courts in *Sanchez–Llamas*, we found it pertinent that the requested relief would not be available under the treaty in any other signatory country. So too here the lack of any basis for supposing that any other country would treat ICJ judgments as directly enforceable as a matter of their domestic law strongly suggests that the treaty should not be so viewed in our courts.

Moreover, the consequences of Medellin's argument give pause. An ICJ judgment, the argument goes, is not only binding domestic law but is also unassailable. As a result, neither Texas nor this Court may look behind a judgment and quarrel with its reasoning or result. (We already know, from *Sanchez–Llamas*, that this Court disagrees with both the reasoning and result in *Avena*.) Medellin's interpretation would allow ICJ judgments to override otherwise binding state law; there is nothing in his logic that would exempt contrary federal law from the same fate. And there is nothing to prevent the ICJ from ordering state courts to annul criminal convictions and sentences, for any reason deemed sufficient by the ICJ. Indeed, that is precisely the relief Mexico requested. . . .

Medellin and the dissent cite Comegys v. Vasse, 26 U.S. 193 (1828), for the proposition that the judgments of international tribunals are automatically binding on domestic courts. That case, of course, involved a different treaty than the ones at issue here; it stands only for the modest principle that the terms of a treaty control the outcome of a case. We do not suggest that treaties can never afford binding domestic effect to international tribunal judgments—only that the U.N. Charter, the Optional Protocol, and the ICJ Statute do not do so. And whether the treaties underlying a judgment are self-executing so that the judgment is directly enforceable as domestic law in our courts is, of course, a matter for this Court to decide.

D

Our holding does not call into question the ordinary enforcement of foreign judgments or international arbitral agreements. Indeed, we agree with Medellin that, as a general matter, "an agreement to abide by the result" of an international adjudication—or what he really means, an agreement to give the result of such adjudication domestic legal effect—can be a treaty obligation like any other, so long as the agreement is consistent with the Constitution. The point is that the particular treaty obligations on which Medellin relies do not of their own force create domestic law.

The dissent worries that our decision casts doubt on some 70–odd treaties under which the United States has agreed to submit disputes to the ICJ according to "roughly similar" provisions. Again, under our established precedent, some treaties are self-executing and some are not, depending on the treaty. That the judgment of an international tribunal might not automatically become domestic law hardly means the underlying treaty is "useless." Such judgments would still constitute international obligations, the proper subject of political and diplomatic negotiations. And Congress could elect to give them wholesale effect (rather than the judgment-by-judgment approach hypothesized by the dissent) through implementing legislation, as it regularly has.

Further, that an ICJ judgment may not be automatically enforceable in domestic courts does not mean the particular underlying treaty is not. Indeed, we have held that a number of the "Friendship, Commerce, and Navigation" Treaties cited by the dissent are self-executing—based on "the language of the[se] Treat[ies]." See *Sumitomo Shoji America, Inc.*, supra, at 180, 189–90. . . . Contrary to the dissent's suggestion, neither our approach nor our cases require that a treaty provide for self-execution in so many talismanic words; that is a caricature of the Court's opinion. Our cases simply require courts to decide whether a treaty's terms reflect a determination by the President who negotiated it and the Senate that confirmed it that the treaty has domestic effect.

In addition, Congress is up to the task of implementing non-self-executing treaties, even those involving complex commercial disputes. The judgments of a number of international tribunals enjoy a different status because of implementing legislation enacted by Congress. . . . Such language [in the relevant statutes] demonstrates that Congress knows how to accord domestic effect to international obligations when it desires such a result.

Further, Medellin frames his argument as though giving the *Avena* judgment binding effect in domestic courts simply conforms to the proposition that domestic courts generally give effect to foreign judgments. But Medellin does not ask us to enforce a foreign-court judgment settling a typical commercial or property dispute. Rather, Medellin argues that the *Avena* judgment has the effect of enjoining the operation of state law. . . .

. . . For the reasons we have stated, the *Avena* judgment is not domestic law. . . . The judgment of the Texas Court of Criminal Appeals is affirmed.

It is so ordered.

■ JUSTICE BREYER, with whom JUSTICE SOUTER and JUSTICE GINSBURG join, dissenting. . . .

[T]his Court has frequently held or assumed that particular treaty provisions are self-executing, automatically binding the States without more. . . .

Of particular relevance to the present case, the Court has held that the United States may be obligated by treaty to comply with the judgment of an international tribunal interpreting that treaty, despite the absence of any congressional enactment specifically requiring such compliance. See *Comegys v. Vasse*, 26 U.S. 193, 211–12 (1828) (holding that decision of tribunal rendered pursuant to a United States–Spain treaty, which obliged the parties to "undertake to make satisfaction" of treaty-based rights, was "conclusive and final" and "not re-examinable" in American courts); see also Meade v. United States, 76 U.S. 691, 725 (1870) (holding that decision of tribunal adjudicating claims arising under United States–Spain treaty "was final and conclusive, and bar[red] a recovery upon the merits" in American court). . . .

. . . I would find the relevant treaty provisions self-executing as applied to the ICJ judgment before us (giving that judgment domestic legal effect) for the following reasons, taken together.

First, the language of the relevant treaties strongly supports direct judicial enforceability, at least of judgments of the kind at issue here. The Optional Protocol bears the title "Compulsory Settlement of Disputes," thereby emphasizing the mandatory and binding nature of the procedures it sets forth. The body of the Protocol says specifically that "any party" that has consented to the ICJ's "compulsory jurisdiction" may bring a "dispute" before the court against any other such party. And the Protocol contrasts proceedings of the compulsory kind with an alternative "conciliation procedure," the recommendations of which a party may decide "not" to "accep[t]." Thus, the Optional Protocol's basic objective is not just to provide a forum for *settlement* but to provide a forum for *compulsory* settlement.

Moreover, in accepting Article 94(1) of the Charter, "[e]ach Member . . . undertakes to comply with the decision" of the ICJ "in any case to which it is a party." And the ICJ Statute (part of the U.N. Charter) makes clear that, a decision of the ICJ between parties that have consented to the ICJ's compulsory jurisdiction has *"binding force . . .* between the parties and in respect of that particular case." Enforcement of a court's judgment that has "binding force" involves quintessential judicial activity. . . .

I . . . recognize, as the majority emphasizes, that the U.N. Charter says that "[i]f any party to a case fails to perform the obligations incumbent upon it under a judgment rendered by the [ICJ], the other party may have recourse to the Security Council." And when the Senate ratified the charter, it took comfort in the fact that the United States has a veto in the Security Council.

But what has that to do with the matter? To begin with, the Senate would have been contemplating politically significant ICJ decisions, not, e.g., the bread-and-butter commercial and other matters that are the typical subjects of self-executing treaty provisions. And in any event, both the Senate debate and U.N. Charter provision discuss and describe what happens (or does not happen) when a nation decides *not* to carry out an ICJ decision. The debates refer to remedies for a breach of our promise to carry out an ICJ decision. The Senate understood, for example, that Congress (unlike legislatures in other nations that do not permit domestic legislation to trump treaty obligations) can block through legislation self-executing, as well as non-self-executing determinations. The debates nowhere refer to the method we use for affirmatively carrying out an ICJ obligation that no political branch has decided to dishonor, still less to a decision that the President (without congressional dissent) seeks to enforce. . . .

The upshot is that treaty language says that an ICJ decision is legally binding, but it leaves the implementation of that binding legal obligation to the domestic law of each signatory nation. In this Nation, the Supremacy Clause, as long and consistently interpreted, indicates that ICJ decisions rendered pursuant to provisions for binding adjudication must be domestically legally binding and enforceable in domestic courts *at least sometimes.* And for purposes of this argument, that conclusion is all that I need. The remainder of the discussion will explain why, if ICJ judgments *sometimes* bind domestic courts, then they have that effect here.

Second, the Optional Protocol here applies to a dispute about the meaning of a Vienna Convention provision that is itself self-executing and judicially enforceable. The Convention provision is about an individual's "rights," namely, his right upon being arrested to be informed of his separate right to contact his nation's consul. The provision language is precise. The dispute arises at the intersection of an individual right with ordinary rules of criminal procedure; it consequently concerns the kind of matter with which judges are familiar. The provisions contain judicially enforceable standards. And the judgment itself requires a further hearing of a sort that is typically judicial. . . .

Third, logic suggests that a treaty provision providing for "final" and "binding" judgments that "settl[e]" treaty-based disputes is self-executing insofar as the judgment in question concerns the meaning of an underlying treaty provision that is itself self-executing. Imagine that two parties to a contract agree to binding arbitration about whether a contract provision's word "grain" includes rye. They would expect that, if the arbitrator decides that the word "grain" does include rye, the arbitrator will then simply read the relevant provision as if it said "grain including rye." They would also expect the arbitrator to issue a binding award that embodies whatever relief would be appropriate under that circumstance.

Why treat differently the parties' agreement to binding ICJ determination about, e.g., the proper interpretation of the Vienna Convention clauses containing the rights here at issue? Why not simply read the relevant Vienna Convention provisions as if (between the parties and in respect to the 51 individuals at issue) they contain words that encapsulate the ICJ's decision? Why would the ICJ judgment not bind in precisely the same way those words would bind if they appeared in the relevant Vienna Convention provisions—just as the ICJ says, for purposes of this case, that they do? . . .

I am not aware of any satisfactory answer to these questions. It is no answer to point to the fact that in Sanchez–Llamas v. Oregon, 548 U.S. 331 (2006), this Court interpreted the relevant Convention provisions differently from the ICJ in *Avena.* This Court's *Sanchez–Llamas* interpretation binds our courts with respect to individuals whose rights were not espoused by a state party in *Avena*. Moreover, as the Court itself recognizes, and as the President recognizes, see President's Memorandum, the question here is the very different question of applying the ICJ's *Avena* judgment to the very parties whose interests Mexico and the United States espoused in the ICJ *Avena* proceeding. It is in respect to these individuals that the United States has promised the ICJ decision will have binding force. . . .

Nor does recognition of the ICJ judgment as binding with respect to the individuals whose claims were espoused by Mexico in any way derogate from the Court's holding in *Sanchez–Llamas*. This case does not implicate the general interpretive question answered in *Sanchez–Llamas*: whether the Vienna Convention displaces state procedural rules. We are instead confronted with the discrete question of Texas' obligation to comply with a binding judgment issued by a tribunal with undisputed jurisdiction to adjudicate the rights of the individuals named therein. . . .

Fourth, the majority's very different approach has seriously negative practical implications. The United States has entered into at least 70 treaties that contain provisions for ICJ dispute settlement similar to the Protocol before us. Many of these treaties contain provisions similar to those this Court has previously found self-executing—provisions that involve, for example, property rights, contract and commercial rights, trademarks, civil liability for personal injury, rights of foreign diplomats, taxation, domestic-court jurisdiction, and so forth. If the Optional Protocol here, taken together with the U.N. Charter and its annexed ICJ Statute, is insufficient to warrant enforcement of the ICJ judgment before us, it is difficult to see how one could reach a different conclusion in any of these other instances. And the consequence is to undermine longstanding efforts in those treaties to create an effective international system for interpreting and applying many, often commercial, self-executing treaty provisions . . .

Nor can the majority look to congressional legislation for a quick fix. Congress is unlikely to authorize automatic judicial enforceability of *all* ICJ judgments, for that could include some politically sensitive judgments and others better suited for enforcement by other branches: for example, those touching upon military hostilities, naval activity, handling of nuclear material, and so forth. Nor is Congress likely to have the time available, let alone the will, to legislate judgment-by-judgment enforcement of, say, the ICJ's (or other international tribunals') resolution of non-politically-sensitive commercial disputes. And as this Court's prior case law has avoided laying down bright-line rules but instead has adopted a more complex approach, it seems unlikely that Congress will find it easy to develop legislative bright lines that pick out those provisions (addressed to the Judicial Branch) where self-execution seems warranted. But, of course, it is not necessary for Congress to do so—at least not if one believes that this Court's Supremacy Clause cases *already* embody criteria likely to work reasonably well. It is those criteria that I would apply here.

Fifth, other factors, related to the particular judgment here at issue, make that judgment well suited to direct judicial enforcement. The specific issue before the ICJ concerned " 'review and reconsideration' " of the "possible prejudice" caused in each of the 51 affected cases by an arresting State's failure to provide the defendant with rights guaranteed by the Vienna Convention. This review will call for an understanding of how criminal procedure works, including whether, and how, a notification failure may work prejudice. As the ICJ itself recognized, "it is the judicial process that is suited to this task." Courts frequently work with criminal procedure and related prejudice. Legislatures do not. Judicial standards are readily available for working in this technical area. Legislative standards are not readily available. Judges typically determine such matters, deciding, for example, whether further hearings are necessary, after reviewing a record in an individual case. Congress does not normally legislate in respect to individual cases. Indeed, to repeat what I said above, what kind of special legislation does the majority believe Congress ought to consider?

Sixth, to find the United States' treaty obligations self-executing as applied to the ICJ judgment (and consequently to find that judgment enforceable) does not threaten constitutional conflict with other branches; it does not require us to engage in nonjudicial activity; and it does not require us to create a new cause of action. The only question before us concerns the application of the ICJ judgment as binding law applicable to the parties in a particular criminal proceeding that Texas law creates independently of the treaty. . . .

Seventh, neither the President nor Congress has expressed concern about direct judicial enforcement of the ICJ decision. To the contrary, the President favors enforcement of this judgment. Thus, insofar as foreign policy impact, the interrelation of treaty provisions, or any other matter within the President's special treaty, military, and foreign affairs responsibilities might prove relevant, such factors *favor,* rather than militate against, enforcement of the judgment before us. . . .

In sum, a strong line of precedent . . . indicates that the treaty provisions before us and the judgment of the International Court of Justice address themselves to the Judicial Branch and consequently are self-executing. In reaching a contrary conclusion, the Court has failed to take proper account of that precedent and, as a result, the Nation may well break its word even though the President seeks to live up to that word and Congress has done nothing to suggest the contrary.

For the reasons set forth, I respectfully dissent.

———————

NOTES ON INTERNATIONAL TRIBUNALS

1. Judicial Enforcement of Treaties. Article II of the Constitution provides that the President has the authority to make treaties "by and with the Advice and Consent of the Senate ... provided two thirds of the Senators present concur." The Supremacy Clause provides that such treaties (along with the Constitution itself and "Laws of the United States") "shall be the supreme Law of the Land; and the Judges in every State shall be bound thereby, any Thing in the Constitution or Laws of any State to the Contrary notwithstanding." And Article III provides that the judicial power shall extend to all cases arising under treaties.

Despite these provisions, it has long been settled that U.S. courts will enforce a treaty only if it is "self-executing." The doctrine of treaty self-execution is usually traced to Foster v. Neilson, 27 U.S. (2 Pet.) 253 (1829). That case involved an 1819 treaty between the United States and Spain that ceded certain disputed territory east of the Mississippi to the United States. The petitioners claimed title to a tract of land within that territory based on an 1804 grant from Spain, and on that basis sought to eject the respondent from the tract. The treaty provided in relevant part that all grants of land made by Spain in the ceded territory prior to the treaty "shall be ratified and confirmed to the persons in possession of the lands to the same extent that the same grants would be valid if the territories had remained under the dominion" of Spain. In concluding that U.S. courts should not give effect to the land grants protected by the treaty, the Court, in an opinion by Chief Justice Marshall, reasoned as follows:

> A treaty is in its nature a contract between two nations, not a legislative act. It does not generally effect, of itself, the object to be accomplished, especially so far as its operation is infra-territorial; but is carried into execution by the sovereign power of the respective parties to the instrument.
>
> In the United States a different principle is established. Our constitution declares a treaty to be the law of the land. It is, consequently, to be regarded in courts of justice as equivalent to an act of the legislature, whenever it operates of itself without the aid of any legislative provision. But when the terms of the stipulation import a contract, when either of the parties engages to perform a particular act, the treaty addresses itself to the political, not the judicial department; and the legislature must execute the contract before it can become a rule for the Court.
>
> The article [of the treaty] under consideration does not declare that all the grants made by [Spain] before the [treaty] shall be valid to the same extent as if the ceded territories had remained under [its] dominion. It does not say that those grants are hereby confirmed. Had such been its language, it would have acted directly on the subject, and would have repealed those acts of Congress which were repugnant to it; but its language is that those grants shall be ratified and confirmed to the persons in possession, etc. By whom shall they be ratified and confirmed? This seems to be the language of contract; and if it is, the ratification and confirmation

which are promised must be the act of the Legislature. Until such act shall be passed, the Court is not at liberty to disregard the existing laws on the subject.

Several years after *Foster*, the Supreme Court changed its mind about the effect of the treaty provision at issue there. After examining the Spanish version of the provision, the English translation of which provided that the grants of land "shall remain ratified and confirmed," the Court concluded that the provision was in fact self-executing. See United States v. Percheman, 32 U.S. (7 Pet.) 51, 88–89 (1833).

For additional discussion of the doctrine of treaty self-execution, see Curtis A. Bradley, Self–Execution and Treaty Duality, 2008 Supreme Court Review 131; Carlos Manuel Vázquez, Treaties as Law of the Land: The Supremacy Clause and the Judicial Enforcement of Treaties, 122 Harv. L. Rev. 599 (2008); Tim Wu, Treaties' Domains, 93 Va. L. Rev. 571 (2007).

2.   The International Court of Justice. The International Court of Justice (ICJ) is a fifteen-judge court that sits in The Hague, in the Netherlands. The ICJ was established by a treaty, the United Nations Charter, and is declared by the Charter to be the "principal judicial organ of the United Nations." Under Article 94(1) of the UN Charter, "[e]ach Member of the United Nations undertakes to comply with the decision of the International Court of Justice in any case to which it is a party." Under Article 94(2) of the Charter, if a party fails to perform the obligations imposed by an ICJ judgment, "the other party may have recourse to the [UN] Security Council, which may, if it deems necessary, make recommendations or decide upon measures to be taken to give effect to the judgment." The jurisdiction of the ICJ is regulated by another, related treaty— the Statute of the International Court of Justice. The United States became a party to both the Charter and the Statute in 1945.

The ICJ hears only disputes between nation-states, and only if the parties to the dispute have consented to the ICJ's jurisdiction. Nations can consent to the ICJ's jurisdiction in any one of three ways: by filing a declaration with the United Nations agreeing to be generally subject to the ICJ's jurisdiction "in relation to any other state accepting the same obligation"; by agreeing in a treaty to have disputes under the treaty resolved by the ICJ; or by agreeing at the time of a dispute to refer the dispute to the ICJ for resolution. For many years, the United States consented generally to the ICJ's jurisdiction, subject to certain limitations. The United States withdrew this general consent in 1985, however, after the ICJ exercised jurisdiction over a controversial case involving U.S. covert activities in Nicaragua.[a] Nevertheless, the United States is still a party to

---

a. The ICJ proceeded to rule against the United States on the merits in the Nicaragua case. The D.C. Circuit subsequently held that the obligation under Article 94 of the UN Charter to comply with the ICJ's judgment in that case was not self-executing. See Committee of United States Citizens Liv-

approximately 70 treaties that have clauses providing for ICJ jurisdiction over disputes arising under the treaties.

3. The Vienna Convention Litigation. The Vienna Convention on Consular Relations is a treaty that regulates the establishment and functions of consulates and the immunity of consular officials.[b] Article 36 of the Convention provides that, when one party country arrests someone from another party country, the arrested individual shall have the right to have their consulate notified of their arrest and to communicate with their consulate. It further provides that the arresting authorities "shall inform the person concerned without delay" of these rights. Finally, it provides that these rights "shall be exercised in conformity with the laws and regulations of the receiving State, subject to the proviso, however, that the said laws and regulations must enable full effect to be given to the purposes for which the[se] rights . . . are intended." The United States became a party to the Vienna Convention in 1969. At the same time, the United States also became a party to an Optional Protocol to the Convention that gives the ICJ jurisdiction to hear disputes arising under the Convention. Today, approximately 171 nations are parties to the Vienna Convention, and approximately 47 are parties to the Optional Protocol.

State and local law enforcement personnel in the United States have often failed to provide arrested foreign nationals with the notice required by Article 36 of the Vienna Convention. Starting in the late 1990s, a series of cases were brought against the United States in the ICJ seeking relief for these treaty violations. The first case was brought by Paraguay on behalf of Angel Breard, a Paraguayan national on death row in Virginia. Although the ICJ issued a preliminary order in that case requesting that the United States "take all measures at its disposal" to stay the execution while the ICJ adjudicated the dispute, Breard was executed on schedule, and Paraguay subsequently abandoned its suit. In declining to stay Breard's execution, the Supreme Court found that Breard had procedurally defaulted his Vienna Convention claim by failing to raise it in state courts. In Breard v. Greene, 523 U.S. 371, 375 (1998), the Court explained:

> [W]hile we should give respectful consideration to the interpretation of an international treaty rendered by an international court with jurisdiction to interpret such, it has been recognized in international law that, absent a clear and express statement to the contrary, the procedural rules of the forum State govern the implementation of the treaty in that State. This proposition is embodied in the Vienna Convention itself, which provides that the

ing in Nicaragua v. Reagan, 859 F.2d 929, 937–38 (D.C. Cir. 1988).

   b. Like embassies, consulates are official outposts of a nation (the "sending state") located in the territory of another nation (the "receiving state"). Whereas embassies handle political relations and are typically located in the receiving state's capital, consulates typically handle economic and trade issues, and also provide certain assistance to the sending state's nationals, and they often have locations outside the capital.

rights expressed in the Convention "shall be exercised in conformity with the laws and regulations of the receiving State," provided that "said laws and regulations must enable full effect to be given to the purposes for which the rights accorded under this Article are intended." It is the rule in this country that assertions of error in criminal proceedings must first be raised in state court in order to form the basis for relief in habeas. Claims not so raised are considered defaulted. By not asserting his Vienna Convention claim in state court, Breard failed to exercise his rights under the Vienna Convention in conformity with the laws of the United States and the Commonwealth of Virginia. Having failed to do so, he cannot raise a claim of violation of those rights now on federal habeas review.

The second case was brought by Germany on behalf of two German brothers on death row in Arizona, Walter and Karl LaGrand. Once again, the executions were carried out before the ICJ had resolved the dispute. Germany nevertheless persisted in its suit, and the ICJ eventually issued a final decision. In its decision, the ICJ held that the United States had violated the Vienna Convention and that in future situations in which German nationals "have been subjected to prolonged detention or convicted and sentenced to severe penalties," the United States would be required "to allow the review and reconsideration of the conviction and sentence by taking account of the violation of the rights set forth in the Convention." The ICJ also suggested that state authorities were responsible for any procedural default of the Vienna Convention claims, since they had failed to provide the requisite notice under Article 36. See LaGrand Case (Germany v. U.S.), ICJ, No. 104 (June 27, 2001), 40 I.L.M. 1069.

The third case, *Avena*, was brought by Mexico on behalf of 54 Mexican nationals on death row in a number of U.S. states. This time none of the individuals in question was executed during the pendency of the case. The ICJ ultimately concluded that the United States had violated the Vienna Convention with respect to 51 of the Mexican nationals. As in *LaGrand*, the ICJ held that, when there has been a violation of the Convention and severe penalties have been imposed, the United States is obligated to provide "review and reconsideration" of the defendant's conviction and sentence. The ICJ further explained that such review and reconsideration should "guarantee that the violation and the possible prejudice caused by that violation will be fully examined and taken into account in the review and reconsideration process." The ICJ also said that this review and reconsideration "should occur within the overall judicial proceedings relating to the individual defendant concerned." Finally, the ICJ suggested that U.S. procedural default rules should not be applied to bar review and reconsideration, at least in certain circumstances, because the application of such rules would deprive the rights in Article 36 from being given "full effect." See Case Concerning Avena and Other Mexican Nationals (Mexico v. U.S.), ICJ, No. 128 (Mar. 31, 2004), 43 I.L.M. 581.

Some months after the *Avena* decision, in February 2005, President Bush wrote a memorandum to the Attorney General stating that:

> I have determined, pursuant to the authority vested in me as President by the Constitution and the laws of the United States of America, that the United States will discharge its international obligations under the decision of the International Court of Justice in [*Avena*], by having State courts give effect to the decision in accordance with general principles of comity in cases filed by the 51 Mexican nationals addressed in that decision.

Shortly thereafter, the United States announced that it was withdrawing from the Optional Protocol that had given the ICJ jurisdiction to hear the Vienna Convention cases.

4. *Sanchez–Llamas v. Oregon.* In Sanchez–Llamas v. Oregon, 548 U.S. 331 (2006), the Court considered two consolidated cases involving foreign nationals who had not been advised of their rights under Article 36 of the Vienna Convention. In one of the cases, a Mexican national, Moises Sanchez–Llamas, was seeking to have incriminating evidence suppressed as a result of the treaty violation. In the other case, a Honduran national, Mario Bustillo, was seeking to obtain review and reconsideration of his conviction and sentence, despite state procedural default rules that would normally have barred the claim because it was not raised either at trial or on direct appeal. Neither Sanchez–Llamas nor Bustillo was among the 51 individuals directly covered by the *Avena* judgment.

In an opinion by Chief Justice Roberts, the Court held that, even assuming that Article 36 of the Vienna Convention is self-executing and confers judicially enforceable rights, suppression of evidence is not an appropriate remedy for violation of the Convention, and a state may apply its regular procedural default rules to a claim brought under the Convention. With respect to the suppression issue, the Court reasoned that "it would be startling if the Convention were read to require suppression," given that the exclusionary rule as applied in the United States "is an entirely American legal creation." The Court also reasoned that the justifications for the exclusionary rule are not substantially implicated in the consular notice context, since a violation of the treaty is unlikely to produce unreliable confessions, and the police will not be tempted to violate the treaty in order to obtain practical advantages. The Court further made clear that the creation of a suppression remedy in this context did not fall within the Court's supervisory powers, since the Court does not have supervisory power over the state courts. As a result, said the Court, "our authority to create a judicial remedy applicable in state court must lie, if anywhere, in the treaty itself."

With respect to the procedural default issue, the Court relied on its decision in *Breard* for the proposition that procedural default rules are not inconsistent with the Vienna Convention. The Court also rejected the argument that it was bound by the ICJ's conclusion in *LaGrand* and *Avena* that Article 36 of the Vienna Convention overrides procedural default rules. The Court explained:

> Under our Constitution, "[t]he judicial Power of the United States" is "vested in one supreme Court, and in such inferior Courts as the Congress may from time to time ordain and establish." Art. III, § 1. That "judicial Power ... extend[s] to ... Treaties." *Id.*, § 2. And, as Chief Justice Marshall famously explained, that judicial power includes the duty "to say what the law is." Marbury v. Madison, 1 Cranch 137, 5 U.S. 137, 160 (1803). If treaties are to be given effect as federal law under our legal system, determining their meaning as a matter of federal law "is emphatically the province and duty of the judicial department," headed by the "one supreme Court" established by the Constitution. Ibid. ... It is against this background that the United States ratified, and the Senate gave its advice and consent to, the various agreements that govern referral of Vienna Convention disputes to the ICJ.
>
> Nothing in the structure or purpose of the ICJ suggests that its interpretations were intended to be conclusive on our courts. The ICJ's decisions have *"no binding force* except between the parties and in respect of that particular case," Statute of the International Court of Justice, Art. 59 (1945) (emphasis added). Any interpretation of law the ICJ renders in the course of resolving particular disputes is thus not binding precedent *even as to the ICJ itself;* there is accordingly little reason to think that such interpretations were intended to be controlling on our courts. The ICJ's principal purpose is to arbitrate particular disputes between national governments. ... While each member of the United Nations has agreed to comply with decisions of the ICJ "in any case to which it is a party," United Nations Charter, Art. 94(1) (1945), the Charter's procedure for noncompliance—referral to the Security Council by the aggrieved state—contemplates quintessentially *international* remedies, Art. 94(2).
>
> In addition, "[w]hile courts interpret treaties for themselves, the meaning given them by the departments of government particularly charged with their negotiation and enforcement is given great weight." Kolovrat v. Oregon, 366 U.S. 187, 194 (1961). Although the United States has agreed to "discharge its international obligations" in having state courts give effect to the decision in *Avena*, it has not taken the view that the ICJ's interpretation of Article 36 is binding on our courts. Moreover, shortly after *Avena*, the United States withdrew from the Optional Protocol concerning Vienna Convention disputes. Whatever the effect of *Avena* and *LaGrand* before this withdrawal, it is doubtful that our courts should give decisive weight to the interpretation of a tribunal

whose jurisdiction in this area is no longer recognized by the United States.

The reasoning in *LaGrand* and *Avena* therefore were entitled only to "respectful consideration," said the Court. Even with that consideration, the Court concluded that the best interpretation of Article 36 was one that allowed for the application of procedural default rules.

Justice Breyer dissented, joined by Justices Stevens and Souter and joined in part by Justice Ginsburg. Breyer argued that suppression of evidence should not be ruled out as a remedy for a violation of Article 36 because it may sometimes be the only effective remedy, and Article 36 requires effective remedies. He further argued, based on the text and drafting history of Article 36 and the ICJ's decisions in *LaGrand* and *Avena*, that Article 36 should be interpreted as sometimes displacing state procedural default rules. *Breard* was not dispositive, he contended, because it concerned a federal rather than state procedural default rule, it predated *LaGrand* and *Avena*, and it was a per curiam decision issued under a compressed time schedule. While Justice Breyer accepted the "respectful consideration" standard applied by the majority, he suggested that the majority had failed to take sufficient account of the ICJ's expertise in matters of treaty interpretation and the desirability of having a uniform treaty interpretation.

5. Questions and Comments on *Medellin v. Texas*. Unlike *Sanchez–Llamas*, *Medellin* concerned an individual who was specifically covered by the ICJ's judgment in *Avena*. Should that difference have led to a different outcome? Note that, whereas the United States was not under a treaty obligation to accept the ICJ's *reasoning* in *Avena*, it was undisputed that it was under a treaty obligation to comply with the ICJ's *judgment*, which required that review and reconsideration be provided in the 51 cases covered by the judgment.

The majority in *Medellin* acknowledged that the ICJ's judgment in *Avena* was binding on the United States internationally, but it concluded that the judgment did not have domestic legal force because the treaty provisions requiring the United States to comply with the judgment were non-self-executing. On what basis did the Court find a lack of self-execution? Does the phrase "undertakes to comply" in Article 94(1) of the UN Charter suggest that the issue of compliance was to be determined by the political branches rather than the courts? Does the provision in Article 94(2) for enforcement of ICJ decisions by the Security Council suggest this?

In addition to finding textual and other evidence of non-self-execution, the majority in *Medellin* expressed concern about the policy implications of allowing ICJ judgments to have direct effect in U.S. courts. The Court noted that "Medellin's interpretation would allow ICJ judgments to override otherwise binding state law" and that "there is nothing in his logic that would exempt contrary federal law from the same fate." The Court further observed that "there is nothing to prevent the ICJ from ordering state courts to annul criminal convictions and sentences, for any reason deemed sufficient by the ICJ." If Article 94(1) of the UN Charter were construed to be self-executing, would these implications necessarily follow? Even if they would, did the United States in effect agree to give the ICJ this authority when the United States consented to allow the ICJ to resolve disputes arising under the Vienna Convention, which is a treaty and thus part of the supreme law of the land?

As discussed in Section 3 of this Chapter, in a series of domestic cases the Supreme Court has staked out rather uncertain boundaries on the proper use of non-Article III tribunals. International courts like the ICJ are non-Article III tribunals in the sense that their judges are not appointed pursuant to the senatorial consent process in the Constitution and do not have the tenure and salary protections of federal judges. Moreover, as *Sanchez–Llamas* and *Medellin* illustrate, the jurisdictional authority of these tribunals sometimes overlaps with the jurisdictional authority of the federal courts. What implications, if any, do the domestic non-Article III tribunal decisions have for the constitutionality of delegations of adjudicative authority to international tribunals like the ICJ? More generally, does the growth of international tribunals present a threat to the power and independence of the federal judiciary?

Medellin was executed by the State of Texas in August 2008, after the Supreme Court denied him a stay of execution. In denying the stay, the Court observed in a per curiam opinion that "[i]t is up to Congress whether to implement obligations undertaken under a treaty which (like this one) does not itself have the force and effect of domestic law sufficient to set aside the judgment or the ensuing sentence, and Congress has not progressed beyond the bare introduction of a bill in the four years since the ICJ ruling and the four months since our ruling. . . ." The Court also noted: "The Department of Justice of the United States is well aware of these proceedings and has not chosen to seek our intervention. Its silence is no surprise: The United States has not wavered in its position that petitioner was not prejudiced by his lack of consular access." See Medellin v. Texas, 554 U.S. 491 (2008).

For additional discussion of *Medellin* and its implications, see Curtis A. Bradley, Intent, Presumptions, and Non–Self–Executing Treaties, 102 Am. J. Int'l L. 540 (2008); Julian G. Ku, *Medellin*'s Clear Statement Rule: A Solution for International Delegations, 77 Fordham L. Rev. 609 (2008); Janet Koven Levit, Does *Medellin* Matter?, 77 Fordham L. Rev. 617 (2008); John T. Parry, A Primer on Treaties and § 1983 After *Medellin v. Texas*, 13 Lewis & Clark L. Rev. 35 (2009); Jordan J. Paust, *Medellin*, *Avena*, the Supremacy of Treaties, and Relevant Executive Authority, 31 Suffolk Transnat'l L. Rev. 301 (2008); John Quigley, President Bush's Directive to Foreigners Under Arrest: A Critique of *Medellin v. Texas*, 22 Emory Int'l L. Rev. 423 (2008); Paul B. Stephan, Open Doors, 13 Lewis & Clark L. Rev. 11 (2009); D.A. Jeremy Telman, *Medellin* and Originalism, 68 Md. L. Rev. 377

(2009); Carlos Manuel Vazquez, Less Than Zero?, 102 Am. J. Int'l L. 563 (2008).

6. The World Trade Organization. Another important international tribunal is the Dispute Settlement Body (DSB) of the World Trade Organization (WTO), which adjudicates trade disputes between the member countries using appointed panels and a standing Appellate Body. The DSB's decisions are binding, and, if the losing party does not comply with a decision, the DSB may authorize the prevailing party to impose trade sanctions on the losing party. The United States is a party to the relevant WTO treaties, and it regularly participates in cases before the DSB, both as a plaintiff and as a defendant. As defendant, the United States has lost a number of significant cases, including a case challenging clean air regulations issued by the Environmental Protection Agency, a case challenging U.S. limits on shrimp imports designed to protect sea turtles, and a case challenging U.S. tax treatment of foreign sales corporations. In 1994, while the United States was considering the WTO treaties, Congress approved a "Statement of Administrative Action," which provides that WTO decisions "have no binding effect under the law of the United States and do not represent an expression of U.S. foreign or trade policy." In subsequent legislation implementing the WTO treaties, Congress deemed this Statement "an authoritative expression by the United States concerning the interpretation and application of the [WTO] Agreements and this Act in any judicial proceeding in which a question arises concerning such interpretation or application." As a result, WTO decisions are regarded as non-self-executing in the U.S. legal system.[c]

In the absence of such legislative guidance, should courts (a) presume that international decisions are self-executing, (b) presume that such decisions are not self-executing, or (c) apply no presumption one way or the other? What, if anything, does *Medellin* suggest about this question?

7. NAFTA Arbitration. In 1993, the United States became a party, along with Canada and Mexico, to the North American Free Trade Agreement (NAFTA). NAFTA provides for two types of arbitration that may raise constitutional issues. First, Chapter 19 of NAFTA allows certain import decisions of member countries (relating to the application of "antidumping laws" and the imposition of "countervailing duties") to be reviewed by binational arbitral panels. These panels apply the standard of review and substantive law of the importing country, and their decisions are binding and final. Thus, in the case of the United States, the panels can

---

c. An additional complication with the WTO treaties is that, like the NAFTA treaty discussed in Note 7, infra, they were concluded as "congressional-executive agreements"—that is, they were concluded for the United States by the President and a majority of Congress, not the President and two-thirds of the Senate as specified in Article II. While there has been academic debate over the legitimacy of the congressional-executive agreement process, this process has been used for the vast majority of international agreements concluded by the United States since the late 1930s.

exercise final review over the application of U.S. trade law by the International Trade Commission (a federal administrative agency), whose decisions would otherwise be subject to review by the Court of International Trade, an Article III court. In situations in which a matter is referred by a panel back to the International Trade Commission, the Commission is bound by federal statute to "take action not inconsistent with the decision" of the panel. The panel members, however, need not be Article III judges, and their selection is not subject to the appointments process for such judges.

Does this scheme violate constitutional limitations on the use of non-Article III courts? Does it fall within the "public rights" category discussed in *Northern Pipeline*? Does the narrow and specialized nature of its jurisdiction help avoid constitutional concerns? The Chapter 19 arrangement has been challenged in U.S. courts on Article III and other constitutional grounds, but the challenges have to date been dismissed for lack of standing, see American Coalition for Competitive Trade v. Clinton, 128 F.3d 761 (D.C. Cir. 1997), and for lack of jurisdiction, see Coalition for Fair Lumber Imports v. United States, 471 F.3d 1329 (D.C. Cir. 2006).

Second, Chapter 11 of NAFTA requires each country to accord investors of the other two countries certain minimum standards of treatment, including protection against uncompensated expropriation. Investors who allege a violation of Chapter 11 may submit claims to a panel of three private arbitrators who can award monetary damages but not injunctive relief. A particularly interesting Chapter 11 case, brought in the late 1990s and resolved in 2003, concerned the treatment that a Canadian company, The Loewen Group, had received from Mississippi state courts. In that case, the owner of a funeral home in Mississippi had sued Loewen in a Mississippi trial court for unfair and deceptive trading practices and breach of contract. The plaintiff sought approximately $26 million in damages, but the jury awarded a total of $500 million, which included $400 million in punitive damages. Under Mississippi state law, Loewen was required to post a bond in the amount of 125 per cent of the judgment (i.e., $625 million) in order to appeal, and the Mississippi Supreme Court refused to waive that requirement. Loewen settled the case for $175 million.

In its Chapter 11 proceeding, Loewen alleged that the plaintiffs' attorneys in the Mississippi case had been allowed to appeal to anti-Canadian, racial, and class biases, and that these biases had affected the verdict. Loewen argued that the unfairness of the Mississippi proceedings and the bond requirement violated Chapter 11 because they constituted an expropriation of property, unequal treatment of a foreign company, and a denial of justice. Loewen sought damages in the amount of $725 million, which included not only what it paid out in the settlement but also compensation for business losses allegedly sustained as a result of the verdict. It sought these damages directly from the U.S. government rather than from Mississippi, since the United States, not Mississippi, is a party to

NAFTA, and nations are generally responsible under international law for the actions of their constituent states.

In a preliminary ruling on jurisdiction, the arbitration panel held that a nation's judicial proceedings may be challenged under Chapter 11. The panel noted that Chapter 11 applies to "measures adopted or maintained by a party," and that "measure" is defined by NAFTA as "any law, regulation, procedure, requirement or practice." The panel reasoned that these terms could reasonably be read as encompassing judicial decisions:

> "Law" comprehends judge-made as well as statute-based rules. "Procedure" is apt to include judicial as well as legislative procedure. "Requirement" is capable of covering a court order which requires a party to do an act or to pay a sum of money, while "practice" is capable of denoting the practice of courts as well as the practice of other bodies.

The panel further reasoned that allowing for challenges to judicial decisions would be consistent with the purposes of NAFTA, since judicial decisions, like other governmental acts, have the potential to undermine free trade and investment. Finally, the panel noted that construing Chapter 11 in this way would be consistent with international law principles, which generally hold nations responsible for the actions of their judicial organs. See Decision on Hearing of Respondent's Objection to Competence and Jurisdiction, The Loewen Group, Inc. and United States of America, Case No. ARB(AF)/98/3 (Jan. 5, 2001), at http://www.state.gov/documents/organization/3921.pdf.

The arbitration panel ultimately ruled in favor of the United States, however, because it concluded that Loewen's assignment of its NAFTA claims to a Canadian corporation owned and controlled by a United States corporation had destroyed the diversity of nationality required for NAFTA arbitration. The panel also concluded that the claims should be dismissed on the merits because the claimants had failed to show that they had no reasonably available and adequate remedy under United States law. While concluding that the trial and verdict in the Mississippi case "were clearly improper and discreditable and cannot be squared with minimum standards of international law and fair and equitable treatment," the panel noted that Loewen had failed to appeal the Mississippi trial court's decision either to the Mississippi Supreme Court or the U.S. Supreme Court, and it reasoned that "a court decision which can be challenged through the judicial process does not amount to a denial of justice at the international level." See Award, The Loewen Group, Inc. and United States of America, Case No. ARB(AF)/98/3 (June 26, 2003), at http://www.state.gov/documents/organization/22094.pdf.

When applied to review the fairness of U.S. judicial proceedings, does Chapter 11 constitute a delegation of Article III judicial power to an international body? Does it constitute a displacement of the Supreme

Court's role in the U.S. judicial system? Does it improperly undermine state judicial authority?

8. Other International Arbitration. In a number of instances throughout history, the United States has participated in international arbitration to resolve disputes with other countries. These disputes have sometimes concerned claims by the nations themselves and at other times have concerned claims by citizens of the respective nations. An early example of the use of such arbitration occurred in connection with the Jay Treaty of 1794, which established several arbitral tribunals to resolve claims between the United States and Great Britain, including claims by British creditors. Another prominent example was the Alabama Claims Arbitration after the Civil War, in which the United States sought damages against Great Britain for allowing British ports to be used during the War for the construction of Confederate ships. A more recent example was the establishment in 1981 of the Iran–United States Claims Tribunal, which, as part of the resolution of the Iranian hostage crisis, was charged with resolving various claims by U.S. citizens and companies against Iran as well as certain claims by Iran against the United States. In Dames & Moore v. Regan, 453 U.S. 654 (1981), the Supreme Court upheld presidential authority to suspend claims pending in U.S. courts and require that the claims be presented to this claims tribunal.

The dissent in *Medellin* refers to Comegys v. Vasse, 26 U.S. 193 (1828). In that case, Spain had agreed by treaty (in a different provision of the same treaty at issue in *Foster v. Neilson*, discussed above in Note 1) to pay up to a total of $5 million to resolve various damage claims by U.S. citizens. The treaty provided that the allocation of damage awards would be made by an arbitral commission consisting of three U.S. citizens, appointed by the President with the advice and consent of the Senate, that would sit in Washington, D.C. In *Comegys*, the Court observed, in an opinion by Justice Story, that:

> The object of the treaty was to invest the commissioners with full power and authority to receive, examine, and decide upon the amount and validity of the asserted claims upon Spain, for damages and injuries. Their decision, within the scope of this authority, is conclusive and final. If they pronounce the claim valid or invalid, if they ascertain the amount, their award in the premises is not re-examinable. The parties must abide by it, as the decree of a competent tribunal of exclusive jurisdiction. A rejected claim cannot be brought again under review, in any judicial tribunal; an amount once fixed, is a final ascertainment of the damages or injury.

Are the circumstances of that case distinguishable from those of *Medellin*?

Private parties also frequently agree to resolve their disputes through arbitration. The Federal Arbitration Act, 9 U.S.C. § 1 et seq., states that arbitration agreements are to be enforced like other contracts and provides for expedited judicial review to enforce arbitration awards. The Supreme Court has described this Act as "establish[ing] a national policy favoring arbitration when the parties contract for that mode of dispute resolution." Preston v. Ferrer, 552 U.S. 346 (2008). The United States is also a party to the New York Convention on the Recognition and Enforcement of Foreign Arbitral Awards, pursuant to which it is obligated to enforce arbitration judgments issued in the territory of other party nations, subject to narrow exceptions. Is dispute resolution by the ICJ analogous to such private-party arbitration, as suggested by the dissent in *Medellin*? For discussion of this issue, see Mark L. Movsesian, International Commercial Arbitration and International Courts, 18 Duke J. Comp. & Int'l L. 423 (2008), and Ernest A. Young, Supranational Rulings as Judgments and Precedents, 18 Duke J. Comp. & Int'l L. 477 (2008).

9. Enforcement of Foreign Judgments. Federal and state courts in the United States often enforce the civil judgments of other countries as a matter of comity. Before *Erie,* the standards for enforcing foreign civil judgments were regarded as part of the "general common law" that could be applied differently by federal and state courts. Today, the standards are generally regarded as matters of state law, which means that, pursuant to *Erie,* federal district courts asked to enforce foreign civil judgments look to the law of the state in which they sit. More than half the states have adopted the Uniform Foreign Money Judgments Recognition Act, which broadly allows for the enforcement of foreign civil judgments, subject to modest procedural and jurisdictional requirements. Other states enforce foreign civil judgments as a matter of state common law. Both in the Act and as a matter of common law, states may decline to enforce a foreign civil judgment if it violates some fundamental public policy of the state. For example, courts have declined to enforce libel awards from Great Britain because British libel law accords less protection to free speech than does the First Amendment (as it has been construed by the Supreme Court). See, e.g., Matusevitch v. Telnikoff, 877 F.Supp. 1 (D.D.C. 1995); Bachchan v. India Abroad Publications Inc., 585 N.Y.S.2d 661 (N.Y. Sup. Ct. 1992).

Are foreign civil judgments distinguishable from the judgments of international tribunals? If so, how? What does the majority say about this in *Medellin*? Should there be a public policy limitation on the enforcement of the judgments of international tribunals? Would such a limitation have addressed some of the concerns of the majority in *Medellin*?

Unlike foreign civil judgments, U.S. courts do not enforce foreign penal or revenue judgments. Judge Learned Hand explained the basis for this limitation:

> Even in the case of ordinary municipal liabilities, a court will not recognize those arising in a foreign state, if they run counter to the "settled public policy" of its own. Thus a scrutiny of the liability is necessarily always in reserve, and the possibility that it will be found not to accord with the policy of the domestic state.

This is not a troublesome or delicate inquiry when the question arises between private persons, but it takes on quite another face when it concerns the relations between the foreign state and its own citizens or even those who may be temporarily within its borders. To pass upon the provisions for the public order of another state is, or at any rate should be, beyond the powers of a court; it involves the relations between the states themselves, with which courts are incompetent to deal, and which are intrusted to other authorities. It may commit the domestic state to a position which would seriously embarrass its neighbor. Revenue laws fall within the same reasoning; they affect a state in matters as vital to its existence as its criminal laws. No court ought to undertake an inquiry which it cannot prosecute without determining whether those laws are consonant with its own notions of what is proper.

Moore v. Mitchell, 30 F.2d 600, 604 (2d Cir. 1929) (Hand, J., concurring), aff'd on other grounds, 281 U.S. 18 (1930). Is this explanation persuasive? For a critique of this limitation on the enforcement of foreign judgments, see William S. Dodge, Breaking the Public Law Taboo, 43 Harv. Int'l L.J. 161 (2002).

10. Bibliography. Ernest Young contends that insights about the proper relationship between domestic and international courts can be gleaned from the principles governing Federal Courts law, which have been developed to regulate the somewhat analogous relationship between federal and state courts. Ernest A. Young, Institutional Settlement in a Globalizing Judicial System, 54 Duke L.J. 1143 (2005). Young suggests that "[i]f we are now to graft another layer of courts onto this system—the ICJ, NAFTA and WTO panels, perhaps an International Criminal Court (ICC)—then we will need to develop a comparable set of tools to mediate the new set of conflicts that will surely arise." Young argues in particular that, in thinking about the relationship between international and domestic courts, more attention should be paid to the principle of "institutional settlement"—that is, the principle that "law should allocate decisionmaking to the institutions best suited to decide particular questions, and that the decisions arrived at by those institutions must then be respected by other actors in the system, even if those actors would have reached a different conclusion."

Curtis Bradley suggests that delegations of adjudicative authority to international institutions are more likely to raise constitutional issues than delegations of legislative or regulatory authority. "[W]hereas delegations of legislative or regulatory authority involve voluntary transfers of authority from the branches of government that would normally exercise that authority, with adjudicative delegations the political branches are delegating another branch's (i.e., the judiciary's) authority" and therefore "[a]rguments about institutional consent and accountability for the initial delegation are ... less applicable here." Curtis A. Bradley, The Federal Judicial Power and the International Legal Order, 2006 Sup. Ct. Rev. 59, 88.

Bradley also contends that, "as a predictive matter, one can expect that the federal courts will be more solicitous in preventing the loss of their own authority than that of the other branches. In other modern contexts, the Supreme Court has resisted what it has perceived as political branch challenges to its judicial authority."

Henry Monaghan argues, by contrast, that arbitral tribunals, such as the panels used under NAFTA "raise no serious problems under Article III and are sanctioned by an ancient lineage," and that the Supreme Court is unlikely to find that the Constitution limits international judicial review. Henry Paul Monaghan, Article III and Supranational Judicial Review, 107 Colum. L. Rev. 833, 842 (2007). He adds:

> While in the beginning of our constitutional history it was quite possible to claim that Our Federalism invested our national government with less legal authority in the international sphere than that possessed by other nation-states, any such conception has no purchase now. Indeed, the Court insists that the national government possesses an apparently freestanding "foreign affairs" power. That being the case, *and assuming here the general validity of supranational lawmaking*, it seems unlikely that the Court will understand the Constitution to seriously impede the manner by which supranational disputes are resolved. [Emphasis in original.]

Monaghan also observes that "the history of our jurisprudence governing the rise of the modern administrative state demonstrates that the factfinding and law-application functions of the district courts (except in criminal and common law trials) can be curtailed." While he notes that "one important systemic role for the Article III courts remains: the power to confine other organs of government within the bounds of their authority," he argues that "[i]f NAFTA-like arbitration processes compromise that function, they do so only at the margin."

For additional discussion of the issues raised by delegations of adjudicative authority to international tribunals, see Curtis A. Bradley, International Delegations, the Structural Constitution, and Non–Self–Execution, 55 Stan. L. Rev. 1557 (2003); Jim C. Chen, Appointments with Disaster: The Unconstitutionality of Binational Arbitral Review Under the United States–Canada Free Trade Agreement, 49 Wash. & Lee L. Rev. 1455 (1992); David M. Golove, The New Confederalism: Treaty Delegations of Legislative, Executive, and Judicial Authority, 55 Stan. L. Rev. 1697 (2003); Brian F. Havel, The Constitution in an Era of Supranational Adjudication, 78 N.C.L. Rev. 257 (2000); Julian G. Ku, The Delegation of Federal Power to International Organizations: New Problems with Old Solutions, 85 Minn. L. Rev. 71 (2000); Jenny S. Martinez, Towards an International Judicial System, 56 Stan. L. Rev. 429 (2003); Mark L. Movsesian, Judging International Judgments, 48 Va. J. Int'l L. 65 (2007); A. Mark Weisburd, International Courts and American Courts, 21 Mich. J. Int'l L. 877 (2000).

Page 350, delete Section 4, pages 350–75, and replace with the following:

SECTION 5: THE POWER TO REGULATE FEDERAL RULES OF DECISION AND JUDGMENTS

Plaut v. Spendthrift Farm, Inc.

Supreme Court of the United States, 1995.
514 U.S. 211.

■ JUSTICE SCALIA delivered the opinion of the Court.

The question presented in this case is whether § 27A(b) of the Securities Exchange Act of 1934, to the extent that it requires federal courts to reopen final judgments in private civil actions under § 10(b) of the Act, contravenes the Constitution's separation of powers or the Due Process Clause of the Fifth Amendment.

I

In 1987, petitioners brought a civil action against respondents in the United States District Court for the Eastern District of Kentucky. The complaint alleged that in 1983 and 1984 respondents had committed fraud and deceit in the sale of stock in violation of § 10(b) of the Securities Exchange Act of 1934 and Rule 10b–5 of the Securities and Exchange Commission. The case was mired in pretrial proceedings in the District Court until June 20, 1991, when we decided Lampf, Pleva, Lipkind, Prupis & Petigrow v. Gilbertson, 501 U.S. 350 (1991). *Lampf* held that "litigation instituted pursuant to § 10(b) and Rule 10b–5 . . . must be commenced within one year after the discovery of the facts constituting the violation and within three years after such violation." We applied that holding to the plaintiff-respondents in *Lampf* itself, found their suit untimely, and reinstated a summary judgment previously entered in favor of the defendant-petitioners. On the same day we decided James B. Beam Distilling Co. v. Georgia, 501 U.S. 529 (1991), in which a majority of the Court held, albeit in different opinions, that a new rule of federal law that is applied to the parties in the case announcing the rule must be applied as well to all cases pending on direct review. The joint effect of *Lampf* and *Beam* was to mandate application of the 1–year/3–year limitations period to petitioners' suit. The District Court, finding that petitioners' claims were untimely under the *Lampf* rule, dismissed their action with prejudice on August 13, 1991. Petitioners filed no appeal; the judgment accordingly became final 30 days later.

On December 19, 1991, the President signed the Federal Deposit Insurance Corporation Improvement Act of 1991. Section 476 of the Act—a section that had nothing to do with FDIC improvements—became § 27A of the Securities Exchange Act of 1934. It provides:

(a) Effect on pending causes of action

The limitation period for any private civil action implied under section 78j(b) of this title [§ 10(b) of the Securities Exchange Act of 1934] that was commenced on or before June 19, 1991, shall be the limitation period provided by the laws applicable in the jurisdiction, including principles of retroactivity, as such laws existed on June 19, 1991.

reinstates prior S.O.L.

(b) Effect on dismissed causes of action

Any private civil action implied under section 78j(b) of this title that was commenced on or before June 19, 1991—

(1) which was dismissed as time barred subsequent to June 19, 1991, and

(2) which would have been timely filed under the limitation period provided by the laws applicable in the jurisdiction, including principles of retroactivity, as such laws existed on June 19, 1991,

Reopens Fed. of A. Judgmts

shall be reinstated on motion by the plaintiff not later than 60 days after December 19, 1991.

On February 11, 1992, petitioners returned to the District Court and filed a motion to reinstate the action previously dismissed with prejudice. The District Court found that the conditions set out in §§ 27A(b)(1) and (2) were met, so that petitioners' motion was required to be granted by the terms of the statute. It nonetheless denied the motion, agreeing with respondents that § 27A(b) is unconstitutional. The United States Court of Appeals for the Sixth Circuit affirmed. We granted certiorari.

DC →

II

[In this section of its opinion, the Court examined the statutory language and concluded that "there is no reasonable construction on which § 27A(b) does not require federal courts to reopen final judgments in suits dismissed with prejudice by virtue of *Lampf*."]

III

Respondents submit that § 27A(b) violates both the separation of powers and the Due Process Clause of the Fifth Amendment. Because the latter submission, if correct, might dictate a similar result in a challenge to state legislation under the Fourteenth Amendment, the former is the narrower ground for adjudication of the constitutional questions in the case, and we therefore consider it first. We conclude that in § 27A(b) Congress has exceeded its authority by requiring the federal courts to exercise "the judicial Power of the United States," U.S. Const., Art. III,

∏'s Argue →

Violation of Sep. of Powers

§ 1, in a manner repugnant to the text, structure, and traditions of Article III.

Our decisions to date have identified two types of legislation that require federal courts to exercise the judicial power in a manner that Article III forbids. The first appears in United States v. Klein, 80 U.S. (13 Wall.) 128 (1872), where we refused to give effect to a statute that was said "[to] prescribe rules of decision to the Judicial Department of the government in cases pending before it." Whatever the precise scope of *Klein*, however, later decisions have made clear that its prohibition does not take hold when Congress "amend[s] applicable law." Robertson v. Seattle Audubon Soc., 503 U.S. 429, 441 (1992). Section 27A(b) indisputably does set out substantive legal standards for the Judiciary to apply, and in that sense changes the law (even if solely retroactively). The second type of unconstitutional restriction upon the exercise of judicial power identified by past cases is exemplified by Hayburn's Case, 2 U.S. (2 Dall.) 409 (1792), which stands for the principle that Congress cannot vest review of the decisions of Article III courts in officials of the Executive Branch. Yet under any application of § 27A(b) only courts are involved; no officials of other departments sit in direct review of their decisions. Section 27A(b) therefore offends neither of these previously established prohibitions.

We think, however, that § 27A(b) offends a postulate of Article III just as deeply rooted in our law as those we have mentioned. Article III establishes a "judicial department" with the "province and duty . . . to say what the law is" in particular cases and controversies. Marbury v. Madison, 5 U.S. (1 Cranch) 137, 177 (1803). The record of history shows that the Framers crafted this charter of the judicial department with an expressed understanding that it gives the Federal Judiciary the power, not merely to rule on cases, but to *decide* them, subject to review only by superior courts in the Article III hierarchy—with an understanding, in short, that "a judgment conclusively resolves the case" because "a 'judicial Power' is one to render dispositive judgments." Frank Easterbrook, Presidential Review, 40 Case W. Res. L. Rev. 905, 926 (1990). By retroactively commanding the federal courts to reopen final judgments, Congress has violated this fundamental principle.

A

The Framers of our Constitution lived among the ruins of a system of intermingled legislative and judicial powers, which had been prevalent in the colonies long before the Revolution, and which after the Revolution had produced factional strife and partisan oppression. In the 17th and 18th centuries colonial assemblies and legislatures functioned as courts of equity of last resort, hearing original actions or providing appellate review of judicial judgments. Often, however, they chose to correct the judicial process through special bills or other enacted legislation. It was common for such legislation not to prescribe a resolution of the dispute, but rather simply to set aside the judgment and order a new trial or appeal. ...

The vigorous, indeed often radical, populism of the revolutionary legislatures and assemblies increased the frequency of legislative correction of judgments. ... Voices from many quarters, official as well as private, decried the increasing legislative interference with the private-law judgments of the courts. ...

This sense of a sharp necessity to separate the legislative from the judicial power, prompted by the crescendo of legislative interference with private judgments of the courts, triumphed among the Framers of the new Federal Constitution. The Convention made the critical decision to establish a judicial department independent of the Legislative Branch by providing that "the judicial Power of the United States shall be vested in one supreme Court, and in such inferior Courts as the Congress may from time to time ordain and establish." ...

B

Section 27A(b) effects a clear violation of the separation-of-powers principle we have just discussed. It is, of course, retroactive legislation, that is, legislation that prescribes what the law *was* at an earlier time, when the act whose effect is controlled by the legislation occurred—in this case, the filing of the initial Rule 10b–5 action in the District Court. When retroactive legislation requires its own application in a case already finally adjudicated, it does no more and no less than "reverse a determination once made, in a particular case." The Federalist No. 81, p. 545 (J. Cooke ed. 1961). Our decisions stemming from *Hayburn's Case*—although their precise holdings are not strictly applicable here—have uniformly provided fair warning that such an act exceeds the powers of Congress. [E.g.,] Pennsylvania v. Wheeling & Belmont Bridge Co., 59 U.S. (18 How.) 421, 431 (1856) ("It is urged, that the act of Congress cannot have the effect and operation to annul the judgment of the court already rendered, or the rights determined thereby.... This, as a general proposition, is certainly not to be denied, especially as it respects adjudication upon the private rights of parties. When they have passed into judgment the right becomes absolute, and it is the duty of the court to enforce it"). Today those clear statements must either be honored, or else proved false.

It is true, as petitioners contend, that Congress can always revise the judgments of Article III courts in one sense: When a new law makes clear that it is retroactive, an appellate court must apply that law in reviewing judgments still on appeal that were rendered before the law was enacted, and must alter the outcome accordingly. See United States v. Schooner Peggy, 5 U.S. (1 Cranch) 103 (1801); Landgraf v. USI Film Products, 511 U.S. 244 (1994). Since that is so, petitioners argue, federal courts must apply the "new" law created by § 27A(b) in finally adjudicated cases as well; for the line that separates lower court judgments that are pending on appeal (or may still be appealed), from lower court judgments that are final, is determined by statute, see, e.g., 28 U.S.C. § 2107(a) (30–day time limit for appeal to federal court of appeals), and so cannot possibly be a *constitutional* line. But a distinction between judgments from which all appeals have been forgone or completed, and judgments that remain on appeal (or subject to being appealed), is implicit in what Article III creates: not a batch of unconnected courts, but a judicial *department* composed of "inferior Courts" and "one supreme Court." Within that hierarchy, the decision of an inferior court is not (unless the time for appeal has expired) the final word of the department as a whole. It is the obligation of the last court in the hierarchy that rules on the case to give effect to Congress's latest enactment, even when that has the effect of overturning the judgment of an inferior court, since each court, at every level, must "decide according to existing laws." *Schooner Peggy,* supra, at 109. Having achieved finality, however, a judicial decision becomes the last word of the judicial department with regard to a particular case or controversy, and Congress may not declare by retroactive legislation that the law applicable *to that very case* was something other than what the courts said it was. Finality of a legal judgment is determined by statute, just as entitlement to a government benefit is a statutory creation; but that no more deprives the former of its constitutional significance for separation-of-powers analysis than it deprives the latter of its significance for due process purposes.

To be sure, § 27A(b) reopens (or directs the reopening of) final judgments in a whole class of cases rather than in a particular suit. We do not see how that makes any difference. The separation-of-powers violation here, if there is any, consists of depriving judicial judgments of the conclusive effect that they had when they were announced, not of acting in a manner—viz., with particular rather than general effect—that is unusual (though, we must note, not impossible) for a legislature. To be sure, a general statute such as this one may reduce the perception that legislative interference with judicial judgments was prompted by individual favoritism; but it is legislative interference with judicial judgments nonetheless. Not favoritism, nor even corruption, but *power* is the object of the separation-of-powers prohibition. The prohibition is violated when an individual final judgment is legislatively rescinded for even the *very best* of reasons, such as the legislature's genuine conviction (supported by all the law professors in the land) that the judgment was wrong; and it is violated 40 times over when 40 final judgments are legislatively dissolved.

It is irrelevant as well that the final judgments reopened by § 27A(b) rested on the bar of a statute of limitations. The rules of finality, both statutory and judge made, treat a dismissal on statute-of-limitations grounds the same way they treat a dismissal for failure to state a claim, for failure to prove substantive liability, or for failure to prosecute: as a judgment on the merits. Petitioners suggest, directly or by implication, two reasons why a merits judgment based on this particular ground may be uniquely subject to congressional nullification. First, there is the fact that the length and indeed even the very existence of a statute of limitations upon a federal cause of action is entirely subject to congressional control. But virtually *all* of the reasons why a final judgment on the merits is rendered on a federal claim are subject to congressional control. Congress can eliminate, for example, a particular element of a cause of action that plaintiffs have found it difficult to establish; or an evidentiary rule that has often excluded essential testimony; or a rule of offsetting wrong (such as contributory negligence) that has often prevented recovery. To distinguish statutes of limitations on the ground that they are mere creatures of Congress is to distinguish them not at all. The second supposedly distinguishing characteristic of a statute of limitations is that it can be extended, without violating the Due Process Clause, after the cause of the action arose and even after the statute itself has expired. But that also does not set statutes of limitations apart. To mention only one other broad category of judgment-producing legal rule: Rules of pleading and proof can similarly be altered after the cause of action arises, *Landgraf* v. *USI Film Products,* supra, and even, if the statute clearly so requires, after they have been applied in a case but before final judgment has been entered. Petitioners' principle would therefore lead to the conclusion that final judgments rendered on the basis of a stringent (or, alternatively, liberal) rule of pleading or proof may be set aside for retrial under a new liberal (or, alternatively, stringent) rule of pleading or proof. This alone provides massive scope for undoing final judgments and would substantially subvert the doctrine of separation of powers. . . .

C

Apart from the statute we review today, we know of no instance in which Congress has attempted to set aside the final judgment of an Article III court by retroactive legislation. That prolonged reticence would be amazing if such interference were not understood to be constitutionally proscribed. The closest analogue that the Government has been able to put forward is the statute at issue in United States v. Sioux Nation, 448 U.S. 371 (1980). That law required the Court of Claims, " 'notwithstanding any other provision of law . . . [to] review on the merits, without regard to the defense of res judicata or collateral estoppel,' " a Sioux claim for just compensation from the United States—even though the Court of Claims had previously heard and rejected that very claim. We considered and rejected separation-of-powers objections to the statute based upon *Hayburn's Case* and *United States v. Klein.* The basis for our rejection was a line of precedent (starting with Cherokee Nation v. United States, 270 U.S. 476 (1926)) that stood, we said, for the proposition that "Congress has the power to waive the res judicata effect of a prior judgment entered in the Government's favor on a claim against the United States." . . .

The Solicitor General suggests that even if *Sioux Nation* is read in accord with its holding, it nonetheless establishes that Congress may require Article III courts to reopen their final judgments, since "if res judicata were compelled by Article III to safeguard the structural independence of the courts, the doctrine would not be subject to waiver by any party litigant." Brief for United States 27. But the proposition that legal defenses based upon doctrines central to the courts' structural independence can never be waived simply does not accord with our cases. Certainly one such doctrine consists of the "judicial Power" to disregard an unconstitutional statute, see *Marbury*, 5 U.S., at 177; yet none would suggest that a litigant may never waive the defense that a statute is unconstitutional. What may follow from our holding that the judicial power unalterably includes the power to render final judgments is not that waivers of res judicata are always impermissible, but rather that, as many federal Courts of Appeals have held, waivers of res judicata need not always be accepted—that trial courts may in appropriate cases raise the res judicata bar on their own motion. Waiver subject to the control of the courts themselves would obviously raise no issue of separation of powers, and would be precisely in accord with the language of the decision that the Solicitor General relies upon. . . .

Petitioners also rely on a miscellany of decisions upholding legislation that altered rights fixed by the final judgments of non-Article III courts, see, e.g., Sampeyreac v. United States, 32 U.S. (7 Pet.) 222, 238 (1833); Freeborn v. Smith, 69 U.S. (2 Wall.) 160 (1865), or administrative agencies, Paramino Lumber Co. v. Marshall, 309 U.S. 370 (1940), or that altered the prospective effect of injunctions entered by Article III courts, *Wheeling & Belmont Bridge Co.*, supra. These cases distinguish themselves; nothing in our holding today calls them into question. Petitioners rely on general statements from some of these cases that legislative annulment of final judgments is not an exercise of judicial power. But even if it were our practice to decide cases by weight of prior dicta, we would find the many dicta that reject congressional power to revise the judgments of Article III courts to be the more instructive authority.

Finally, petitioners liken § 27A(b) to Federal Rule of Civil Procedure 60(b), which authorizes courts to relieve parties from a final judgment for grounds such as excusable neglect, newly discovered evidence, fraud, or "any other reason justifying relief. . . ." We see little resemblance. Rule 60(b), which authorizes discretionary judicial revision of judgments in the listed situations and in other "extraordinary circumstances," does not impose any legislative mandate to reopen upon the courts, but merely reflects and confirms the courts' own inherent and discretionary power, "firmly established in English practice long before the foundation of our Republic," to set aside a judgment whose enforcement would work inequity. Hazel–Atlas Glass Co. v. Hartford–Empire Co., 322 U.S. 238, 244 (1944). Thus, Rule 60(b), and the tradition that it embodies, would be relevant refutation of a claim that reopening a final judgment is always a denial of property without due process; but they are irrelevant to the claim that legislative instruction to reopen impinges upon the independent constitutional authority of the courts.

Dissent ↓

The dissent promises to provide "[a] few contemporary examples" of statutes retroactively requiring final judgments to be reopened, "to demonstrate that [such statutes] are ordinary products of the exercise of legislative power." That promise is not kept. The relevant retroactivity, of course, consists not of the requirement that there be set aside a judgment that has been rendered *prior to its being setting aside*—for example, a statute passed today which says that all default judgments rendered in the future may be reopened within 90 days after their entry. In that sense, *all* requirements to reopen are "retroactive," and the designation is superfluous. Nothing we say today precludes a law such as that. The finality that a court can pronounce is no more than what the law in existence at the time of judgment will permit it to pronounce. If the law then applicable says that the judgment may be reopened for certain reasons, that limitation is built into the judgment itself, and its finality is so conditioned. The present case, however, involves a judgment that Congress subjected to a reopening requirement which did not exist when the judgment was pronounced. The dissent provides not a single clear prior instance of such congressional action. . . .

The dissent sets forth a number of hypothetical horribles flowing from our assertedly "rigid holding"—for example, the inability to set aside a civil judgment that has become final during a period when a natural disaster prevented the timely filing of a certiorari petition. That is horrible not because of our holding, but because the underlying statute *itself* enacts a "rigid" jurisdictional bar to entertaining untimely civil petitions. Congress could undoubtedly enact *prospective* legislation permitting, or indeed requiring, this Court to make equitable exceptions to an otherwise applicable rule of finality, just as district courts do pursuant to Rule 60(b). It is no indication whatever of the invalidity of the constitutional rule which we announce, that it produces unhappy consequences when a legislature lacks foresight, and acts belatedly to remedy a deficiency in the law. That is a routine result of constitutional rules. . . .

Produces inequitable results? Tough, talk to Congress.

Finally, we may respond to the suggestion of the concurrence that this case should be decided more narrowly. . . . Ultimately, the concurrence agrees with our judgment only "because the law before us embodies risks of the very sort that our Constitution's 'separation of powers' prohibition seeks to avoid." But the doctrine of separation of powers is a *structural safeguard* rather than a remedy to be applied only when specific harm, or risk of specific harm, can be identified. In its major features (of which the conclusiveness of judicial judgments is assuredly one) it is a prophylactic device, establishing high walls and clear distinctions because low walls and vague distinctions will not be judicially defensible in the heat of interbranch conflict. . . . Separation of powers, a distinctively American political doctrine, profits from the advice authored by a distinctively American poet: Good fences make good neighbors.

* * *

We know of no previous instance in which Congress has enacted retroactive legislation requiring an Article III court to set aside a final judgment, and for good reason. The Constitution's separation of legislative and judicial powers denies it the authority to do so. Section 27A(b) is unconstitutional to the extent that it requires federal courts to reopen final judgments entered before its enactment. The judgment of the Court of Appeals is affirmed.

It is so ordered.

[Justice Breyer concurred in the judgment, arguing that "the separation of powers inherent in our Constitution means that at least *sometimes* Congress lacks the power under Article I to reopen an otherwise closed court judgment," and that "[t]hree features of [§ 27A(B)]—its exclusively retroactive effect, its application to a limited number of individuals, and its reopening of closed judgments—taken together, show that Congress here impermissibly tried to *apply*, as well as *make*, the law." Justice Breyer noted, however, that "if Congress enacted legislation that reopened an otherwise closed judgment but in a way that mitigated some of the here relevant 'separation-of-powers' concerns, by also providing some of the assurances against 'singling out' that ordinary legislative activity normally provides—say, prospectivity and general applicability—we might have a different case."]

■ JUSTICE STEVENS, with whom JUSTICE GINSBURG joins, dissenting. . . .

Section 27A is a statutory amendment to a rule of law announced by this Court. The fact that the new rule announced in *Lampf* was a product of judicial, rather than congressional, lawmaking should not affect the separation-of-powers analysis. We would have the same issue to decide had Congress enacted the *Lampf* rule but, as a result of inadvertence or perhaps a scrivener's error, failed to exempt pending cases, as is customary when limitations periods are shortened. In my opinion, if Congress had retroactively restored rights its own legislation had inadvertently or unfairly impaired, the remedial amendment's failure to exclude dismissed cases from the benefited class would not make it invalid. The Court today faces a materially identical situation and, in my view, reaches the wrong result.

Throughout our history, Congress has passed laws that allow courts to reopen final judgments. Such laws characteristically apply to judgments entered before as well as after their enactment. When they apply retroactively, they may raise serious due process questions,[2] but the Court has

---

2. Because the Court finds a separation-of-powers violation, it does not reach respondents' alternative theory that § 27A(b) denied them due process under the Fifth Amendment. . . . Given the existence of statutes and rules, such as Rule 60(b), that allow courts to reopen apparently "final" judg-

ments in various circumstances, respondents cannot assert an inviolable "vested right" in the District Court's post-*Lampf* dismissal of petitioners' claims. In addition, § 27A(b) did not upset any "settled expectations" of respondents. . . . Before 1991 no one could have relied either on the yet to be announced rule

never invalidated such a law on separation-of-powers grounds until today. . . .

The most familiar remedial measure that provides for reopening of final judgments is Rule 60(b) of the Federal Rules of Civil Procedure. That Rule both codified common-law grounds for relieving a party from a final judgment and added an encompassing reference to "any other reason justifying relief from the operation of the judgment." Not a single word in its text suggests that it does not apply to judgments entered prior to its effective date. On the contrary, the purpose of the Rule, its plain language, and the traditional construction of remedial measures all support construing it to apply to past as well as future judgments. Indeed, because the Rule explicitly abolished the common-law writs it replaced, an unintended gap in the law would have resulted if it did not apply retroactively.

Other examples of remedial statutes that resemble § 27A include the Soldiers' and Sailors' Civil Relief Act of 1940, which authorizes members of the Armed Forces to reopen judgments entered while they were on active duty; the Handicapped Children's Protection Act of 1986, which provided for recovery of attorney's fees under the Education for All Handicapped Children Act of 1975; and the federal habeas corpus statute, 28 U.S.C. § 2255, which authorizes federal courts to reopen judgments of conviction. The habeas statute, similarly to Rule 60(b), replaced a common-law writ, and thus necessarily applied retroactively. State statutes that authorize the reopening of various types of default judgments and judgments that became final before a party received notice of their entry, as well as provisions for motions to reopen based on newly discovered evidence, further demonstrate the widespread acceptance of remedial statutes that allow courts to set aside final judgments. As in the case of Rule 60(b), logic dictates that these statutes be construed to apply retroactively to judgments that were final at the time of their enactments. All of these remedial statutes announced generally applicable rules of law as well as establishing procedures for reopening final judgments.[5]

In contrast, in the examples of colonial legislatures' review of trial courts' judgments on which today's holding rests, the legislatures issued directives in individual cases without purporting either to set forth or to apply any legal standard. . . .

The Framers' disapproval of such a system of ad hoc legislative review of individual trial court judgments has no bearing on remedial measures

in *Lampf* or on the Court's unpredictable decision to apply that rule retroactively. All of the reliance interests that ordinarily support a presumption against retroactivity militate in favor of allowing retroactive application of § 27A.

5. The Court offers no explanation of why the Constitution should be construed to interpose an absolute bar against these statutes' retroactive application. Under the Court's reasoning, for example, an amendment that broadened the coverage of Rule 60(b) could not apply to any inequitable judgments entered prior to the amendment. The Court's rationale for this formalistic restriction remains elusive.

such as Rule 60(b) or the 1991 amendment at issue today. The history on which the Court relies provides no support for its holding. . . .

Section 27A shares several important characteristics with the remedial statutes discussed above. It does not decide the merits of any issue in any litigation but merely removes an impediment to judicial decision on the merits. The impediment it removes would have produced inequity because the statute's beneficiaries did not cause the impediment. It requires a party invoking its benefits to file a motion within a specified time and to convince a court that the statute entitles the party to relief. Most important, § 27A(b) specifies both a substantive rule to govern the reopening of a class of judgments—the pre-*Lampf* limitations rule—and a procedure for the courts to apply in determining whether a particular motion to reopen should be granted. These characteristics are quintessentially legislative. They reflect Congress' fealty to the separation of powers and its intention to avoid the sort of ad hoc excesses the Court rightly criticizes in colonial legislative practice. In my judgment, all of these elements distinguish § 27A from "judicial" action and confirm its constitutionality. A sensible analysis would at least consider them in the balance.

Instead, the Court myopically disposes of § 27A(b) by holding that Congress has no power to "require an Article III court to set aside a final judgment." That holding must mean one of two things. It could mean that Congress may not impose a mandatory duty on a court to set aside a judgment even if the court makes a particular finding, such as a finding of fraud or mistake, that Congress has not made. Such a rule, however, could not be correct. Although Rule 60(b), for example, merely authorizes federal courts to set aside judgments after making appropriate findings, Acts of Congress characteristically set standards that judges are obligated to enforce. Accordingly, Congress surely could add to Rule 60(b) certain instances in which courts *must* grant relief from final judgments if they make particular findings—for example, a finding that a member of the jury accepted a bribe from the prevailing party. The Court, therefore, must mean to hold that Congress may not *unconditionally* require an Article III court to set aside a final judgment. That rule is both unwise and beside the point of this case. . . .

The majority's rigid holding unnecessarily hinders the Government from addressing difficult issues that inevitably arise in a complex society. This Court, for example, lacks power to enlarge the time for filing petitions for certiorari in a civil case after 90 days from the entry of final judgment, no matter how strong the equities. See 28 U.S.C. § 2101(c). If an Act of God, such as a flood or an earthquake, sufficiently disrupted communications in a particular area to preclude filing for several days, the majority's reasoning would appear to bar Congress from addressing the resulting inequity. If Congress passed remedial legislation that retroactively granted movants from the disaster area extra time to file petitions or motions for extensions of time to file, today's holding presumably would compel us to strike down the legislation as an attack on the finality of judgments. Such a ruling, like today's holding, would gravely undermine federal courts' traditional power "to set aside a judgment whose enforcement would work inequity." ...

We have the authority to hold that Congress has usurped a judicial prerogative, but even if this case were doubtful I would heed Justice Iredell's admonition in Calder v. Bull, 3 U.S. (3 Dall.) 386, 399 (1798), that "the Court will never resort to that authority, but in a clear and urgent case." An appropriate regard for the interdependence of Congress and the judiciary amply supports the conclusion that § 27A(b) reflects constructive legislative cooperation rather than a usurpation of judicial prerogatives.

Accordingly, I respectfully dissent.

Miller v. French

Supreme Court of the United States, 2000.
530 U.S. 327.

■ JUSTICE O'CONNOR delivered the opinion of the Court.

The Prison Litigation Reform Act of 1995 (PLRA) establishes standards for the entry and termination of prospective relief in civil actions challenging prison conditions. If prospective relief under an existing injunction does not satisfy these standards, a defendant or intervenor is entitled to "immediate termination" of that relief. And under the PLRA's "automatic stay" provision, a motion to terminate prospective relief "shall operate as a stay" of that relief during the period beginning 30 days after the filing of the motion (extendable to up to 90 days for "good cause") and ending when the court rules on the motion. The superintendent of the Pendleton Correctional Facility, which is currently operating under an ongoing injunction to remedy violations of the Eighth Amendment regarding conditions of confinement, filed a motion to terminate prospective relief under the PLRA. Respondent prisoners moved to enjoin the operation of the automatic stay provision of § 3626(e)(2), arguing that it is unconstitutional. The District Court enjoined the stay, and the Court of Appeals for the Seventh Circuit affirmed. We must decide whether a district court may enjoin the operation of the PLRA's automatic stay provision and, if not, whether that provision violates separation of powers principles.

I

A

This litigation began in 1975, when four inmates at what is now the Pendleton Correctional Facility brought a class action under 42 U.S.C. § 1983, on behalf of all persons who were, or would be, confined at the facility against the predecessors in office of petitioners (hereinafter State).

After a trial, the District Court found that living conditions at the prison violated both state and federal law, including the Eighth Amendment's prohibition against cruel and unusual punishment, and the court issued an injunction to correct those violations. While the State's appeal was pending, this Court decided Pennhurst State School and Hospital v. Halderman, 465 U.S. 89 (1984), which held that the Eleventh Amendment deprives federal courts of jurisdiction over claims for injunctive relief against state officials based on state law. Accordingly, the Court of Appeals for the Seventh Circuit remanded the action to the District Court for reconsideration. On remand, the District Court concluded that most of the state law violations also ran afoul of the Eighth Amendment, and it issued an amended remedial order to address those constitutional violations. The order also accounted for improvements in living conditions at the Pendleton facility that had occurred in the interim.

The Court of Appeals affirmed the amended remedial order as to those aspects governing overcrowding and double celling, the use of mechanical restraints, staffing, and the quality of food and medical services, but it vacated those portions pertaining to exercise and recreation, protective custody, and fire and occupational safety standards. This ongoing injunctive relief has remained in effect ever since, with the last modification occurring in October 1988, when the parties resolved by joint stipulation the remaining issues related to fire and occupational safety standards.

B

In 1996, Congress enacted the PLRA. As relevant here, the PLRA establishes standards for the entry and termination of prospective relief in civil actions challenging conditions at prison facilities. Specifically, a court "shall not grant or approve any prospective relief unless the court finds that such relief is narrowly drawn, extends no further than necessary to correct the violation of a Federal right, and is the least intrusive means necessary to correct the violation of the Federal right." 18 U.S.C. § 3626(a)(1)(A). The same criteria apply to existing injunctions, and a defendant or intervenor may move to terminate prospective relief that does not meet this standard. In particular, § 3626(b)(2) provides:

> In any civil action with respect to prison conditions, a defendant or intervener shall be entitled to the immediate termination of any prospective relief if the relief was approved or granted in the absence of a finding by the court that the relief is narrowly drawn, extends no further than necessary to correct the violation of the Federal right, and is the least intrusive means necessary to correct the violation of the Federal right.

A court may not terminate prospective relief, however, if it "makes written findings based on the record that prospective relief remains necessary to correct a current and ongoing violation of the Federal right, extends no further than necessary to correct the violation of the Federal right, and that the prospective relief is narrowly drawn and the least intrusive means necessary to correct the violation." § 3626(b)(3). The PLRA also requires courts to rule "promptly" on motions to terminate prospective relief, with mandamus available to remedy a court's failure to do so. § 3626(e)(1).

Finally, the provision at issue here, § 3626(e)(2), dictates that, in certain circumstances, prospective relief shall be stayed pending resolution of a motion to terminate. Specifically, subsection (e)(2), entitled "Automatic Stay," states:

> Any motion to modify or terminate prospective relief made under subsection (b) shall operate as a stay during the period—
>
>> (A)(i) beginning on the 30th day after such motion is filed, in the case of a motion made under paragraph (1) or (2) of subsection (b); . . . and
>>
>> (B) ending on the date the court enters a final order ruling on the motion.

As one of several 1997 amendments to the PLRA, Congress permitted courts to postpone the entry of the automatic stay for not more than 60 days for "good cause," which cannot include general congestion of the court's docket. § 123, 111 Stat. 2470, codified at 18 U.S.C. § 3626(e)(3).

C

On June 5, 1997, the State filed a motion under § 3626(b) to terminate the prospective relief governing the conditions of confinement at the Pendleton Correctional Facility. In response, the prisoner class moved for a temporary restraining order or preliminary injunction to enjoin the operation of the automatic stay, arguing that § 3626(e)(2) is unconstitutional as both a violation of the Due Process Clause of the Fifth Amendment and separation of powers principles. The District Court granted the prisoners' motion, enjoining the automatic stay. The State appealed, and the United States intervened pursuant to 28 U.S.C. § 2403(a) to defend the constitutionality of § 3626(e)(2).

The Court of Appeals for the Seventh Circuit affirmed the District Court's order, concluding that although § 3626(e)(2) precluded courts from exercising their equitable powers to enjoin operation of the automatic stay, the statute, so construed, was unconstitutional on separation of powers grounds. The court reasoned that Congress drafted § 3626(e)(2) in unequivocal terms, clearly providing that a motion to terminate under § 3626(b)(2) "*shall* operate" as a stay during a specified time period. While acknowledging that courts should not lightly assume that Congress meant to restrict the equitable powers of the federal courts, the Court of Appeals found "it impossible to read this language as doing anything less than that." Turning to the constitutional question, the court characterized § 3626(e)(2) as "a self-executing legislative determination that a specific decree of a federal court . . . must be set aside at least for a period of time."

As such, it concluded that § 3626(e)(2) directly suspends a court order in violation of the separation of powers doctrine under Plaut v. Spendthrift Farm, Inc., 514 U.S. 211 (1995), and mandates a particular rule of decision, at least during the pendency of the § 3626(b)(2) termination motion, contrary to United States v. Klein, 80 U.S. (13 Wall.) 128 (1872). Having concluded that § 3626(e)(2) is unconstitutional on separation of powers grounds, the Court of Appeals did not reach the prisoners' due process claims. Over the dissent of three judges, the court denied rehearing en banc.

We granted certiorari, to resolve a conflict among the Courts of Appeals as to whether § 3626(e)(2) permits federal courts, in the exercise of their traditional equitable authority, to enjoin operation of the PLRA's automatic stay provision and, if not, to review the Court of Appeals' judgment that § 3626(e)(2), so construed, is unconstitutional. . . .

II

We address the statutory question first. Both the State and the prisoner class agree, as did the majority and dissenting judges below, that § 3626(e)(2) precludes a district court from exercising its equitable powers to enjoin the automatic stay. The Government argues, however, that § 3626(e)(2) should be construed to leave intact the federal courts' traditional equitable discretion to "stay the stay," invoking two canons of statutory construction. First, the Government contends that we should not interpret a statute as displacing courts' traditional equitable authority to preserve the status quo pending resolution on the merits "absent the clearest command to the contrary." Califano v. Yamasaki, 442 U.S. 682, 705 (1979). Second, the Government asserts that reading § 3626(e)(2) to remove that equitable power would raise serious separation of powers questions, and therefore should be avoided under the canon of constitutional doubt. Like the Court of Appeals, we do not lightly assume that Congress meant to restrict the equitable powers of the federal courts, and we agree that constitutionally doubtful constructions should be avoided where "fairly possible." Communications Workers v. Beck, 487 U.S. 735, 762 (1988). But where Congress has made its intent clear, "we must give effect to that intent." Sinclair Refining Co. v. Atkinson, 370 U.S. 195, 215 (1962). . . .

[The Court concluded that § 3626(e)(2) could not reasonably be construed to permit federal courts, in the exercise of their traditional equitable authority, to enjoin operation of the PLRA's automatic stay provision.]

III

The Constitution enumerates and separates the powers of the three branches of Government in Articles I, II, and III, and it is this "very structure" of the Constitution that exemplifies the concept of separation of powers. INS v. Chadha, 462 U.S. 919, 946 (1983). While the boundaries between the three branches are not "'hermetically' sealed," see id. at 951, the Constitution prohibits one branch from encroaching on the central prerogatives of another. . . . The powers of the Judicial Branch are set forth in Article III, § 1, which states that the "judicial Power of the United States shall be vested in one supreme Court and in such inferior Courts as Congress may from time to time ordain and establish," and provides that these federal courts shall be staffed by judges who hold office during good behavior, and whose compensation shall not be diminished during tenure in office. As we explained in *Plaut v. Spendthrift Farm, Inc.*, Article III "gives the Federal Judiciary the power, not merely to rule on cases, but to *decide* them, subject to review only by superior courts in the Article III hierarchy."

Respondent prisoners contend that § 3626(e)(2) encroaches on the central prerogatives of the Judiciary and thereby violates the separation of powers doctrine. It does this, the prisoners assert, by legislatively suspending a final judgment of an Article III court in violation of *Plaut* and *Hayburn's Case*, 2 U.S. (2 Dall.) 409 (1792). According to the prisoners, the remedial order governing living conditions at the Pendleton Correctional Facility is a final judgment of an Article III court, and § 3626(e)(2) constitutes an impermissible usurpation of judicial power because it commands the district court to suspend prospective relief under that order, albeit temporarily. An analysis of the principles underlying *Hayburn's Case* and *Plaut*, as well as an examination of § 3626(e)(2)'s interaction with the other provisions of § 3626, makes clear that § 3626(e)(2) does not offend these separation of powers principles. . . .

Unlike the situation in *Hayburn's Case*, § 3626(e)(2) does not involve the direct review of a judicial decision by officials of the Legislative or Executive Branches. Nonetheless, the prisoners suggest that § 3626(e)(2) falls within *Hayburn's* prohibition against an indirect legislative "suspension" or reopening of a final judgment, such as that addressed in *Plaut*. . . .

Plaut, however, was careful to distinguish the situation before the Court in that case—legislation that attempted to reopen the dismissal of a suit seeking money damages—from legislation that "altered the prospective effect of injunctions entered by Article III courts." We emphasized that "nothing in our holding today calls . . . into question" Congress' authority to alter the prospective effect of previously entered injunctions. Prospective relief under a continuing, executory decree remains subject to alteration due to changes in the underlying law. This conclusion follows from our decisions in Pennsylvania v. Wheeling & Belmont Bridge Co., 54 U.S. (13 How.) 518 (1852) (*Wheeling Bridge I*) and Pennsylvania v. Wheeling & Belmont Bridge Co., 59 U.S. (18 How.) 421 (1856) (*Wheeling Bridge II*). . . .

Applied here, the principles of *Wheeling Bridge II* demonstrate that the automatic stay of § 3626(e)(2) does not unconstitutionally "suspend" or reopen a judgment of an Article III court. Section § 3626(e)(2) does not by itself "tell judges when, how, or what to do." French v. Duckworth, 178

F.3d 437, 449 (7th Cir. 1999) (Easterbrook, J., dissenting from denial of rehearing en banc). Instead, § 3626(e)(2) merely reflects the change implemented by § 3626(b), which does the "heavy lifting" in the statutory scheme by establishing new standards for prospective relief. Section 3626 prohibits the continuation of prospective relief that was "approved or granted in the absence of a finding by the court that the relief is narrowly drawn, extends no further than necessary to correct the violation of the Federal right, and is the least intrusive means to correct the violation," § 3626(b)(2), or in the absence of "findings based on the record that prospective relief remains necessary to correct a current and ongoing violation of a Federal right, extends no further than necessary to correct the violation of the Federal right, and that the prospective relief is narrowly drawn and the least intrusive means necessary to correct the violation," § 3626(b)(3). Accordingly, if prospective relief under an existing decree had been granted or approved absent such findings, then that prospective relief must cease, see § 3626(b)(2), unless and until the court makes findings on the record that such relief remains necessary to correct an ongoing violation and is narrowly tailored, see § 3626(b)(3). The PLRA's automatic stay provision assists in the enforcement of §§ 3626(b)(2) and (3) by requiring the court to stay any prospective relief that, due to the change in the underlying standard, is no longer enforceable, i.e., prospective relief that is not supported by the findings specified in §§ 3626(b)(2) and (3).

By establishing new standards for the enforcement of prospective relief in § 3626(b), Congress has altered the relevant underlying law. The PLRA has restricted courts' authority to issue and enforce prospective relief concerning prison conditions, requiring that such relief be supported by findings and precisely tailored to what is needed to remedy the violation of a federal right. We note that the constitutionality of § 3626(b) is not challenged here; we assume, without deciding, that the new standards it pronounces are effective. As *Plaut* and *Wheeling Bridge II* instruct, when Congress changes the law underlying a judgment awarding prospective relief, that relief is no longer enforceable to the extent it is inconsistent with the new law. Although the remedial injunction here is a "final judgment" for purposes of appeal, it is not the "last word of the judicial department." *Plaut,* 514 U.S. at 227. The provision of prospective relief is subject to the continuing supervisory jurisdiction of the court, and therefore may be altered according to subsequent changes in the law. . . .

The entry of the automatic stay under § 3626(e)(2) helps to implement the change in the law caused by §§ 3626(b)(2) and (3). If the prospective relief under the existing decree is not supported by the findings required under § 3626(b)(2), and the court has not made the findings required by § 3626(b)(3), then prospective relief is no longer enforceable and must be stayed. The entry of the stay does not reopen or "suspend" the previous judgment, nor does it divest the court of authority to decide the merits of the termination motion. Rather, the stay merely reflects the changed legal circumstances—that prospective relief under the existing decree is no longer enforceable, and remains unenforceable unless and until the court makes the findings required by § 3626(b)(3).

For the same reasons, § 3626(e)(2) does not violate the separation of powers principle articulated in United States v. Klein, 80 U.S. (13 Wall.) 128 (1872). ...

... As we noted in *Plaut*, ... "whatever the precise scope of *Klein*, ... later decisions have made clear that its prohibition does not take hold when Congress 'amends applicable law.'" The prisoners concede this point but contend that, because § 3626(e)(2) does not itself amend the legal standard, *Klein* is still applicable. As we have explained, however, § 3626(e)(2) must be read not in isolation, but in the context of § 3626 as a whole. Section 3626(e)(2) operates in conjunction with the new standards for the continuation of prospective relief; if the new standards of § 3626(b)(2) are not met, then the stay "shall operate" unless and until the court makes the findings required by § 3626(b)(3). Rather than prescribing a rule of decision, § 3626(e)(2) simply imposes the consequences of the court's application of the new legal standard.

Finally, the prisoners assert that, even if § 3626(e)(2) does not fall within the recognized prohibitions of *Hayburn's Case*, *Plaut*, or *Klein*, it still offends the principles of separation of powers because it places a deadline on judicial decisionmaking, thereby interfering with core judicial functions. Congress' imposition of a time limit in § 3626(e)(2), however, does not in itself offend the structural concerns underlying the Constitution's separation of powers. For example, if the PLRA granted courts 10 years to determine whether they could make the required findings, then certainly the PLRA would raise no apprehensions that Congress had encroached on the core function of the Judiciary to decide "cases and controversies properly before them." United States v. Raines, 362 U.S. 17 (1960). Respondents' concern with the time limit, then, must be its relative brevity. But whether the time is so short that it deprives litigants of a meaningful opportunity to be heard is a due process question, an issue that is not before us. We leave open, therefore, the question whether this time limit, particularly in a complex case, may implicate due process concerns.

In contrast to due process, which principally serves to protect the personal rights of litigants to a full and fair hearing, separation of powers principles are primarily addressed to the structural concerns of protecting the role of the independent Judiciary within the constitutional design. In this action, we have no occasion to decide whether there could be a time constraint on judicial action that was so severe that it implicated these structural separation of powers concerns. The PLRA does not deprive courts of their adjudicatory role, but merely provides a new legal standard for relief and encourages courts to apply that standard promptly. ...

Through the PLRA, Congress clearly intended to make operation of the automatic stay mandatory, precluding courts from exercising their equitable powers to enjoin the stay. And we conclude that this provision does not violate separation of powers principles. Accordingly, the judgment of the Court of Appeals for the Seventh Circuit is reversed, and the action is remanded for further proceedings consistent with this opinion.

It is so ordered.

[Justice Breyer dissented, joined by Justice Stevens. He argued for "a more flexible interpretation of the statute" whereby the federal courts would have the authority to suspend the automatic stay "when a party, in accordance with traditional equitable criteria, has demonstrated a need for such an exception."]

■ JUSTICE SOUTER, with whom JUSTICE GINSBURG joins, concurring in part and dissenting in part.

I agree that 18 U.S.C. § 3626(e)(2) is unambiguous and join Parts I and II of the majority opinion. I also agree that applying the automatic stay may raise the due process issue, of whether a plaintiff has a fair chance to preserve an existing judgment that was valid when entered. But I believe that applying the statute may also raise a serious separation-of-powers issue if the time it allows turns out to be inadequate for a court to determine whether the new prerequisite to relief is satisfied in a particular case. I thus do not join Part III of the Court's opinion and on remand would require proceedings consistent with this one. I respectfully dissent from the terms of the Court's disposition.

A prospective remedial order may rest on at least three different legal premises: the underlying right meant to be secured; the rules of procedure for obtaining relief, defining requisites of pleading, notice, and so on; and, in some cases, rules lying between the other two, such as those defining a required level of certainty before some remedy may be ordered, or the permissible scope of relief. At issue here are rules of the last variety.

Congress has the authority to change rules of this sort by imposing new conditions precedent for the continuing enforcement of existing, prospective remedial orders and requiring courts to apply the new rules to those orders. Cf. Plaut v. Spendthrift Farm, Inc., 514 U.S. 211, 232 (1995). If its legislation gives courts adequate time to determine the applicability of a new rule to an old order and to take the action necessary to apply it or to vacate the order, there seems little basis for claiming that Congress has crossed the constitutional line to interfere with the performance of any judicial function. But if determining whether a new rule applies requires time (say, for new factfinding) and if the statute provides insufficient time for a court to make that determination before the statute invalidates an extant remedial order, the application of the statute raises a serious question whether Congress has in practical terms assumed the judicial function. In such a case, the prospective order suddenly turns unenforceable not because a court has made a judgment to terminate it due to changed law or fact, but because no one can tell in the time allowed whether the new rule requires modification of the old order. One way to view this result is to see the Congress as mandating modification of an order that may turn out to be perfectly enforceable under the new rule, depending on judicial factfinding. If the facts are taken this way, the new statute might well be treated as usurping the judicial function of determining the applicability of a general rule in particular factual circumstances.[3] Cf. United States v. Klein, 80 U.S. (13 Wall.) 128 (1872).

Whether this constitutional issue arises on the facts of this action, however, is something we cannot yet tell, for the District Court did not address the sufficiency of the time provided by the statute to make the findings required by § 3626(b)(3) in this particular action. Absent that determination, I would not decide the separation-of-powers question, but simply remand for further proceedings. If the District Court determined both that it lacked adequate time to make the requisite findings in the period before the automatic stay would become effective, and that applying the stay would violate the separation of powers, the question would then be properly presented.

NOTES ON CONGRESSIONAL REGULATION OF FEDERAL RULES OF DECISION AND JUDGMENTS

1. ***Hayburn's Case.*** A 1792 statute authorized pensions for disabled veterans of the Revolutionary War. The statute provided that the federal circuit courts were to determine the appropriate disability payments, but that the Secretary of War had the discretion either to adopt or reject the courts' findings. The Supreme Court did not address the constitutionality of this arrangement, but the views of several circuit courts (reflecting the views of five Supreme Court Justices) were reported with the case, and these courts reasoned that the statute was unconstitutional because it asked the federal courts to do something that was not "judicial." See Hayburn's Case, 2 U.S. 408, 2 Dall. 409 (1792). In *Plaut v. Spendthrift Farm*, excerpted above, the Supreme Court said that *Hayburn's Case* "stands for the principle that Congress cannot vest review of the decisions

---

3. The constitutional question inherent in these possible circumstances does not seem to be squarely addressed by any of our cases. Congress did not engage in discretionary review of a particular judicial judgment, cf. Plaut v. Spendthrift Farm, Inc., 514 U.S. 211, 218, 226 (1995) (characterizing Hayburn's Case, [2 U.S. 408], 2 Dall. 409 (1792)), or try to modify a final, non-prospective judgment, cf. 514 U.S. at 218–19. Nor would a stay result from the judicial application of a change in the underlying law, cf. Pennsylvania v. Wheeling & Belmont Bridge Co., 59 U.S. (18 How.) 421 (1856); *Plaut*, supra, at 218 (characterizing United States v. Klein, 80 U.S. (13 Wall.) 128 (1872)). Instead, if the time is insufficient for a court to make a judicial determination about the applicability of the new rules, the stay would result from the inability of the Judicial Branch to exercise the judicial power of determining whether the new rules applied at all. Cf. Marbury v. Madison, 5 U.S. (1 Cranch) 137, 177 (1803) ("It is emphatically the province and duty of the judicial department to say what the law is").

of Article III courts in officials of the Executive Branch." *Hayburn's Case* is also often cited for the more general proposition that Article III courts may not issue advisory opinions.

2. *Pennsylvania v. Wheeling & Belmont Bridge Co.* In the late 1840s, the state of Virginia (which at that time included what is now West Virginia) chartered a private company to build a bridge across the Ohio River. The state of Pennsylvania subsequently sued the company directly in the Supreme Court under the Court's original jurisdiction, arguing that the bridge would interfere with navigation on the river and seeking an injunction requiring that the bridge either be removed or elevated. The Court granted the requested injunction, concluding that the bridge was "an obstruction and nuisance." See Pennsylvania v. Wheeling & Belmont Bridge Co., 54 U.S. 518, 626–27 (1852) *(Wheeling Bridge I)*. Congress subsequently enacted a statute declaring the bridge to be a "lawful structure" and designating it as a "post road" for the passage of mail. Congress further stated that the bridge could be maintained at its present elevation "anything in the law or laws of the United States to the contrary notwithstanding." About two years later, the bridge was blown down in a storm, and the company began to rebuild it to its prior height. Pennsylvania returned to the Supreme Court, seeking to have the company held in contempt for violating the Court's injunction.

The Supreme Court denied the contempt motion and dissolved the injunction it had issued in *Wheeling Bridge I*. See Pennsylvania v. Wheeling & Belmont Bridge Co., 59 U.S. (18 How.) 421 (1856) *(Wheeling Bridge II)*. The Court acknowledged that, "as a general proposition, [it] is certainly not to be denied" that an act of Congress "cannot have the effect and operation to annul the judgment of the court already rendered." Thus, the Court noted that, "if the remedy in this case had been an action at law, and a judgment rendered in favor of the plaintiff for damages, the right to these would have passed beyond the reach of the power of Congress." The Court explained, however, that the injunction at issue here was "executory, a continuing decree" that was based on the violation of a public right of free navigation, and that this public right was no longer being violated now that Congress had approved the bridge. In light of Congress's enactment, said the Court, "[t]here is no longer any interference with the enjoyment of the public right inconsistent with law."

Does this decision mean that Congress has unlimited authority to overturn injunctions issued by Article III courts? What if an injunction is based on the violation of a constitutional right? What if the injunction is based on the violation of a private property right?

3. *United States v. Klein.* During the Civil War, Congress authorized the Treasury Department to seize abandoned property in rebellious states. It also gave individuals the right to petition in the Court of Claims to recover the property or its proceeds if they could show that they had been loyal to the Union during the rebellion. Union agents subsequently

seized 600 bales of cotton belonging to Victor Wilson. Although there was
evidence that Wilson had provided support to the Confederacy early in the
War, he obtained a pardon pursuant to a proclamation issued by President
Lincoln. Wilson died in 1865, and the administrator of his estate, John
Klein, filed a petition in the Court of Claims seeking recovery of the
proceeds from the Union's sale of the cotton.

In an unrelated but similar case, the Supreme Court held that a
presidential pardon constituted sufficient evidence of loyalty during the
rebellion, because a person covered by a pardon "is as innocent as if he had
never committed the offence." United States v. Padelford, 76 U.S. 531, 542
(1870). Based on that precedent, the Court of Claims held in favor of Klein,
awarding him $125,300. The government appealed the case to the Supreme
Court. While the appeal was pending, Congress passed a statute that
provided that in these property seizure cases a presidential pardon should
not be treated as evidence of loyalty. The statute further provided that,
when the pardon recited involvement in the rebellion or other acts of
disloyalty, the pardon should be treated as "conclusive evidence that such
person did take part in, and give aid and comfort to, the late rebellion."
The statute also had two jurisdictional provisions. First, it provided that in
cases in which a claimant had prevailed in the Court of Claims based on a
presidential pardon, "the Supreme Court shall, on appeal, have no further
jurisdiction of the cause, and shall dismiss the same for want of jurisdiction." Second, it provided that when proof of disloyalty was shown through
the facts recited in a pardon, the jurisdiction of the Court of Claims over
the case "shall cease, and the court shall forthwith dismiss the suit of such
claimant." Based on this statute, the government sought to have the
Supreme Court remand the case back to the Court of Claims with a
mandate that the case be dismissed for lack of jurisdiction.

The Supreme Court concluded that the statute was unconstitutional,
and it proceeded to affirm the Court of Claims' award in favor of Klein. See
United States v. Klein, 80 U.S. (13 Wall.) 128 (1872). The Court first
concluded that Klein still owned the property at the time of the pardon:

> We conclude . . . that the title to the proceeds of the property
> which came to the possession of the government by capture or
> abandonment . . . was in no case divested out of the original
> owner. It was for the government itself to determine whether
> these proceeds should be restored to the owner or not. The
> promise of restoration of all rights of property decides that ques-
> tion affirmatively as to all persons who availed themselves of the
> proferred pardon. It was competent for the President to annex to
> his offer of pardon any conditions or qualifications he should see
> fit; but after those conditions and qualifications had been satisfied,
> the pardon and its connected promises took full effect. The resto-
> ration of the proceeds became the absolute right of the persons

pardoned, on application within two years from the close of the war.

It then considered whether the denial of jurisdiction in the Supreme Court should "be regarded as an exercise of the power of Congress to make 'such exceptions from the appellate jurisdiction' as should seem to it expedient." The Court responded:

> [T]he language of the [statute] shows plainly that it does not intend to withhold jurisdiction except as a means to an end. Its great and controlling purpose is to deny to pardons granted by the President the effect which this Court had adjudged them to have. [T]he denial of jurisdiction to this Court, as well as the Court of Claims, is founded solely on the application of a rule of decision, in cases pending, prescribed by Congress. The court has jurisdiction of the cause to a given point; but when it ascertains that a certain state of things exists, its jurisdiction is to cease and it is required to dismiss the cause for want of jurisdiction.
>
> It seems to us that this is not an exercise of the acknowledged power of Congress to make exceptions and prescribe regulations to the appellate power.
>
> The court is required to ascertain the existence of certain facts and thereupon to declare that its jurisdiction on appeal has ceased, by dismissing the bill. What is this but to prescribe a rule for the decision of a cause in a particular way? In the case before us, the Court of Claims has rendered judgment for the claimant and an appeal has been taken to this Court. We are directed to dismiss the appeal, if we find that the judgment must be affirmed, because of a pardon granted to the intestate of the claimants. Can we do so without allowing one party to the controversy to decide it in its own favor? Can we do so without allowing that the legislature may prescribe rules of decision to the judicial department of the government in cases pending before it? We think not. . . .

The Court distinguished *Wheeling Bridge II* on the ground that:

> No arbitrary rule of decision was prescribed in that case, but the Court was left to apply its ordinary rules to the new circumstances created by the act. In the case before us no new circumstances have been created by legislation. But the Court is forbidden to give the effect to evidence which, in its own judgment, such evidence should have, and is directed to give it an effect precisely contrary.
>
> We must think that Congress has inadvertently passed the limit which separates the legislative from the judicial power. . . . Congress has already provided that the Supreme Court shall have jurisdiction of the judgments of the Court of Claims on appeal. Can it prescribe a rule in conformity with which the Court must deny to itself the jurisdiction thus conferred, because and only because

*Court could look to see if it had JD →
if No, dismiss. If yes, find for gov't.*

2010 SUPPLEMENT   **113**

its decision, in accordance with settled law, must be adverse to the government and favorable to the suitor? This question seems to us to answer itself.

At this point, the Court shifted ground. It began by observing that "[t]he rule prescribed is also liable to just exception as impairing the effect of a pardon, and thus infringing the constitutional power of the executive." It continued:

Legislative/ Executive Encroachment

> It is the intention of the Constitution that each of the great co-ordinate departments of the government—the legislative, the executive, and the judicial—shall be, in its sphere, independent of the others. To the executive alone is intrusted the power of pardon; and it is granted without limit. Pardon includes amnesty. It blots out the offence pardoned and removes all its penal consequences. It may be granted on conditions. In these particular pardons, that no doubt might exist as to their character, restoration of property was expressly pledged, and the pardon was granted on condition that the person who availed himself of it should take and keep a prescribed oath.

> Now it is clear that the legislature cannot change the effect of such a pardon any more than the executive can change a law. Yet this is attempted by the provision under consideration. The court is required to receive special pardons as evidence of guilt and to treat them as null and void. It is required to disregard pardons granted by proclamation on condition, though the condition has been fulfilled, and to deny them their legal effect. This certainly impairs the executive authority and directs the court to be instrumental to that end.

Justice Miller, joined by Justice Bradley, dissented. He pointed out that the pardon in *Padelford* occurred *before* the property was seized by the government, whereas Klein's pardon came *after* the seizure. In his view, this made all the difference:

DISSENT

> I have not been able to bring my mind to concur in the proposition that, under the act concerning captured and abandoned property, there remains in the former owner, who had given aid and comfort to the rebellion, any interest whatever in the property or its proceeds when it had been sold and paid into the treasury or had been converted to the use of the public under that act. ... I hold now that as long as the possession or title of property remains in the party, the pardon or the amnesty remits all right in the government to forfeit or confiscate it. But where the property has already been seized and sold, and the proceeds paid into the treasury, and it is clear that the statute contemplates no further proceeding as necessary to divest the right of the former owner, the pardon does not and cannot restore that which has thus completely passed away.

4. Questions and Comments on *Klein*. As many scholars have noted, it is difficult to parse the Court's reasoning in *Klein*. In fact, one scholar remarked that *"Klein* is sufficiently impenetrable that calling it opaque is a compliment." Barry Friedman, The History of the Countermajoritarian Difficulty, Part II: Reconstruction's Political Court, 91 Geo. L.J. 1, 34 (2002). Another scholar observed that the vague statements in *Klein* have allowed the decision "to be viewed as nearly all things to all men." Gordon G. Young, Congressional Regulation of Federal Courts' Jurisdiction and Processes: *United States v. Klein* Revisited, 1981 Wis. L. Rev. 1189, 1195.

Consider the following theories about what *Klein* stands for:

"[I]f Congress directs an Article III court to decide a case ... Article III [places] a limitation on the power of Congress to tell the court *how* to decide it." Henry M. Hart, Jr., The Power of Congress to Limit the Jurisdiction of Federal Courts: An Exercise in Dialectic, 66 Harv. L. Rev. 1362, 1373 (1953).

"The particular holding in *Klein* prohibits Congress from using its jurisdictional powers to manipulate federal courts so as to reach decisions which, if addressed in terms of substantive law, would be forbidden by the Constitution." Young, supra, at 1260.

"Congress may withhold jurisdiction. But it may not choose how much of the 'whole supreme law' an Article III court may apply to a case it has told the court to decide. Nor may it tell a court how to interpret that law. Nor, at the point when the court's constitutionally mandated choice of law and independent judgment are about to generate a decision and relief, may Congress pull the jurisdictional plug." James S. Liebman & William F. Ryan, "Some Effectual Power": The Quantity and Quality of Decisionmaking Required of Article III Courts, 98 Colum. L. Rev. 696, 822 (1998).

"The judiciary will not allow itself to be made to speak and act against its own best judgment on matters within its competence which have great consequence for our political community." Lawrence G. Sager, *Klein's* First Principle: A Proposed Solution, 86 Geo. L.J. 2525, 2529 (1998).

"[W]hatever the breadth of Congress's power to regulate federal court jurisdiction, it may not exercise that power in a way that requires a federal court to act unconstitutionally." Daniel J. Meltzer, Congress, Courts, and Constitutional Remedies, 86 Geo. L.J. 2537, 2549 (1998).

"[T]he judiciary has the constitutional power and obligation to assure that Congress has not deceived the electorate as to the manner in which its legislation actually alters the preexisting legal, political, social, or economic topography." Martin H. Redish & Christopher R. Pudelski, Legislative Deception, Separation of

Powers, and the Democratic Process: Harnessing the Political Theory of *United States v. Klein*, 100 Nw. U. L. Rev. 437, 438–39 (2006).

Do these theories exhaust the possible meanings of *Klein*? Is *Klein*, in the end, nothing more or less than a reaffirmation of the unremarkable principle derived from *Marbury* that Congress may not regulate federal court jurisdiction in a way that causes a court to act unconstitutionally? Note that the government asked the Supreme Court to deny its own jurisdiction, but at the same time remand to the Court of Claims with a direction that it dismiss the case too. Could the Court have set aside the Court of Claims judgment without examining the merits and, in effect, resolving the case in an unconstitutional manner?

5. *United States v. Sioux Nation*. In 1868, the United States entered into a treaty with the Sioux Nation tribes granting them territory in South Dakota as a reservation, including the Black Hills. In 1877, after gold was discovered in the Black Hills, Congress enacted a law removing the Black Hills from the territory of the reservation. In 1923, the Sioux Nation tribes petitioned the Court of Claims, arguing that the Black Hills had been taken from them without just compensation, in violation of the Fifth Amendment. The Court of Claims eventually dismissed this claim in 1942. Some years later, when the Sioux Nation tribes attempted to resubmit their takings claim, the Court of Claims held that it was barred by res judicata. In 1978, Congress directed the Court of Claims to consider the claim without regard to the defense of res judicata, and, acting pursuant to that statute, the Court of Claims held in favor of the tribes.

The Supreme Court affirmed, concluding that Congress's waiver of res judicata did not violate the doctrine of separation of powers. See United States v. Sioux Nation, 448 U.S. 371 (1980). The Court relied on a line of precedent, starting with Cherokee Nation v. United States, 270 U.S. 476 (1926), that stood for the proposition that "Congress has the power to waive the res judicata effect of a prior judgment entered in the Government's favor on a claim against the United States." The Court also distinguished *Klein* as follows:

> First, of obvious importance to the *Klein* holding was the fact that Congress was attempting to decide the controversy at issue in the Government's own favor. Thus, Congress' action could not be grounded upon its broad power to recognize and pay the Nation's debts. Second, and even more important, the proviso at issue in *Klein* had attempted "to prescribe a rule for the decision of a cause in a particular way." 80 U.S. at 146. The amendment at issue in the present case, however, like the Special Act at issue in *Cherokee Nation*, waived the defense of res judicata so that a legal claim could be resolved on the merits. Congress made no effort in either instance to control the Court of Claims' ultimate decision of that claim.

Consider these distinctions of *Klein* when reviewing the questions about *Plaut* in Note 7 below.

6. *Robertson v. Seattle Audubon Society.* Various groups brought lawsuits challenging the way in which the U.S. Forest Service was managing timber harvesting in the Pacific Northwest, with some groups (such as the Seattle Audubon Society) arguing that the Forest Service's approach provided too little protection to the spotted owl, and other groups (such as the Washington Contract Loggers Association) arguing that the approach provided too much protection. Seattle Audubon alleged violations of several federal statutes—the Migratory Bird Treaty Act, the National Environmental Policy Act, and the National Forest Management Act. In response to this litigation, Congress enacted the Northwest Timber Compromise, a statute that regulated timber harvesting in certain forests known to contain spotted owls. Subsection (b)(6)(A) of the Compromise provided that the regulations in the Compromise were "adequate consideration for the purpose of meeting the statutory requirements that are the basis for the consolidated cases captioned Seattle Audubon Society et al. v. F. Dale Robertson, Civil No. 89–160 and Washington Contract Loggers Assoc. et al., v. F. Dale Robertson, Civil No. 89–99 (order granting preliminary injunction) and the case Portland Audubon Society et al. v. Manuel Lujan, Jr., Civil No. 87–1160–FR."

The Seattle Audubon argued that subsection (b)(6)(A) violated *Klein* because it directed particular results in pending cases, and the U.S. Court of Appeals for the Ninth Circuit agreed. The Supreme Court reversed, reasoning that subsection (b)(6)(A) "compelled changes in law, not findings or results under old law." Robertson v. Seattle Audubon Society, 503 U.S. 429, 438 (1992). Although subsection (b)(6)(A) referred to specific cases, the Court concluded that these references were made in order to identify the statutory provisions being modified. As a result, explained the Court, "[t]o the extent that subsection (b)(6)(A) affected the adjudication of the cases, it did so by effectively modifying the provisions at issue in those cases." The Court concluded by stating:

> We have no occasion to address any broad question of Article III jurisprudence. The Court of Appeals held that subsection (b)(6)(A) was unconstitutional under *Klein* because it directed decisions in pending cases without amending any law. Because we conclude that subsection (b)(6)(A) *did* amend applicable law, we need not consider whether this reading of *Klein* is correct.

How is this case different from *Klein*? Why wasn't *Klein* also a case of amending applicable law? Is the only difference that in *Klein* Congress lacked the constitutional authority to make the amendment?

7. Questions and Comments on *Plaut*. What was the specific constitutional problem in *Plaut*? To what extent were the decisions in *Hayburn's Case* and *Klein* relevant to the Court's analysis? How is *Plaut* distinguishable from *Wheeling Bridge II*? The Court in *Plaut* acknowledges that Congress has the authority to change the law that applies to a case while the case is pending, even while the case is pending on appeal after a judgment in the district court. Why is that sort of change allowed, but not the one in *Plaut*? Does the Court's holding deprive Congress of needed flexibility in remedying inequities, as argued by the dissent?

Consider Rule 60(b) of the Federal Rules of Civil Procedure, which provides:

> On motion and just terms, the court may relieve a party or its legal representative from a final judgment, order, or proceeding for the following reasons:
>
> (1) mistake, inadvertence, surprise, or excusable neglect;
>
> (2) newly discovered evidence that, with reasonable diligence, could not have been discovered in time to move for a new trial under Rule 59(b);
>
> (3) fraud (whether previously called intrinsic or extrinsic), misrepresentation, or misconduct by an opposing party;
>
> (4) the judgment is void;
>
> (5) the judgment has been satisfied, released, or discharged; it is based on an earlier judgment that has been reversed or vacated; or applying it prospectively is no longer equitable; or
>
> (6) any other reason that justifies relief.

A motion under Rule 60(b) "must be made within a reasonable time—and for reasons (1), (2), and (3) no more than a year after the entry of the judgment or order or the date of the proceeding." Why doesn't this rule offend the principle of finality applied by the Court in *Plaut*? Because it is discretionary with the court? Is the dissent correct in arguing that "Congress surely could add to Rule 60(b) certain instances in which courts *must* grant relief from final judgments if they make particular findings—for example, a finding that a member of the jury accepted a bribe from the prevailing party"?

The majority in *Plaut* states that "the doctrine of separation of powers is a *structural safeguard* rather than a remedy to be applied only when specific harm, or risk of specific harm, can be identified." How does this conception of separation of powers differ from the one suggested by the concurrence and the dissent?

8. Statutory Retroactivity. At the backdrop of *Plaut* are more general issues concerning statutory retroactivity. As the Supreme Court has explained, a number of constitutional provisions limit statutory retroactivity:

> The Ex Post Facto Clause flatly prohibits retroactive application of penal legislation. Article I, § 10, cl. 1, prohibits States from passing another type of retroactive legislation, laws "impairing the

Obligation of Contracts." The Fifth Amendment's Takings Clause prevents the Legislature (and other government actors) from depriving private persons of vested property rights except for a "public use" and upon payment of "just compensation." The prohibitions on "Bills of Attainder" in Art. I, §§ 9–10, prohibit legislatures from singling out disfavored persons and meting out summary punishment for past conduct. The Due Process Clause also protects the interests in fair notice and repose that may be compromised by retroactive legislation. . . .

Landgraf v. USI Film Products, 511 U.S. 244, 266 (1994).

These constitutional limits are strongest with respect to criminal legislation. In the civil area, constitutional restrictions on retroactive legislation have been viewed as less robust, especially since the New Deal. In determining whether it is constitutional to apply a civil statute retroactively, courts will balance the public and private interests and will consider, among other things, whether retroactive application of the statute would interfere with settled expectations or reasonable reliance interests. Even when constitutional limits are not implicated, however, courts will presume that statutes do not operate retroactively, and thus will require that Congress "first make its intention clear" before a statute will be applied to conduct occurring prior to its enactment. *Landgraf*, 511 U.S. at 268. This presumption only applies, however, if the law "attaches new legal consequences to events completed before its enactment," id. at 269–70, and thus will not necessarily apply to jurisdictional and procedural changes.

Because the majority in *Plaut* found that the statute there violated the separation of powers, it did not address whether the statute was consistent with due process. Justice Stevens, in footnote 2 of his dissent, argued that the statute did not violate due process. Is his reasoning persuasive? Note that the majority in *Plaut* acknowledges that a statute of limitations "can be extended, without violating the Due Process Clause, after the cause of the action arose and even after the statute itself has expired." See also Chase Securities Corp. v. Donaldson, 325 U.S. 304, 316 (1945) ("[C]ertainly it cannot be said that lifting the bar of a statute of limitation so as to restore a remedy lost through mere lapse of time is per se an offense against the Fourteenth Amendment."). For additional discussion of statutory retroactivity, with an emphasis on the historic distinction between public and private rights, see Ann Woolhandler, Public Rights, Private Rights, and Statutory Retroactivity, 94 Geo. L.J. 1015 (2006).

9. Questions and Comments on *Miller*. In what ways is *Miller* distinguishable from *Plaut*? The Court in *Miller* reasons that Congress in the Prison Litigation Reform Act (PLRA) was simply changing applicable law, similar to what Congress had done in *Robertson*. But wasn't the applicable law in *Miller* the Eighth Amendment prohibition against cruel and unusual punishments (as applied to the states through the Due Process Clause of the Fourteenth Amendment)? If so, was Congress in effect amending the Constitution? Under the PLRA, prospective relief may be continued if the court finds that the relief "remains necessary to correct a current and ongoing violation of the Federal right, extends no further than necessary to correct the violation of the Federal right, and that the prospective relief is narrowly drawn and the least intrusive means necessary to correct the violation." Does this allowance remove the concern about congressional amendment of the Constitution?

The Court in *Miller* leaves open the question whether the time limit on judicial decisionmaking associated with the automatic stay provision in the PLRA might violate due process under certain circumstances. Could such a time limit also raise separation of powers concerns, as argued by Justice Souter in his partial dissent? For a discussion of constitutional issues raised by time limits on judicial decisionmaking, see William F. Ryan, Rush to Judgment: A Constitutional Analysis of Time Limits on Judicial Decisions, 77 B.U. L. Rev. 761 (1997).

10. The Terri Schiavo Controversy. In 1990, Terri Schiavo, a Florida resident, suffered severe brain damage and was subsequently diagnosed as being in a persistent vegetative state. Her husband sought to have her disconnected from a life-sustaining feeding tube, but her parents opposed this action. Years of litigation ensued in the Florida state courts. In 2005, in response to a Florida court order to have the feeding tube removed, Congress enacted the "Act for the Relief of the Parents of Theresa Marie Schiavo," which purported to give a federal district court in Florida jurisdiction to hear "a suit or claim by or on behalf of Theresa Marie Schiavo for the alleged violation of any right of Theresa Marie Schiavo under the Constitution or laws of the United States relating to the withholding or withdrawal of food, fluids, or medical treatment necessary to sustain her life." The Act also purported to confer standing to Schiavo's parents, call for a de novo determination of the issues notwithstanding the state court proceedings, disallow judicial abstention, and remove any requirement the parents might have had to exhaust state remedies. Finally, the Act provided that "[n]othing in this Act shall be construed to create substantive rights not otherwise secured by the Constitution and laws of the United States or of the several States."

Notwithstanding the Act, the district court in Florida and the U.S. Court of Appeals for the Eleventh Circuit allowed the feeding tube to be removed, and Terri Schiavo died. The Eleventh Circuit also denied a motion for rehearing en banc. In concurring in the denial of rehearing, Judge Stanley Birch expressed the view that the Act was unconstitutional. Citing *Klein* and other cases, Judge Birch reasoned that, because the Act "constitute[s] legislative dictation of how a federal court should exercise its judicial functions (known as a 'rule of decision'), [it] invades the province of the judiciary and violates the separation of powers principle." Schiavo ex rel. Schindler v. Schiavo, 404 F.3d 1270, 1273–74 (11th Cir. 2005) (Birch, J., concurring).

Is it constitutionally problematic for Congress to override judicial doctrines such as issue preclusion, abstention, or exhaustion? Even if not normally problematic, does it become problematic if the override is directed at a single specified case? For discussion of these and other constitutional issues associated with the Schiavo controversy, see Michael P. Allen, Congress and Terri Schiavo: A Primer on the American Constitutional Order?, 108 W. Va. L. Rev. 309 (2005); Evan Caminker, *Schiavo* and *Klein*, 22 Const. Comm. 529 (2005); Edward A. Hartnett, Congress Clears its Throat, 22 Const. Comm. 553 (2005); Steven G. Calabresi, The Terri Schiavo Case: In Defense of the Special Law Enacted by Congress and President Bush, 100 Nw. U. L. Rev. 151 (2006).

11. The Military Commissions Act of 2006. After the September 11, 2001, terrorist attacks, the Bush administration established military commissions to try terrorist detainees being held at the Guantanamo Bay naval base. In 2006, the Supreme Court concluded that this military commission system was invalid because it violated statutory requirements that had been imposed by Congress for the use of military commissions. See Hamdan v. Rumsfeld, 548 U.S. 557 (2006). One of these statutorily-imposed requirements, the Court found, was that the commissions had to comply with the international laws of war, which the Court said included at least "common Article 3" of the Geneva Conventions—a provision common to all four of the Geneva Conventions that establishes certain minimum protections for detainees in a "non-international armed conflict," including a prohibition on "[t]he passing of sentences and the carrying out of executions without previous judgment pronounced by a regularly constituted court affording all the judicial guarantees which are recognized as indispensable by civilized peoples." Congress responded to this decision by enacting the Military Commissions Act of 2006, which authorized the use of military commissions to try certain detainees in the war on terrorism, and regulated the procedures of these commissions and the crimes that could be tried before them.

One of the provisions in the Military Commissions Act of 2006 provided as follows:

A military commission established under this chapter is a regularly constituted court, affording all the necessary "judicial guarantees which are recognized as indispensable by civilized peoples" for purposes of common Article 3 of the Geneva Conventions.

Under the "last in time rule," when there is a conflict between a federal statute and a treaty provision, U.S. courts will apply the statute if it is enacted after the treaty. See, e.g., Edye v. Robertson (The Head Money Cases), 112 U.S. 580, 599 (1884). Thus, Congress has the ability to override common Article 3 of the Geneva Conventions for purposes of U.S. litigation. The above provision in the Military Commissions Act, however, did not purport to do this. Instead, it simply stated that the military commission system that Congress was authorizing satisfied the requirements of common Article 3. Was this provision binding on the courts? If the provision was intended to direct courts how to construe common Article 3, did it violate *Klein*? For discussion of this issue, see Curtis A. Bradley, The Military Commissions Act, Habeas Corpus, and the Geneva Conventions, 101 Am. J. Int'l L. 322, 341–42 (2007). (In 2009, Congress enacted a revised Military Commissions Act, and this revised version does not contain the provision quoted above.)

CHAPTER IV

JUSTICIABILITY

Page 400, add to the citations in the first full paragraph:

Tara Leigh Grove, Standing as An Article II Nondelegation Doctrine, 11 U. Pa. J. Const. L. 781 (2009); F. Andrew Hessick, Standing, Injury in Fact, and Private Rights, 93 Corn. L. Rev. 275 (2008); Eugene Kontorovich, What Standing Is Good For, 93 Va. L. Rev. 1663 (2007); Richard Murphy, Abandoning Standing: Trading a Rule of Access for a Rule of Deference, 60 Admin. L. Rev. 943 (2008); Heather Elliott, The Functions of Standing, 61 Stan. L. Rev. 459 (2008); Jonathan R. Siegel, A Theory of Justiciability, 86 Tex. L. Rev. 73 (2007).

Page 419, add a footnote at the end of Note 4:

e. For commentary on this decision, see Kimberly N. Brown, Justiciable Generalized Grievances, 68 Md. L. Rev. 221 (2008); Bradford Mank, Should States Have Greater Standing Rights Than Ordinary Citizens?: *Massachusetts v. EPA*'s New Standing Test for States, 49 Wm & Mary L. Rev. 1701 (2008); Bradford Mank, Standing and Future Generations: Does *Massachusetts v. EPA* Open Standing for Generations to Come?, 34 Colum. J. Environ. L. 1 (2009); Calvin Massey, State Standing After *Massachusetts v. EPA*, 61 Fla. L. Rev. 249 (2009).

Page 420, add at the end of Note 5:

See also Radha A. Pathak, Statutory Standing and the Tyranny of Labels, 62 Okla. L. Rev. 89 (2009) (examining confusion in the concept of "statutory standing" and concluding that some lower courts have erred by treating it as something separate from the merits of the case rather than as simply a question of this plaintiff's statutory right to recovery).

Page 446, add a footnote at the end of the Note on Taxpayer Standing:

a. For an amusing "dialogue" on *Hein* and taxpayer standing, see Eric J. Segall, The Taxing Law of Taxpayer Standing, 43 Tulsa L. Rev. 673 (2008), and for additional commentary on *Hein*, see Craig A. Stern, Another Sign from *Hein*: Does the Generalized Grievance Fail a Constitutional or a Prudential Test of Federal Standing to Sue?, 12 Lewis & Clark L. Rev. 1169 (2008).

Page 463, add a new Note 6:

6. Assignee Standing. In the words of the Supreme Court, the question presented in Sprint Communications Co. v. APCC Services, Inc., 554 U.S. 269 (2008), was "whether an assignee of a legal claim for money owed has standing to pursue that claim in federal court, even when the assignee has promised to remit the proceeds of the litigation to the assignor." The assignors were payphone operators that were owed money for calls placed to toll-free numbers. The assignees were "aggregators," who aggregated such claims and sued to collect them from Sprint and other carriers that sponsored toll-free numbers. Recoveries were promised to the assignors, who then paid the aggregators a fee.

Speaking through Justice Breyer, the Court found that the aggregators had standing. This conclusion rested squarely on history: "[H]istory and precedent are clear on the question before us: Assignees of a claim, including assignees for collection, have long been permitted to bring suit." Given the historical tradition of allowing suits by assignees, the Court looked for a "convincing reason" to do otherwise and, finding none, upheld standing. Controversy focused on the redressability requirement, for the aggregators were required to remit any recovery to the payphone operators. In the Court's view, however, redressability focused

> on whether the *injury* that a plaintiff alleges is likely to be redressed through the litigation—not on what the plaintiff ultimately intends to do with the money he recovers. Here, a legal victory would unquestionably redress the *injuries* for which the aggregators bring suit. . . . [I]f the aggregators prevail in this litigation, the long-distance carriers would write a check to the aggregators for the amount of . . . compensation owed. What does it matter what the aggregators do with the money afterward? The injuries would be redressed whether the aggregators remit the litigation proceeds to the payphone operators, donate them to charity, or use them to build new corporate headquarters.

In dissent, Chief Justice Roberts, speaking for himself and for Justices Scalia, Thomas, and Alito, joined issue on this and other points. With respect to redressability, the dissenters said the following:

> The Court goes awry when it asserts that the standing inquiry focuses on whether the *injury* is likely to be redressed, not whether the *complaining party's* injury is likely to be redressed. That could not be more wrong. We have never approved federal-court jurisdiction over a claim where the entire relief requested will run to a party not before the court. Never. . . .

> The majority's view of the Article III redressability requirement is also incompatible with what we said in Raines v. Byrd, 521 U.S. 811 (1997). In that case, we held that individual Members of Congress lacked standing to contest the constitutionality of the Line Item Veto Act. We observed that the Congressmen "do not claim that they have been deprived of something to which they *personally* are entitled." Rather, the Members sought to enforce a right that ran to their office, not to their person. . . . We therefore held that the individual Members did "not have a sufficient 'personal stake' in th[e] dispute" to maintain their challenge. . . .

The majority finds that respondents have a sufficient stake in this litigation because the substantive recovery will initially go to them, and [w]hat does it matter what the aggregators do with the money afterward? The majority's assertion implies, incorrectly, that respondents have, or ever had, a choice of what to do with the recovery. It may be true that a plaintiffs *independent* decision to pledge his recovery to another . . . would not divest the plaintiff of Article III standing. But respondents never had the right to direct the disposition of the recovery; they have only the right to sue. The hypothetical plaintiff who chooses to pledge her recovery to charity, by contrast, will secure a personal benefit from the recovery. . . . In that situation, the Article III requirement that a plaintiff demonstrate a personal stake in the outcome of the litigation is satisfied.

Who has the better of this exchange? Can *Sprint* be reconciled with *Raines* on redressability? More generally, what role should history play in such determinations? Should a long (though not uncomplicated) tradition of allowing suit by assignees suffice, or should historical practices be subjected to rigorous review under modern standing doctrine?

The majority also observed that, "as a practical matter, . . . it would be particularly unwise for us to abandon history and precedent in resolving the question before us" because a denial of standing "could easily be overcome." The majority noted, for example, that "the Agreement could be rewritten to give the aggregator a tiny portion of the assigned claim itself, perhaps only a dollar or two." The dissent responded that, while the majority might be right that there would be standing in that situation, "Article III is worth a dollar" and that, in any event, "the ease with which respondents can comply with the requirements of Article III is not a reason to abandon our precedents; it is a reason to adhere to them." Which view is more persuasive? Is there a value to insisting on standing requirements even if they can easily be bypassed, or does such insistence improperly elevate form over substance?

Page 480, add a new Note 4 and renumber the remaining Notes:

4. ***Davis v. FEC.*** The same rationale was used to reject a mootness challenge in Davis v. Federal Election Commission, 554 U.S. ___ (2008). Jack Davis twice ran for Congress and spent so much of his own money that he became subject to the "Millionaire's Amendment" to federal election laws in the Bipartisan Campaign Reform Act of 2002. Basically, the law provides that a candidate planning to spend more than $350,000 of his own money must file certain notices and disclosures about that intention. Once personal spending reaches that level, the candidate's opponent is allowed to receive campaign contributions at three times the normal limit, until the advantage of self-financing is offset, at which point the usual limits are reimposed.

Davis ran for Congress in 2004 and again in 2006. In 2006, he filed suit against the Federal Election Commission in a three-judge district court, seeking to have these provisions declared unconstitutional. He asked that the case be decided before the election, but the FEC opposed the accelerated schedule. It was therefore after the election that the three-judge district court rejected Davis's claims on the merits. On his appeal to the Supreme Court, the FEC claimed that the case should be dismissed for mootness and lack of standing, but the Supreme Court unanimously rejected both claims. The Court found that Davis's injury at the time of the complaint gave him standing to challenge both the disclosure requirements and the increased contribution limits that became applicable to his opponent. On mootness, the Court based its ruling squarely on the exception for cases "capable of repetition but evading review," citing a similar ruling in FEC v. Wisconsin Right to Life, 551 U.S. 449 (2007). It was sufficient, said the Court, that no election campaign would last long enough for the issue to be resolved on the merits and that Davis had announced his intention to run again as a self-financed candidate.[c]

Page 497, add a footnote at the end of Note 4:

c. Cf. Matthew I. Hall, The Partially Prudential Doctrine of Mootness, 77 Geo. Wash. L. Rev. 562 (2009), which argues that mootness is properly considered prudential insofar as it concerns whether *this plaintiff* still has the necessary personal stake to raise a live issue, but is properly considered constitutional (and hence not subject to exceptions) when it concerns whether the *issue* itself remains live.

Page 521, add at the end of the Bibliography Note:

For an effort to achieve an integrated understanding of standing, the political question doctrine, procedural due process, and non-Article III courts, see John Harrison, The Relation Between Limitations on and Requirements of Article III Adjudication, 95 Cal. L. Rev. 1367 (2007).

c. Although unanimous on standing and mootness, the Court split on the merits. Speaking through Justice Alito, a majority ruled that, by making adverse consequences turn on the expenditure of personal funds, the Millionaire's Amendment burdened Davis's First Amendment right to use personal funds for campaign speech. Justices Stevens, Souter, Ginsburg, and Breyer dissented.

CHAPTER V

SUBJECT MATTER JURISDICTION

Page 524, add a footnote at the end of the last sentence on the page:

d. The lore is that the federal claim over which federal jurisdiction is asserted must be "substantial," that is, non-frivolous. The traditional citation for this proposition is Bell v. Hood, 327 U.S. 678 (1946). For an attack on the *Bell* principle, see Howard M. Wasserman, Jurisdiction, Merits, and Substantiality, 42 Tulsa L. Rev. 579 (2007).

Page 526, add at the end of footnote d:

For exploration of the broader implications of *Holmes* by the same author, see Christopher A. Cotropia, Counterclaims, the Well–Pleaded Complaint, and Federal Jurisdiction, 33 Hofstra L. Rev. 1 (2004). For discussion of *Holmes* in the larger context of Supreme Court development of a federal common law of federal question jurisdiction, see F. Andrew Hessick III, The Common Law of Federal Question Jurisdiction, 60 Ala. L. Rev. 895 (2009).

Page 530, add to the sentence beginning "For discussion of these issues" in footnote i:

Deborah J. Challener and John B. Howell, III, Remand and Appellate Review When a District Court Declines to Exercise Supplemental Jurisdiction under 28 U.S.C. Section 1367(c), 81 Temp. L. Rev. 1067 (2008);

Page 533, add at the end of footnote n:

For discussion of whether failure to comply with the limits of § 1441(b) and other related limitations on removal jurisdiction are properly considered "procedural" errors that are lost if not timely raised or "jurisdictional" errors that courts must enforce whenever noticed, see Scott Dodson, In Search of Removal Jurisdiction, 102 Nw. U. L. Rev. 55 (2008).

Page 538, add at the end of footnote b:

For an historical analysis concluding that the Holmes view in *Smith v. Kansas City Title & Trust Co.* was the anomaly, not the position of the majority, see Ann Woolhandler and Michael G. Collins, Federal Question Jurisdiction and Justice Holmes, 84 Notre Dame L. Rev. 2151 (2009). Indeed, they say, that "cases along the model of *Smith* were, historically, quite familiar to the federal courts and may even have been a primary focus of the 1875 federal question statute."

Page 549, add to citations in the first sentence of the last paragraph of Note 2:

Richard D. Freer, Of Rules and Standards: Reconciling Statutory Limitations on "Arising Under" Jurisdiction, 82 Indiana L.J. 309 (2007); Rachel M. Janutis, The Road Forward from *Grable*: Separation of Powers and the Limits of "Arising Under" Jurisdiction, 69 La. L. Rev. 99 (2008);

Page 549, add at the end of Note 2:

And see Robert J. Pushaw, Jr., A Neo–Federalist Analysis of Federal Question Jurisdiction, 95 Cal. L. Rev. 1515 (2007), which argues for an expansive interpretation of federal question jurisdiction to encompass all cases "that will likely depend on the resolution of a genuine dispute over the interpretation, application, or enforcement of federal law" and a contraction of jurisdiction over cases that are likely only to involve state law.

Finally, for a fresh attempt to bring order to the Supreme Court's decisions on the scope of § 1331 jurisdiction, see Lumen N. Mulligan, A Unified Theory of U.S.C. Section 1331 Jurisdiction, 61 Vand. L. Rev. 1667 (2008). Mulligan argues that "§ 1331 jurisdiction is best understood as a function of the viability of the federal right a plaintiff asserts in relation to other indicia of congressional permission to bring such a claim in federal court, which is often expressed by the creation of causes of action." This offers, he asserts, an appropriate focus on congressional intent, a means of reconciling existing precedent, and "greater clarity for adjudicating tough cases."

Page 557, add a new Note 4 and renumber existing Note 4:

 4. **Arbitration Analogy?:** *Vaden v. Discover Bank.* Discover Bank filed an action in state court against Vaden, seeking to recover past due charges on a credit card. The action arose entirely under state law. Vaden counterclaimed, asserting that Discover's finance charges, late fees, and interest violated state law. Vaden's counterclaim was styled as a class action. Discover then filed a petition in federal court seeking an order under a clause in the credit card agreement to compel arbitration of the issues raised in the counterclaim.[a] The District Court accepted jurisdiction and ordered arbitration. The Circuit Court affirmed. The Supreme Court granted certiorari in Vaden v. Discover Bank, 556 U.S. ___ (2009), and reversed. The majority opinion was written by Justice Ginsburg.

Section 4 of the Federal Arbitration Act, 9 U.S.C.§ 4, provides:

 A party aggrieved by the alleged failure, neglect, or refusal of another to arbitrate under a written agreement for arbitration may petition any United States district court which, save for such agreement, would have jurisdiction under title 28, in a civil action or in admiralty of the subject matter of a suit arising out of the controversy between the parties, for an order directing that such arbitration proceed in the manner provided for in such agreement.

To supply the federal question to demonstrate that a federal court "would have jurisdiction" over the controversy, Discover argued that the issues

---

 a. One reason Discover wanted arbitration is that the arbitration clause in the credit card agreement contained a provision precluding presentation of "any claims as a representative or member of a class."

raised in Vaden's counterclaim were preempted by provisions of the Federal Deposit Insurance Act (FDIA). To be successful, therefore, Discover argued—and Vaden ultimately agreed—that Vaden's counterclaims would have to rely on federal law. But even if it was appropriate to recharacterize Vaden's counterclaims as arising under federal law, Justice Ginsburg said, the case seemed to present a classic "face of the complaint" issue:

> A *complaint* purporting to rest on state law, we have recognized, can be recharacterized as one "arising under" federal law if the law governing the complaint is exclusively federal. See Beneficial Nat. Bank v. Anderson, 539 U.S. 1, 8 (2003). Under this so-called "complete preemption doctrine," a plaintiff's "state cause of action [may be recast] as a federal claim for relief, making [its] removal [by the defendant] proper on the basis of federal question jurisdiction." 14B Wright & Miller § 3722.1, p. 511. A state-law-based *counterclaim*, however, even if similarly susceptible to recharacterization, would remain nonremovable. Under our precedent construing § 1331 ... counterclaims, even if they rely exclusively on federal substantive law, do not qualify a case for federal-court cognizance.[b]

In dissent, joined by Justices Stevens, Breyer, and Alito, Chief Justice Roberts nonetheless argued in favor of district court jurisdiction based on the language of § 4:

> The statute provides a clear and sensible answer: The court may consider the § 4 petition if the court "would have" jurisdiction over "the subject matter of a suit arising out of the controversy between the parties."

> The § 4 petition in this case explains that the controversy Discover seeks to arbitrate is whether "Discover Bank charged illegal finance charges, interest and late fees." Discover contends in its petition that the resolution of this dispute is controlled by federal law.... Vaden agrees that the legality of Discover's charges and fees is governed by the FDIA.[*] A federal court therefore "would have jurisdiction ... of the subject matter of a suit arising out of the controversy" Discover seeks to arbitrate. That suit could be an action by Vaden asserting that the charges violate the FDIA, or one by Discover seeking a declaratory judg-

b. *Beneficial National Bank* is the next main case, following which the implications of the "complete preemption" doctrine are explored. At the end of the day, the Court found it unnecessary to determine whether the "complete preemption" doctrine applied in this setting.—[Footnote by eds.]

*Vaden has conceded that the FDIA completely pre-empts her state-law counterclaims. What is significant about that concession is not Vaden's agreement on the jurisdictional question of complete pre-emption (which we need not and do not address), but rather her agreement that federal law—the FDIA—governs her allegation that Discover's charges and fees are illegal.

ment that they do not. . . . [This result] is closely analogous to the jurisdictional analysis in a typical declaratory judgment action. See Franchise Tax Bd. of Cal. v. Construction Laborers Vacation Trust for Southern Cal., 463 U.S. 1, 19 (1983) (jurisdiction over a declaratory judgment action exists when, "*if* the declaratory judgment defendant brought a coercive action to enforce its rights, that suit would necessarily present a federal question" (emphasis added)).

But the majority disagreed:

> [W]e read § 4 to convey that a party seeking to compel arbitration may gain a federal court's assistance only if, "save for" the agreement, the entire, actual "controversy between the parties," as they have framed it, could be litigated in federal court. We conclude that the parties' actual controversy here precipitated by Discover's state-court suit for the balance due on Vaden's account, is not amenable to federal-court adjudication. Consequently, the § 4 petition Discover filed in the United States District Court . . . must be dismissed.

Justice Ginsburg explained:

> Under the well-pleaded complaint rule, a completely preempted counterclaim remains a counterclaim and thus does not provide a key capable of opening a federal court's door. . . . There is a fundamental flaw in the dissent's analysis: In lieu of focusing on the whole controversy as framed by the parties, the dissent hypothesizes discrete controversies of its own design. As the parties' state-court filings reflect, the originating controversy here concerns Vaden's alleged debt to Discover. Vaden's responsive counterclaims challenging the legality of Discover's charges are a discrete aspect of the whole controversy Discover and Vaden brought to state court. Whether one might imagine a federal-question suit involving the parties' disagreement over Discover's charges is beside the point. The relevant question is whether the whole controversy between the parties—not just a piece broken off from that controversy—is one over which the federal courts would have jurisdiction.

The dissent would have us treat a § 4 petitioner's statement of the issues to be arbitrated as the relevant controversy even when that statement does not convey the full flavor of the parties' entire dispute. Artful dodges by a § 4 petitioner should not divert us from recognizing the actual dimensions of that controversy. The text of § 4 instructs federal courts to determine whether they would have jurisdiction over "a suit arising out of *the* controversy between the parties"; it does not give § 4 petitioners license to recharacterize an existing controversy, or manufacture a new controversy, in an effort to obtain a federal court's aid in compelling arbitration. . . .

In sum, § 4 . . . instructs district courts asked to compel arbitration to inquire whether the court would have jurisdiction, "save for [the arbitration] agreement," over "a suit arising out of the controversy between the parties." We read that prescription in light of the well-pleaded complaint rule and the corollary rule that federal jurisdiction cannot be invoked on the basis of a defense or counterclaim. Parties may not circumvent those rules by asking a federal court to order arbitration of the portion of a controversy that implicates federal law when the court would not have federal-question jurisdiction over the controversy as a whole. It does not suffice to show that a federal question lurks somewhere inside the parties' controversy, or that a defense or counterclaim would arise under federal law. Because the controversy between Discover and Vaden, properly perceived, is not one qualifying for federal-court adjudication, § 4 . . . does not empower a federal court to order arbitration of that controversy, in whole or in part.[19]

Discover, we note, is not left without recourse. Under the Federal Arbitration Act, state courts as well as federal courts are obliged to honor and enforce agreements to arbitrate. Discover may therefore petition a Maryland court for aid in enforcing the arbitration clause of its contracts with Maryland cardholders.[c]

---

19. This Court's declaratory judgment jurisprudence in no way undercuts our analysis. Discover, the dissent implies, could have brought suit in federal court seeking a declaration that its charges conform to federal law. Again, the dissent's position rests on its misconception of "the controversy between the parties." Like § 4 itself, the Declaratory Judgment Act does not enlarge the jurisdiction of the federal courts; it is "procedural only." Aetna Life Ins. Co. v. Haworth, 300 U.S. 227, 240 (1937). Thus, even in a declaratory judgment action, a federal court could not entertain Discover's state-law debt-collection claim. Cf. 10B Wright & Miller § 2758, pp. 519–521 ("The Declaratory Judgment Act was not intended to enable a party to obtain a change of tribunal from a state to federal court, and it is not the function of the federal declaratory action merely to anticipate a defense that otherwise could be presented in a state action.").

c. *Vaden* resolved a Circuit split. A majority of the Circuits had held that a § 4 petition only raised questions about the validity and scope of the agreement to arbitrate.

In *Vaden*, that approach would have involved only questions of state law—whether the agreement to arbitrate was a valid contract, to what issues it extended, whether the agreement had been breached, and the like. The minority position was that it was appropriate, in Justice Ginsburg's words, to "'look through' the petition and grant the requested relief if the court would have federal-question jurisdiction over the underlying controversy." The entire Court concluded that it was appropriate to "look through" the petition. It split over where to look.

For pre-*Vaden* consideration of the Circuit cases, see Richard A. Bales & Jamie L. Ireland, Federal Question Jurisdiction and the Federal Arbitration Act, 80 U. Colo. L. Rev. 89 (2009) (supporting a "look through" approach); Teressa L. Elliott, District Court Subject–Matter Jurisdiction in Suits to Compel Arbitration under the Federal Arbitration Act, 33 Okla. City U. L. Rev. 749 (2008) (opposing a "look through" analysis). For an earlier analysis of the same issue (supporting "look through"), see Imre S. Szalai, The Fed-

Page 572, add at the end of Note 6 and move footnote h to the end of this addition:

Consider the debate initiated by Gil Seinfeld, The Puzzle of Complete Preemption, 155 U. Pa. L. Rev. 537 (2007), responded to in Trevor W. Morrison, Complete Preemption and the Separation of Powers, 155 U. Pa. L. Rev. Pennumbra 186 (2007), http://www.pennumbra.com/responses/02–2007/Morrison.pdf, and in Paul E. McGreal, Defense of Complete Preemption, 155 U. Pa. L. Rev. Pennumbra 147 (2007), http://www.pennumbra.com/responses/09–2007/McGreal.pdf. Seinfeld argues that, out of respect for the core values underlying federal question jurisdiction, "the jurisprudence of complete preemption might stand on firmer ground if the availability of federal defense removal turned on the breadth of the preemptive statute relied upon by the defendant." This requires, in his view, a case-by-case determination that "distinguishes those federal statutes that are so robustly preemptive as to merit special jurisdictional treatment from those that are not." Morrison's response is that "[c]ourts are ill-suited to perform this sort of policy-based balancing. Congress, in contrast, is well suited to the task." McGreal argues that they are both wrong. They conceive the doctrine as an exception to the well-pleaded complaint rule that requires special justification. He believes it is a corollary to that rule, a doctrine that "recharacterizes preempted state law claims according to their true federal nature." He concludes that the complete preemption doctrine "eliminates [a plaintiff's] perverse incentive" and therefore "ought to be retained."

See also Ernest A. Young, Stalking the Yeti: Protective Jurisdiction, Foreign Affairs Removal, and Complete Preemption, 95 Cal. L. Rev. 1775 (2007), and Margaret Tarkington, Rejecting the Touchstone: Complete Preemption and Congressional Intent after *Beneficial National Bank v. Anderson*, 59 S.C.L. Rev. 225 (2008). Young analogizes complete preemption to protective jurisdiction: "Like protective jurisdiction, complete preemption ultimately rests on the notion that 'arising under' federal law should be interpreted expansively to cover not only cases in which federal law provides the rule of decision but also cases in which a federal forum for *state* claims is deemed necessary to protect federal interests stemming from a federal regulatory scheme." Tarkington rejects the Seinfeld position, and aligns herself more closely with Morrison's position. She argues that *Beneficial National Bank* "creates a policy-bankrupt allocation of state and

---

eral Arbitration Act and the Jurisdiction of the Federal Courts, 12 Harv. Negot. L. Rev. 319 (2007).

Another question lurking in the background in *Vaden*, again to use Justice Ginsburg's language, was the " 'antiquated and arcane' ouster notion.... [C]ourts traditionally viewed arbitration clauses as unworthy attempts to 'oust' them of jurisdiction; accordingly, to guard against encroachment on

their domain, they refused to order specific enforcement of agreements to arbitrate." This doctrine was put to rest, the Court concluded, by enactment of the Federal Arbitration Act in 1925. For discussion of an issue not addressed specifically in *Vaden*, namely how arbitration can be regarded as consistent with Article III, see Peter B. Rutledge, Arbitration and Article III, 61 Vand. L. Rev. 1189 (2008)—[Footnote by eds.]

federal jurisdiction" and that the proper "test for complete preemption [should be] based on congressional intent of removability."

Page 574, add a footnote at the end of the Friendly quote:

d. Robert L. Jones, Finishing a Friendly Argument: The Jury and the Historical Origins of Diversity Jurisdiction, 82 N.Y.U. L. Rev. 997 (2007), examines the historical sources at length and concludes that it was the prospect of controlling the composition of federal juries that was the primary motivation for establishing the diversity jurisdiction.

Page 576, add to the "See also" cite in the first paragraph of footnote g:

David Crump, The Case for Restricting Diversity Jurisdiction: The Undeveloped Arguments, from the Race to the Bottom to the Substitution Effect, 62 Me. L. Rev. 1 (2010);

Page 579, add to the first paragraph of footnote k:

Emily J. Sack, The Domestic Relations Exception, Domestic Violence, and Equal Access to Federal Courts, 84 Wash. U. L. Rev. 1441 (2006);

Page 579, add at the end of footnote k:

For discussion of a potential spill-over effect of the domestic relations exception to federal question cases, see Meredith Johnson Harbach, Is the Family a Federal Question? 66 Wash. & Lee L. Rev. 131 (2009).

Pages 579–80, omit the paragraph dealing with corporate citizenship and substitute the following:

Among the many potentially complicated details of diversity jurisdiction is determining the citizenship of a corporation. Section 1332(c) provides that "a corporation shall be deemed to be a citizen of any State by which it has been incorporated and of the State where it has its principal place of business." The circuits diverged in their treatment of the principal place of business, some focusing on the volume of business activity in a state and others looking to the location of the corporate headquarters or "nerve center." In Hertz Corp. v. Friend, 559 U.S. ___ (2010), two California citizens sued Hertz, a Delaware corporation with its headquarters in New Jersey, for violations of California law. Hertz tried to remove the case to federal court, but the court found that, because Hertz did more business in California than in any other single state, California was its principal place of business. The Supreme Court unanimously disagreed. Speaking through Justice Breyer, the Court reasoned that the nerve center approach was consistent with the statutory language referencing a particular place within a state. The business activities test, in contrast, led some courts "to look, not at a particular place within a State, but incorrectly at the State itself, measuring the total amount of business activities that the corporation conducts there and determining whether they are 'significantly larger' than in the next-ranking State." On that analysis, every national retailer would be deemed a citizen of California.

The Court also cited ease of administration. While a corporation's business activities might be scattered across the entire country, focusing on the corporate nerve center suggests a single location. Administrative simplicity was thought particularly important for a jurisdictional statute:

> Complex jurisdictional tests complicate a case, eating up time and money as the parties litigate, not the merits of their claims, but which court is the right court to decide those claims. Complex tests produce appeals and reversals, encourage gamesmanship, and, again, diminish the likelihood that results and settlements will reflect a claim's legal and factual merits. Judicial resources too are at stake. Courts have an independent obligation to determine whether subject-matter jurisdiction exists, even when no party challenges it. So courts benefit from straightforward rules under which they can readily assure themselves of their power to hear a case.

The Court acknowledged that there might be hard cases, but thought that the nerve center approach "nonetheless points courts in a single direction, towards the center of overall direction, control, and coordination."

Page 580, move the second sentence from the top of the page dealing with unincorporated associations and its footnote to the end of the first full paragraph on the page.

Page 580, add at the end of footnote m:

For a discussion of *Wachovia Bank*, see Paul E. Lund, National Banks and Diversity Jurisdiction, 46 U. Louisville L. Rev. 73 (2007).

Page 586, add a new footnote after the sentence "Ordinary principles of statutory construction apply." in the first full paragraph:

a. For an article challenging this statement, see Debra Lyn Bassett, Statutory Interpretation in the Context of Federal Jurisdiction, 76 Geo. Wash. L. Rev. 52 (2007).— [Footnote by eds.]

Page 608, add the following Note after Note 4 and renumber remaining Note:

5. Class Action Fairness Act. In 2005, in response to concerns about abuses of the class action device and the perception that, as a result of limitations on diversity jurisdiction, class actions of nationwide significance were improperly being kept out of the federal courts, Congress enacted the Class Action Fairness Act (CAFA). Subject to certain limitations, the CAFA authorizes federal courts to exercise jurisdiction over class actions based on state law as long as any member of the class has diverse citizenship from any defendant, there are at least 100 class members, and there is at least $5,000,000 in controversy. See 28 U.S.C. § 1332(d). It also allows the claims of the class members to be aggregated in order to satisfy the amount in controversy requirement. In addition, it facilitates removal of these class actions from state to federal court—by, for example, allowing removal even if one or more of the defendants is a citizen of the state in which the suit is brought. See 28 U.S.C. § 1453.

The extensive scholarship on the CAFA includes a valuable set of symposium articles published in the Pennsylvania Law Review. These articles include Stephen B. Burbank, The Class Action Fairness Act of 2005 in Historical Context: A Preliminary View, 156 U. Pa. L. Rev. 1439 (2008); Kevin M. Clermont & Theodore Eisenberg, CAFA Judicata: A Tale of Waste and Politics, 156 U. Pa. L. Rev. 1553 (2008); Geoffrey C. Hazard, Jr., Has the *Erie* Doctrine Been Repealed by Congress?, 156 U. Pa. L. Rev. 1629 (2008); Emery G. Lee III & Thomas E. Willging, The Impact of the Class Action Fairness Act on the Federal Courts: An Empirical Analysis of Filings and Removals, 156 U. Pa. L. Rev. 1723 (2008); Richard L. Marcus, Assessing CAFA's Stated Jurisdictional Policy, 156 U. Pa. L. Rev. 1765 (2008); and Edward A. Purcell, Jr., The Class Action Fairness Act in Perspective: The Old and the New in Federal Jurisdictional Reform, 156 U. Pa. L. Rev. 1823 (2008). For additional articles on the CAFA, see, for example, Nan S. Ellis, The Class Action Fairness Act of 2005: The Story Behind the Statute, 35 J. Legis. 76 (2009), David Marcus, *Erie*, the Class Action Fairness Act, and Some Federalism Implications of Diversity Jurisdiction, 48 Wm. & Mary L. Rev. 1247 (2007), and Mark Moller, A New Look at the Original Meaning of the Diversity Clause, 51 Wm. & Mary L. Rev. 1113 (2009).

Page 608, add to the citations in the second paragraph of Note 5:

C. Douglas Floyd, Three Faces of Supplemental Jurisdiction after the Demise of *United Mine Workers v. Gibbs*, 60 Fla. L. Rev. 277 (2008).

Pages 610–32, replace Section 3 with the following:

SECTION 3: THE SUBSTANCE/PROCEDURE PROBLEM

INTRODUCTORY NOTES ON THE SUBSTANCE/PROCEDURE PROBLEM

1. Background. Two important events occurred in 1938. The Supreme Court held in *Erie* that federal courts were required to apply state substantive law in large categories of cases where federal courts had previously supplied the rules of decision as a matter of general common law. The same year saw the adoption of the Federal Rules of Civil Procedure, which for the first time provided uniform rules of procedure for the federal district courts. Before *Erie*, federal courts had been free under *Swift v. Tyson* to develop independent substantive rules of decision in many cases that would have been controlled by state law if litigated in a state court. As to procedure, the Conformity Act of 1872 had provided that procedure in federal district court, other than in equity and admiralty cases, should "conform, as near as may be" to the procedures of the state in which the court sat. The combined effect of *Erie* and the Federal Rules was, therefore, to reverse former practice with respect to both substance and procedure.

The Federal Rules were adopted pursuant to the 1934 Rules Enabling Act, now found in 28 U.S.C. § 2072, which gave the Supreme Court power to "prescribe general rules of practice and procedure" for the federal courts. It also specified that, "[s]uch rules shall not abridge, enlarge or modify any substantive right... ." Proposed drafts of the Rules were prepared by an Advisory Committee composed of law professors and practicing lawyers. After making some revisions to these proposals, the Supreme Court sent them to Congress. Under the terms of the Enabling Act, the Rules automatically took effect after Congress failed to disapprove them.

These two events created questions about how federal courts should handle issues that were arguably procedural in cases governed by state substantive law. As an initial matter, there is sometimes a fine line between substance and procedure. Even rules that are commonly understood as procedural can affect the outcome of a case. Consequently, if procedural rules vary depending on whether a case is heard in state or federal court, *Erie*'s concerns about forum shopping and inequitable adminstration of the laws might be implicated. Nonetheless, it is clear that the Federal Rules of Civil Procedure, which were promulgated with authorization from Congress, were designed to create a uniform system of procedure for the federal courts.

In deciding what law to apply to an arguably procedural issue in a case otherwise governed by state substantive law, there are at least three questions that a federal court might face. First, does a Federal Rule of Civil Procedure govern the issue? Second, if so, is the Rule valid under the Rules Enabling Act? Third, if the issue is not governed by a Federal Rule, is a federal court required under *Erie* to apply state law?

2. *Sibbach v. Wilson.* Relying on diversity jurisdiction, Sibbach filed a tort action against Wilson & Company in a federal court in Illinois for injuries allegedly sustained in an automobile accident in Indiana. At Wilson's request, and consistent with Rule 35 of the Federal Rules of Civil Procedure, the court ordered the plaintiff to submit to a physical examination by a court-appointed physician, even though an Illinois state court would not have issued such an order. Sibbach sought review in the Supreme Court, arguing that Rule 35 was inconsistent with the Rules Enabling Act because it modified a substantive right.

In Sibbach v. Wilson, 312 U.S. 1 (1941), the Supreme Court upheld the validity of Rule 35. The Court noted that "Congress has undoubted power to regulate the practice and procedure of federal courts, and may exercise that power by delegating to this or other federal courts authority to make rules not inconsistent with the statutes or Constitution of the United States." It concluded that the issue of court-ordered physical examinations was procedural and that, in regulating that issue, Rule 35 did not modify substantive rights in violation of the Rules Enabling Act. The Court said that the right not to undergo a physical examination "is no more important than many others enjoyed by litigants in District Courts sitting in the several states, before the Federal Rules of Civil Procedure altered and abolished old rights or privileges and created new ones in connection with the conduct of litigation." More to the point, the Court rejected the idea that the test for determining whether a right was substantive should turn on whether the right is "important," noting that such an approach would "invite endless litigation and confusion worse confounded." Instead, said the Court, "[t]he test must be whether a rule really regulates procedure—the judicial process for enforcing rights and duties recognized by substantive law, and for justly administering remedy and redress for disregard or infraction of them."

3. *Guaranty Trust Co. v. York*. Although *Sibbach* settled the general validity of the Federal Rules, those rules do not cover all matters that could be termed procedural. Does *Erie* require the federal courts to follow state law on procedural matters not governed by the Federal Rules? In Cities Service Oil Co. v. Dunlap, 308 U.S. 208 (1939), the Court held that a Texas rule on burden of proof (a matter not covered by the Federal Rules) must be followed because it "relate[d] to a substantial right" and was not merely "one of practice." In Palmer v. Hoffman, 318 U.S. 109 (1943), the Court considered whether Rule 8(c), which provides that contributory negligence must be pleaded as an affirmative defense, also meant that the defendant had the burden of proof on that issue. The Court held that "Rule 8(c) covers only the matter of pleading. The question of the burden of establishing contributory negligence is a question of local law which federal courts in diversity of citizenship cases must apply."

These early decisions did not make an effort to develop general guidelines for interpreting the Federal Rules or for administering the line between substance and procedure. The first major decision to do so was Guaranty Trust Co. v. York, 326 U.S. 99 (1945), which involved a class action filed in federal court based on diversity jurisdiction. The suit was brought in equity to recover for an alleged breach of trust in violation of state law. The question was whether the federal court was free, in a suit seeking equitable relief, to ignore the statute of limitations of the state whose substantive law controlled the controversy. *Guaranty Trust* is important for two reasons. First, the Court made it clear that the policy of *Erie* applied to suits in equity as well as law. Second, Justice Frankfurter's opinion for the Court advanced a general test for determining when *Erie* required resort to state law:

> Here we are dealing with a right to recover derived not from the United States but from one of the states. When, because the plaintiff happens to be a non-resident, such a right is enforceable in a federal as well as in a state court, the forms and mode of enforcing the right may at times, naturally enough, vary because

the two judicial systems are not identic. But since a federal court adjudicating a state-created right solely because of the diversity of citizenship of the parties is for that purpose, in effect, only another court of the state, it cannot afford recovery if the right to recover is made unavailable by the state nor can it substantially affect the enforcement of the right as given by the state.

And so the question is not whether a statute of limitations is deemed a matter of "procedure" in some sense. The question is whether such a statute concerns merely the manner and the means by which a right to recover, as recognized by the state, is enforced, or whether such statutory limitation is a matter of substance in the aspect that alone is relevant to our problem, namely, does it significantly affect the result of a litigation for a federal court to disregard a law of a state that would be controlling in an action upon the same claim by the same parties in a state court?

It is therefore immaterial whether statutes of limitation are characterized either as "substantive" or "procedural" in state court opinions in any use of those terms unrelated to the specific issue before us. *Erie R. Co. v. Tompkins* was not an endeavor to formulate scientific legal terminology. It expressed a policy that touches vitally the proper distribution of judicial power between state and federal courts. In essence, the intent of that decision was to insure that, in all cases where a federal court is exercising jurisdiction solely because of the diversity of citizenship of the parties, the outcome of the litigation in the federal court should be substantially the same, so far as legal rules determine the outcome of a litigation, as it would be if tried in a state court. The nub of the policy that underlies *Erie R. Co. v. Tompkins* is that for the same transaction the accident of a suit by a non-resident litigant in a federal court instead of in a state court a block away should not lead to a substantially different result.

The Court concluded that state law should be applied to determine the statute of limitations in a case otherwise governed by state law: "Plainly enough, a statute that would completely bar recovery in a suit if brought in a State court bears on a State-created right vitally, and not merely formally or negligibly. As to consequences that so intimately affect recovery or nonrecovery, a federal court in a diversity case should follow State law."

In attempting to distinguish between substance and procedure, is it useful to focus on whether the rule in question is likely to affect the outcome of the litigation? Could not any rule affect the outcome, if a party failed to comply with it?

4. *Ragan v. Merchants Transfer*. Four years after *Guaranty Trust*, the Court decided a trio of cases that were particularly deferential to state law. Ragan v. Merchants Transfer & Warehouse Co., 337 U.S. 530 (1949); Woods v. Interstate Realty Co., 337 U.S. 535 (1949); Cohen v. Beneficial

Industrial Loan Corporation, 337 U.S. 541 (1949). *Ragan* illustrates the Court's approach.

It involved a suit brought in federal court in Kansas concerning an automobile accident that had occurred on October 1, 1943. Federal Rule of Civil Procedure 3 provides that "a civil action is commenced by filing a complaint with the court." This was done on September 4, 1945, well within the two-year statute of limitations established by Kansas law. A summons was issued on September 7 and duly served, but it was later quashed, presumably because of some irregularity. A valid summons was finally served on December 28, after the statute of limitations had run.

Under Kansas law, the statute of limitations is not tolled until the summons is served. The plaintiff claimed that "the Federal Rules of Civil Procedure determine when an action is commenced in the federal courts—a matter of procedure which the principle of *Erie* does not control." Accordingly, the plaintiff argued, the suit should have been allowed to continue since it was properly filed in federal court within the applicable statute of limitations.

The Supreme Court disagreed. It held that the "theory of *Guaranty Trust*" required the federal court to follow the Kansas rule:

> [T]here can be no doubt that the suit was properly commenced in the federal court. But in the present case we look to local law to find the cause of action on which the suit is brought. Since that cause of action is created by local law, the measure of it is to be found only in local law. It carries the same burden and is subject to the same defenses in federal court as in the state court. It accrues and comes to an end when local law so declares. Where local law qualifies or abridges it, the federal court must follow suit.... We cannot give it longer life in the federal court than it would have had in the state court without adding something to the cause of action. We may not do that consistently with *Erie*.

5. *Byrd v. Blue Ridge*. In part because of considerations relating to the role of the jury in the federal courts, the Court was less deferential to state law in Byrd v. Blue Ridge Rural Elec. Cooperative, Inc., 356 U.S. 525 (1958). On the merits, the question was whether the plaintiff was a "statutory employee" of the defendant under South Carolina law. If so, he could recover only workmen's compensation. If not, he was permitted to sue for negligence. The *Erie* issue was whether the "statutory employee" question should be tried to a jury or, as required by South Carolina law, to the judge. In an opinion by Justice Brennan, the Court began by describing the state rule as "merely a form and mode of enforcing the immunity, and not a rule intended to be bound up with the definition of the rights and obligations of the parties." The Court then turned to the legacy of *Guaranty Trust*:

But cases following *Erie* have evinced a broader policy to the effect that the federal courts should conform as near as may be—in the absence of other considerations—to state rules even of form and mode where the state rules may bear substantially on the question whether the litigation would come out one way in the federal court and another way in the state court if the federal court failed to apply a particular local rule. Concededly the nature of the tribunal which tries issues may be important in the enforcement of the parcel of rights making up a cause of action or defense, and bear significantly upon achievement of uniform enforcement of the right. It may well be that in the instant personal-injury case the outcome would be substantially affected by whether the issue ... is decided by a judge or a jury. Therefore, were "outcome" the only consideration, a strong case might appear for saying that the federal court should follow the state practice.

But there are affirmative countervailing considerations at work here. The federal system is an independent system for administering justice to litigants who properly invoke its jurisdiction. An essential characteristic of that system is the manner in which, in civil common-law actions, it distributed trial functions between judge and jury and, under the influence—if not the command[10]—of the Seventh Amendment, assigns the decisions of disputed questions of fact to the jury. The policy of uniform enforcement of state-created rights and obligations, see, e.g., *Guaranty Trust v. York*, cannot in every case exact compliance with a state rule—not bound up with rights and obligations—which disrupts the federal system of allocating functions between judge and jury.

The Court concluded that the federal court should not follow the state rule in this case, in light of the "strong federal policy against allowing state rules to disrupt the judge-jury relationship in the federal courts" and the fact that it was far from clear that following the federal jury practice would change the outcome.

6. Concluding Comment. To this point, the Court's "substance-procedure" jurisprudence had not clearly distinguished between situations in which the Federal Rules purported to govern an issue and situations in which they did not. In *Hanna v. Plumer*, the Court drew a sharp distinction between these two situations and modified the outcome-determinative test of *Guaranty Trust*.

---

10. Our conclusion makes unnecessary the consideration of—and we intimate no view upon—the constitutional question whether the right of jury trial protected in the federal courts by the Seventh Amendment embraces the factual issue of statutory immunity when asserted, as here, as an affirmative defense in a common-law negligence action.

Hanna v. Plumer

Supreme Court of the United States, 1965.
380 U.S. 460.

■ MR. CHIEF JUSTICE WARREN delivered the opinion of the Court.

The question to be decided is whether, in a civil action where the jurisdiction of the United States district court is based upon diversity of citizenship between the parties, service of process shall be made in the manner prescribed by state law or that set forth in Rule 4(d)(1) of the Federal Rules of Civil Procedure.

On February 6, 1963, petitioner, a citizen of Ohio, filed her complaint in the District Court for the District of Massachusetts, claiming damages in excess of $10,000 for personal injuries resulting from an automobile accident in South Carolina, allegedly caused by the negligence of one Louise Plumer Osgood, a Massachusetts citizen deceased at the time of the filing of the complaint. Respondent, Mrs. Osgood's executor and also a Massachusetts citizen, was named as defendant. On February 8, service was made by leaving copies of the summons and the complaint with respondent's wife at his residence, concededly in compliance with Rule 4(d)(1), which provides:

> The summons and complaint shall be served together. The plaintiff shall furnish the person making service with such copies as are necessary. Service shall be made as follows:
>
> > (1) Upon an individual other than an infant or an incompetent person, by delivering a copy of the summons and of the complaint to him personally or by leaving copies thereof at his dwelling house or usual place of abode with some person of suitable age and discretion then residing therein . . . .

Respondent filed his answer on February 26, alleging, *inter alia*, that the action could not be maintained because it had been brought "contrary to and in violation of the provisions of Massachusetts General Laws (Ter. Ed.) Chapter 197, Section 9." That section provides:

> Except as provided in this chapter, an executor or administrator shall not be held to answer to an action by a creditor of the deceased which is not commenced within one year from the time of his giving bond for the performance of his trust, or to such an action which is commenced within said year unless before the expiration thereof the writ in such action has been served by delivery in hand upon such executor or administrator or service thereof accepted by him or a notice stating the name of the estate, the name and address of the creditor, the amount of the claim and the court in which the action has been brought has been filed in the proper registry of probate. . . .

On October 17, 1963, the District Court granted respondent's motion for summary judgment, citing Ragan v. Merchants Transfer & Warehouse Co., 337 U.S. 530 (1949), and Guaranty Trust Co. v. York, 326 U.S. 99 (1945), in support of its conclusion that the adequacy of the service was to be measured by § 9, with which, the court held, petitioner had not complied. On appeal, petitioner admitted noncompliance with § 9, but argued that Rule 4(d)(1) defines the method by which service of process is to be effected in diversity actions. The Court of Appeals for the First Circuit, finding that "relatively recent amendments [to § 9] evince a clear legislative purpose to require personal notification within the year," concluded that the conflict of state and federal rules was over "a substantive rather than a procedural matter," and unanimously affirmed. Because of the threat to the goal of uniformity of federal procedure posed by the decision below, we granted certiorari.

We conclude that the adoption of Rule 4(d)(1), designed to control service of process in diversity actions, neither exceeded the congressional mandate embodied in the Rules Enabling Act nor transgressed constitutional bounds, and that the Rule is therefore the standard against which the District Court should have measured the adequacy of the service. Accordingly, we reverse the decision of the Court of Appeals.

The Rules Enabling Act, 28 U.S.C. § 2702, provides, in pertinent part:

> The Supreme Court shall have the power to prescribe, by general rules, the forms of process, writs, pleadings, and motions, and the practice and procedure of the district courts of the United States in civil actions.

> Such rules shall not abridge, enlarge or modify any substantive right and shall preserve the right of trial by jury. . . .

Under the cases construing the scope of the Enabling Act, Rule 4(d)(1) clearly passes muster. Prescribing the manner in which a defendant is to be notified that a suit has been instituted against him, it relates to the "practice and procedure of the district courts."

> The test must be whether a rule really regulates procedure,—the judicial process for enforcing rights and duties recognized by substantive law and for justly administering remedy and redress for disregard or infraction of them.

Sibbach v. Wilson & Co., 312 U.S. 1, 14 (1941). . . .

[W]ere there no conflicting state procedure, Rule 4(d)(1) would clearly control. However, respondent, focusing on the contrary Massachusetts rule, calls to the Court's attention another line of cases, a line which—like the Federal Rules—had its birth in 1938. Erie R. Co. v. Tompkins, 304 U.S. 64 (1938), overruling Swift v. Tyson, 41 U.S. (16 Pet.) 1 (1842), held that federal courts sitting in diversity cases, when deciding questions of "substantive" law, are bound by state court decisions as well as state statutes. The broad command of *Erie* was therefore identical to that of the Enabling Act: federal courts are to apply state substantive law and federal procedural law. However, as subsequent cases sharpened the distinction between substance and procedure, the line of cases following *Erie* diverged markedly from the line construing the Enabling Act. *Guaranty Trust Co. v. York* made it clear that *Erie*-type problems were not to be solved by reference to any traditional or common-sense substance-procedure distinction:

> And so the question is not whether a statute of limitations is deemed a matter of "procedure" in some sense. The question is ... does it significantly affect the result of a litigation for a federal court to disregard a law of a state that would be controlling in an action upon the same claim by the same parties in a state court?

326 U.S., at 109.

Respondent, by placing primary reliance on *York* and *Ragan*, suggests that the *Erie* doctrine acts as a check on the Federal Rules of Civil Procedure, that despite the clear command of Rule 4(d)(1), *Erie* and its progeny demand the application of the Massachusetts rule. Reduced to essentials, the argument is: (1) *Erie*, as refined in *York*, demands that federal courts apply state law whenever application of federal law in its stead will alter the outcome of the case. (2) In this case, a determination that the Massachusetts service requirements obtain will result in immediate victory for respondent. If, on the other hand, it should be held that Rule 4(d)(1) is applicable, the litigation will continue, with possible victory for petitioner. (3) Therefore, *Erie* demands application of the Massachusetts rule. The syllogism possesses an appealing simplicity, but is for several reasons invalid.

In the first place, it is doubtful that, even if there were no Federal Rule making it clear that in-hand service is not required in diversity actions, the *Erie* rule would have obligated the District Court to follow the Massachusetts procedure. "Outcome-determination" analysis was never intended to serve as a talisman. Byrd v. Blue Ridge Rural Elec. Cooperative, 356 U.S. 525, 537 (1958). Indeed, the message of *York* itself is that choices between state and federal law are to be made not by application of any automatic, "litmus paper" criterion, but rather by reference to the policies underlying the *Erie* rule.

The *Erie* rule is rooted in part in a realization that it would be unfair for the character or result of a litigation materially to differ because the suit had been brought in a federal court.... The decision was also in part a reaction to the practice of "forum-shopping" which had grown up in response to the rule of *Swift v. Tyson*. That the *York* test was an attempt to effectuate these policies is demonstrated by the fact that the opinion framed the inquiry in terms of "substantial" variations between state and federal litigation. Not only are nonsubstantial, or trivial, variations not likely to raise the sort of equal protection problems which troubled the Court in *Erie*; they are also unlikely to influence the choice of a forum. The "outcome-determination" test therefore cannot be read without reference to the twin aims of the *Erie* rule: discouragement of forum-shopping and avoidance of inequitable administration of the laws.[9]

The difference between the conclusion that the Massachusetts rule is applicable, and the conclusion that it is not, is of course at this point "outcome-determinative" in the sense that if we hold the state rule to apply, respondent prevails, whereas if we hold that Rule 4(d)(1) governs, the litigation will continue. But in this sense *every* procedural variation is "outcome-determinative." For example, having brought suit in a federal court, a plaintiff cannot then insist on the right to file subsequent pleadings in accord with the time limits applicable in the state courts, even though enforcement of the federal timetable will, if he continues to insist that he must meet only the state time limit, result in determination of the controversy against him. So it is here. Though choice of the federal or state rule will at this point have a marked effect upon the outcome of the litigation, the difference between the two rules would be of scant, if any, relevance to the choice of a forum. Petitioner, in choosing her forum, was not presented with a situation where application of the state rule would wholly bar recovery;[10] rather, adherence to the state rule would have resulted only in altering the way in which process was served.[11] Moreover, it is difficult to argue that permitting service of defendant's wife to take the place of in-hand service of defendant himself alters the mode of enforcement of state-created rights in a fashion sufficiently "substantial" to raise the sort of equal protection problems to which the *Erie* opinion alluded.

9. The Court of Appeals seemed to frame the inquiry in terms of how "important" § 9 is to the State. In support of its suggestion that § 9 serves some interest the State regards as vital to its citizens, the court noted that something like § 9 has been on the books in Massachusetts a long time, that § 9 has been amended a number of times, and that § 9 is designed to make sure that executors receive actual notice. The apparent lack of relation among these three observations is not surprising, because it is not clear to what sort of question the Court of Appeals was addressing itself. One cannot meaningfully ask how important something is without first asking "important for what purpose?" *Erie* and its progeny make clear that when a federal court sitting in a diversity case is faced with a question of whether or not to apply state law, the importance of a state rule is indeed relevant, but only in the context of asking whether application of the rule would make so important a difference to the character or result of the litigation that failure to enforce it would unfairly discriminate against citizens of the forum State, or wheth-

er application of the rule would have so important an effect upon the fortunes of one or both of the litigants that failure to enforce it would be likely to cause a plaintiff to choose the federal court.

10. See *Guaranty Trust Co. v. York,* supra; *Ragan v. Merchants Transfer Co.,* supra; Woods v. Interstate Realty Co., 337 U.S. 535 (1949). Similarly, a federal court's refusal to enforce the New Jersey rule involved in Cohen v. Beneficial Loan Corp., 337 U.S. 541 (1949), requiring the posting of security by plaintiffs in stockholders' derivative actions, might well impel a stockholder to choose to bring suit in the federal, rather than the state, court.

11. We cannot seriously entertain the thought that one suing an estate would be led to choose the federal court because of a belief that adherence to Rule 4(d)(1) is less likely to give the executor actual notice than § 9, and therefore more likely to produce a default judgment. Rule 4(d)(1) is well designed to give actual notice, as it did in this case.

There is, however, a more fundamental flaw in respondent's syllogism: the incorrect assumption that the rule of *Erie R. Co. v. Tompkins* constitutes the appropriate test of the validity and therefore the applicability of a Federal Rule of Civil Procedure. The *Erie* rule has never been invoked to void a Federal Rule. It is true that there have been cases where this Court has held applicable a state rule in the face of an argument that the situation was governed by one of the Federal Rules. But the holding of each such case was not that *Erie* commanded displacement of a Federal Rule by an inconsistent state rule, but rather that the scope of the Federal Rule was not as broad as the losing party urged, and therefore, there being no Federal Rule which covered the point in dispute, *Erie* commanded the enforcement of state law.... (Here, of course, the clash is unavoidable; Rule 4(d)(1) says—implicitly, but with unmistakable clarity—that in-hand service is not required in federal courts.) At the same time, in cases adjudicating the validity of Federal Rules, we have not applied the *York* rule or other refinements of *Erie*, but have to this day continued to decide questions concerning the scope of the Enabling Act and the constitutionality of specific Federal Rules in light of the distinction set forth in *Sibbach*.

Nor has the development of two separate lines of cases been inadvertent. The line between "substance" and "procedure" shifts as the legal context change.... It is true that both the Enabling Act and the *Erie* rule say, roughly, that federal courts are to apply state "substantive" law and federal "procedural" law, but from that it need not follow that the tests are identical. For they were designed to control very different sorts of decisions. When a situation is covered by one of the Federal Rules, the question facing the court is a far cry from the typical, relatively unguided *Erie* choice: the court has been instructed to apply the Federal Rule, and can refuse to do so only if the Advisory Committee, this Court, and Congress erred in their prima facie judgment that the Rule in question transgresses neither the terms of the Enabling Act nor constitutional restrictions.

We are reminded by the *Erie* opinion that neither Congress nor the federal courts can, under the guise of formulating rules of decision for federal courts, fashion rules which are not supported by a grant of federal authority contained in Article I or some other section of the Constitution; in such areas state law must govern because there can be no other law. But the opinion in *Erie*, which involved no Federal Rule and dealt with a question which was "substantive" in every traditional sense (whether the railroad owed a duty of care to Tompkins as a trespasser or a licensee), surely neither said nor implied that measures like Rule 4(d)(1) are unconstitutional. For the constitutional provision for a federal court system (augmented by the Necessary and Proper Clause) carries with it congressional power to make rules governing the practice and pleading in those courts, which in turn includes a power to regulate matters which, though falling within the uncertain area between substance and procedure, are rationally capable of classification as either. Cf. M'Culloch v. Maryland, 17 U.S. (4 Wheat.) 316, 421 (1819). Neither *York* nor the cases following it ever suggested that the rule there laid down for coping with situations where no Federal Rule applies is coextensive with the limitation on Congress to which *Erie* had adverted.. . .

Erie and its offspring cast no doubt on the long-recognized power of Congress to prescribe housekeeping rules for federal courts even though some of those rules will inevitably differ from comparable state rules. . . . Thus, though a court, in measuring a Federal Rule against the standards contained in the Enabling Act and the Constitution, need not wholly blind itself to the degree to which the Rule makes the character and result of the federal litigation stray from the course it would follow in state courts, it cannot be forgotten that the *Erie* rule, and the guidelines suggested in *York*, were created to serve another purpose altogether. To hold that a Federal Rule of Civil Procedure must cease to function whenever it alters the mode of enforcing state-created rights would be to disembowel either the Constitution's grant of power over federal procedure or Congress' attempt to exercise that power in the Enabling Act. Rule 4(d)(1) is valid and controls the instant case.

Reversed.

■ MR. JUSTICE BLACK concurs in the result.

■ MR. JUSTICE HARLAN, concurring.

It is unquestionably true that up to now *Erie* and the cases following it have not succeeded in articulating a workable doctrine governing choice of law in diversity actions. I respect the Court's effort to clarify the situation in today's opinion. However, in doing so I think it has misconceived the constitutional premises of *Erie* and has failed to deal adequately with those past decisions upon which the courts below relied.

Erie was something more than an opinion which worried about "forum-shopping and avoidance of inequitable administration of the laws," although to be sure these were important elements of the decision. I have always regarded that decision as one of the modern cornerstones of our federalism, expressing policies that profoundly touch the allocation of judicial power between the state and federal systems. *Erie* recognized that there should not be two conflicting systems of law controlling the primary activity of citizens, for such alternative governing authority must necessarily give rise to a debilitating uncertainty in the planning of everyday affairs.[1] And it recognized that the scheme of our Constitution envisions an allocation of law-making functions between state and federal legislative processes which is undercut if the federal judiciary can make substantive law affecting state affairs beyond the bounds of congressional legislative powers in this regard. Thus, in diversity cases *Erie* commands that it be the state law governing primary private activity which prevails.

---

1. Since the rules involved in the present case are parallel, rather than conflicting, this first rationale does not come into play here.

The shorthand formulations which have appeared in some past decisions are prone to carry untoward results that frequently arise from oversimplification. The Court is quite right in stating that the "outcome-determinative" test of *Guaranty Trust Co. v. York*, if taken literally, proves too much, for any rule, no matter how clearly "procedural," can affect the outcome of litigation if it is not obeyed. In turning from the "outcome" test of *York* back to the unadorned forum-shopping rationale of *Erie*, however, the Court falls prey to like oversimplification, for a simple forum-shopping rule also proves too much; litigants often choose a federal forum merely to obtain what they consider the advantages of the Federal Rules of Civil Procedure or to try their cases before a supposedly more favorable judge. To my mind the proper line of approach in determining whether to apply a state or a federal rule, whether "substantive" or "procedural," is to stay close to basic principles by inquiring if the choice of rule would substantially affect those primary decisions respecting human conduct which our constitutional system leaves to state regulation.[2] If so, *Erie* and the Constitution require that the state rule prevail, even in the face of a conflicting federal rule.

The Court weakens, if indeed it does not submerge, this basic principle by finding, in effect, a grant of substantive legislative power in the constitutional provision for a federal court system (compare *Swift v. Tyson*), and through it, setting up the Federal Rules as a body of law inviolate.... So long as a reasonable man could characterize any duly adopted federal rule as "procedural," the Court, unless I misapprehend what is said, would have it apply no matter how seriously it frustrated a State's substantive regulation of the primary conduct and affairs of its citizens. Since the members of the Advisory Committee, the Judicial Conference, and this Court who formulated the Federal Rules are presumably reasonable men, it follows that the integrity of the Federal Rules is absolute. Whereas the unadulterated outcome and forum-shopping tests may err too far toward honoring state rules, I submit that the Court's "arguably procedural, ergo constitutional" test moves too fast and far in the other direction....

It remains to apply what has been said to the present case. The Massachusetts rule provides that an executor need not answer suits unless in-hand service was made upon him or notice of the action was filed in the proper registry of probate within one year of his giving bond. The evident intent of this statute is to permit an executor to distribute the estate which he is administering without fear that further liabilities may be outstanding for which he could be held personally liable. If the Federal District Court in Massachusetts applies Rule 4(d)(1) of the Federal Rules of Civil Procedure

---

2.   Byrd v. Blue Ridge Rural Elec. Cooperative, Inc., 356 U.S. 525, 536–40 (1958), indicated that state procedures would apply if the State had manifested a particularly strong interest in their employment. However, this approach may not be of constitutional proportions.

instead of the Massachusetts service rule, what effect would that have on the speed and assurance with which estates are distributed? As I see it, the effect would not be substantial. It would mean simply that an executor would have to check at his own house or the federal courthouse as well as the registry of probate before he could distribute the estate with impunity. As this does not seem enough to give rise to any real impingement on the vitality of the state policy which the Massachusetts rule is intended to serve, I concur in the judgment of the Court.

NOTES ON SUBSTANCE AND PROCEDURE AFTER *HANNA*

1. Questions and Comments on *Hanna*. The Court's opinion in *Hanna* addresses two situations. The first is when a Federal Rule of Civil Procedure conflicts with state law. The question then, the Court says, is whether the federal rule is "rationally capable of classification" as procedure. If so, the Federal Rule is valid and must be applied. Is this approach consistent with the Rules Enabling Act? With more general considerations of federalism?

The second situation to which *Hanna* speaks is when there is no Federal Rule of Civil Procedure on point. The Court's discussion of the "twin aims of Erie" in footnote 9 and its accompanying text suggests that the test for determining whether to follow state law in such a situation is twofold. State law is to be followed if

> the rule would make so important a difference to the character or result of the litigation that failure to enforce it would unfairly discriminate against citizens of the forum State, or ... application of the rule would have so important an effect upon the fortunes of one or both of the litigants that failure to enforce it would be likely to cause a plaintiff to choose the federal court.

Is this a meaningful inquiry? Is Justice Harlan correct that this inquiry, like the "outcome" test, "proves too much"? As a thought experiment, what would be wrong with the following approach?

(i) If there is an applicable Federal Rule of Civil Procedure, follow it.

(ii) If not, but there is a discernible federal policy, follow it.

(iii) If there is no applicable federal rule or policy, follow state law.

Would step (i) be consistent with the Rules Enabling Act? Does step (ii) give enough weight to the concerns articulated by the Court in *Erie*?

In the substance-procedure cases that have been decided by the Supreme Court since *Hanna*, there is frequently a dispute over whether a Federal Rule applies. In making this determination, what attitude should the federal courts bring to their interpretation of the Federal Rules? Should the Federal Rules be narrowly construed to avoid conflicts with state law? Or is the desirability of a uniform system of federal procedure—applicable to diversity and federal question cases alike—so strong that the possibility of conflict with state law should be ignored?

2. *Walker v. Armco Steel Corp.* As illustrated by Walker v. Armco Steel Corp., 446 U.S. 740 (1980), considerations of substance vs. procedure can affect the determination of whether a Federal Rule applies to a particular issue. Walker, a carpenter, injured his eye when a nail he was hammering shattered. He filed a federal diversity suit against the manufacturer of the nail. The injury occurred on August 22, 1975. The complaint was filed on August 19, 1977. The record is ambiguous as to whether the summons was issued on August 19 or August 20, but in any event it was not delivered to the marshal for service until December 1, 1977, when it was served on the defendant.

The Oklahoma statute of limitations was two years. Oklahoma law provided that an action was "commenced" for purposes of tolling the statute of limitations by service of the summons, or in the alternative by filing the complaint if the summons was served within 60 days. Rule 3 of the Federal Rules, however, provides that, "A civil action is commenced by filing a complaint with the court." The plaintiff conceded that the Oklahoma law was not followed, but argued that Rule 3 should govern in federal court. The District Court dismissed the complaint, citing *Ragan,* and the Supreme Court agreed in a unanimous opinion by Justice Marshall.

After reviewing *Erie, Guaranty Trust, Ragan,* and *Hanna,* the Court noted that "the instant action is barred by the statute of limitations unless *Ragan* is no longer good law." The Court continued:

> This Court in *Hanna* distinguished *Ragan* rather than overruled it, and for good reason. Application of the *Hanna* analysis is premised on a "direct collision" between the federal rule and the state law. In *Hanna* itself the "clash" between Rule 4(d)(1) and the state in-hand service requirement was "unavoidable." The first question must therefore be whether the scope of the federal rule in fact is sufficiently broad to control the issue before the Court. It is only if that question is answered affirmatively that the *Hanna* analysis applies.[9]
>
> . . . There is no indication that [Rule 3] was intended to toll a state statute of limitations, much less that it purported to displace state tolling rules for purposes of state statutes of limitations. In our view, in diversity actions Rule 3 governs the date from which various timing requirements of the federal rules begin to run, but does not affect state statutes of limitations.
>
> In contrast to Rule 3, the Oklahoma statute is a statement of a substantive decision by that state that actual service on, and

9. This is not to suggest that the Federal Rules of Civil Procedure are to be narrowly construed in order to avoid a "direct collision" with state law. The Federal Rules should be given their plain meaning. If a direct collision with state law arises from that plain meaning, then the analysis developed in *Hanna v. Plumer* applies.

accordingly actual notice by, the defendant is an integral part of the several policies served by the statute of limitations. The statute of limitations establishes a deadline after which the defendant may legitimately have peace of mind; it also recognizes that after a certain period of time it is unfair to require the defendant to attempt to piece together his defense to an old claim. A requirement of actual service promotes both of those functions of the statute. It is these policy aspects which make the service requirement an "integral" part of the statute of limitations both in this case and in *Ragan*. As such, the service rule must be considered part and parcel of the statute of limitations. Rule 3 does not replace such policy determinations found in state law. Rule 3 and [the Oklahoma law] can exist side-by-side, therefore, each controlling its own intended sphere of coverage without conflict.

Since there is no direct conflict between the federal rule and the state law, the *Hanna* analysis does not apply.[14] Instead, the policies behind *Erie* and *Ragan* control the issue whether, in the absence of a federal rule directly on point, state service requirements which are an integral part of the state statute of limitations should control in an action based on state law which is filed in federal court under diversity jurisdiction. The reasons for the application of such a state service requirement in a diversity action in the absence of a conflicting federal rule are well explained in *Erie* and *Ragan,* and need not be repeated here. It is sufficient to note that although in this case failure to apply the state service law might not create any problem of forum shopping,[15] the result would be an "inequitable administration" of the law. *Hanna,* at 468. There is simply no reason why, in the absence of a controlling federal rule, an action based on state law which concededly would be barred in the state courts by the statute of limitations should proceed through litigation to judgment in federal court solely because of the fortuity that there is diversity of citizenship between the litigants. The policies underlying diversity jurisdiction do not support such a distinction between state and federal plaintiffs, and *Erie* and its progeny do not permit it.

Is *Walker* consistent with *Hanna*? What is the Court assuming when interpreting Rule 3? Does *Walker* imply, contrary to the Court's assertion, that the Federal Rules should be narrowly construed to avoid a "direct collision" with state law?

---

14. Since we hold that Rule 3 does not apply, it is unnecessary for us to address the second question posed by the *Hanna* analysis: whether Rule 3, if applied, would be outside the scope of the Rules Enabling Act or beyond the power of Congress under the Constitution.

15. There is no indication that when petitioner filed his suit in federal court he had any reason to believe that he would be unable to comply with the service requirements of Oklahoma law or that he chose to sue in federal court in an attempt to avoid those service requirements.

3. ***Gasperini v. Center for Humanities.*** In Gasperini v. Center for Humanities, 518 U.S. 415 (1996), the Court addressed a situation in which, at least in the view of the majority, no Federal Rule was potentially applicable. As a result, the Court was operating under the "twin aims of *Erie*" analysis articulated in *Hanna.*

Gasperini, a journalist, brought a diversity action against the Center for Humanities in a federal district court in New York, alleging that the Center had lost a set of 300 photographic slides that it had borrowed from him. The Center conceded liability, and the issue of damages was tried before a jury. After hearing expert testimony, the jury awarded Gasperini $1500 for each lost slide, for a total of $450,000. The Circuit Court reversed, concluding that the award was excessive. The court reached this conclusion after applying a New York statute that directs New York appellate courts to review the size of jury verdicts and order new trials when the jury's award "deviates materially from what would be reasonable compensation." This standard is more intrusive than the common law standard traditionally applied by the federal courts in reviewing jury awards, under which the award would not be disturbed unless so exorbitant that it "shocked the conscience of the court."

The Supreme Court vacated the decision below and remanded for further proceedings. In an opinion by Justice Ginsburg, the Court began by observing that "[c]lassification of a law as 'substantive' or 'procedural' for *Erie* purposes is sometimes a challenging endeavor." After reviewing the relevant decisions, it said that "we address the question whether New York's 'deviates materially' standard . . . is outcome affective in this sense: Would 'application of the [standard] . . . have so important an effect upon the fortunes of one or both of the litigants that failure to [apply] it would [unfairly discriminate against citizens of the forum State, or] be likely to cause a plaintiff to choose the federal court?"

The Court noted that even the plaintiff acknowledged that if New York had enacted a statutory cap on damages, this would be "substantive" for purposes of the *Erie* doctrine, and added that the New York law in question "was designed to provide an analogous control." The Court further observed that although New York law "contains a procedural instruction, . . . the State's objective is manifestly substantive." Finally, the Court said that if federal courts ignored the state law standard, there would likely be substantial variations between state and federal monetary judgments. The conclusion, therefore, was that the New York law implicated the twin aims of *Erie* articulated in *Hanna.*

The Court went on to explain, however, that there was a countervailing interest here that stemmed from the Seventh Amendment. This Amendment "bears not only on the allocation of trial functions between judge and jury, the issue in *Byrd*; it also controls the allocation of authority to review verdicts, the issue of concern here." Application of the New York standard by a federal appeals court, it was reasoned, "would be out of sync with the federal system's division of trial and appellate court functions, an allocation weighted by the Seventh Amendment." This concern led to the conclusion that federal district courts, rather than the federal circuit court should apply New York's "deviates materially" standard, subject to review by the circuit court for abuse of discretion.

Justice Scalia dissented, joined by Chief Justice Rehnquist and Justice Thomas. He argued that "changing the standard by which trial judges review jury verdicts ... disrupt[s] the federal system, and is plainly inconsistent with the 'strong federal policy against allowing state rules to disrupt the judge-jury relationship in the federal court.' Byrd v. Blue Ridge Rural Elec. Cooperative, Inc., 356 U.S. 525, 538 (1958)." He rejected the majority's analogy to a statutory cap on damages, arguing that "[t]here is an absolutely fundamental distinction between a *rule of law* such as that, which would ordinarily be imposed upon the jury in the trial court's instructions, and a *rule of review*, which simply determines how closely the jury verdict will be scrutinized for compliance with the instructions." He also accused the majority of "commit[ting] the classic *Erie* mistake of regarding whatever changes the outcome as substantive." Finally, he argued that the Court should not even have reached the *Erie* question because Rule 59 of the Federal Rules of Civil Procedure provides that "[a] new trial may be granted ... for any of the reasons for which new trials have heretofore been granted in actions at law in the courts of the United States." Because "[i]t is simply not possible to give controlling effect both to the federal standard and the state standard in reviewing the jury's award, ... the court has no choice but to apply the Federal Rule."

4. *Semtek International Inc. v. Lockheed Martin Corp.* As in *Gasperini*, the Court in Semtek International Inc. v. Lockheed Martin Corp., 531 U.S. 497 (2001), found that no Federal Rule applied to the issue before it. In that case, Semtek's suit against Lockheed, based on diversity jurisdiction, had been dismissed by a California federal district court as barred by the California two-year statute of limitations. A suit alleging the same claims was then filed in a Maryland state court, based on the Maryland three-year limitations period. The Maryland courts held that the preclusive effect of the California federal court judgment was to be determined by federal law and that, under the applicable federal law, the suit was barred.

The Supreme Court unanimously reversed. In an opinion by Justice Scalia, the Court found no answer in the Federal Rules of Civil Procedure. Although Rule 41(b) deems dismissals such as this one to be a judgment "on the merits," the Court concluded that it does not address the res judicata effect of such judgments. Among other things, the reasoning was that construing Rule 41(a) to give more res judicata effect to dismissals of state law claims than is provided for under the state law in which the federal court sits would arguably violate the Rules Enabling Act by affecting substantive rights, and would run afoul of the twin aims of *Erie* (by creating a claim preclusive judgment in cases removed to federal court but not cases litigated in state court). So instead Rule 41(b) was interpreted as simply barring the return of the losing party *to the same court.*

There was one prior Supreme Court case on point, Dupasseur v. Rochereau, 88 U.S. (21 Wall.) 130 (1875), which held that state law controlled the res judicata effect of a federal trial court exercising diversity jurisdiction. But *Dupasseur* was "not dispositive because it was decided under the Conformity Act of 1872, which required federal courts to apply the procedural law of the forum State in nonequity cases." What, then, to do? The Court's answer was that "federal common law governs the claim-preclusive effect of a dismissal by a federal court sitting in diversity.... It is left to us, then, to determine the appropriate federal rule."

And what should "the appropriate federal rule" be? The answer was:

> [D]espite the sea change that has occurred in the background law since *Dupasseur* was decided—not only repeal of the Conformity Act but also the watershed decision of this Court in *Erie*—we think the result decreed by *Dupasseur* continues to be correct for diversity cases. Since state, rather than federal, substantive law is at issue there is no need for a uniform federal rule. And indeed, nationwide uniformity in the substance of the matter is better served by having the same claim-preclusive rule (the state rule) apply whether the dismissal has been ordered by a state or a federal court. This is, it seems to us, a classic case for adopting, as the federally prescribed rule of decision, the law that would be applied by state courts in the State in which the federal diversity court sits. [A]ny other rule would produce the sort of "forum-shopping ... and ... inequitable administration of the laws" that *Erie* seeks to avoid, Hanna v. Plumer, 380 U.S. 460, 468 (1965), since filing in, or removing to, federal court would be encouraged by the divergent effects that the litigants would anticipate from likely grounds of dismissal.
>
> This federal reference to state law will not obtain, of course, in situations in which the state law is incompatible with federal interests. If, for example, state law did not accord claim-preclusive effect to dismissals for willful violation of discovery orders, federal courts' interest in the integrity of their own processes might justify a contrary federal rule. No such conflict with potential federal interests exists in the present case. Dismissal of this state cause of action was decreed by the California federal court only because the California statute of limitations so required; and there is no conceivable federal interest in giving that time bar more effect in other courts than the California courts themselves would impose.

The case was accordingly remanded so that the Maryland courts could determine the applicable California preclusion rules.[1]

---

1. In Taylor v. Sturgell, 553 U.S. 880 (2008), the Court observed that "[f]or judg- ments in federal-question cases ... federal courts participate in developing 'uniform fed-

5. *Shady Grove Orthopedic Associates v. Allstate Insurance Co.*

The Court returned to the first part of the *Hanna* analysis, which governs what to do when a Federal Rule is potentially applicable, in Shady Grove Orthopedic Associates v. Allstate Insurance Co., 559 U.S. ___ (2010). After Shady Grove provided medical care to Sonia Galvez, it was assigned her rights to insurance benefits under a policy issued in New York by Allstate Insurance Co. Shady Grove tendered its claim to Allstate, which under New York law had 30 days in which to pay it. Allstate eventually paid, but not on time, and it refused to pay the statutory interest mandated by New York law. Shady Grove then filed a diversity class action in federal court in New York, alleging that Allstate routinely refused to pay interest on overdue benefits. After concluding that statutory interest constituted a "penalty," the District Court dismissed the suit on the basis of a New York law providing that "[u]nless a statute creating or imposing a penalty ... specifically authorizes the recovery thereof in a class action, an action to recover a penalty ... created or imposed by statute may not be maintained as a class action." The court reached this conclusion notwithstanding Rule 23 of the Federal Rules of Civil Procedure, which provides that "[a] class action may be maintained" if certain conditions, all of which were satisfied, are met.

(i) Interpretive Principles. In an opinion by Justice Scalia, a five to four majority described the starting point of its analysis:

> We must first determine whether Rule 23 answers the question in dispute. If it does, it governs—New York's law notwithstanding—unless it exceeds statutory authorization or Congress's rulemaking power. We do not wade into *Erie*'s murky waters unless the federal rule is inapplicable or invalid.

The first question, therefore, was whether Rule 23 applied, and in particular whether it should be interpreted in light of the potential conflict with New York law. The Court began its discussion of this issue as follows:

> The question in dispute is whether Shady Grove's suit may proceed as a class action. Rule 23 provides an answer.... By its terms [it] creates a categorical rule entitling a plaintiff whose suit meets the specified criteria to pursue his claim as a class action. [It] provides a one-size-fits-all formula for deciding the class-action question. Because [New York law] attempts to answer the same question—i.e., it states that Shady Grove's suit "may *not* be maintained as a class action" (emphasis added) because of the relief it seeks—it cannot apply in diversity suits unless Rule 23 is ultra vires.

> Joined by Justices Kennedy, Breyer, and Alito, Justice Ginsburg argued in dissent that there was no conflict between Rule 23 and the New

eral rule[s]' of res judicata, which this Court
has ultimate authority to determine and declare."

York law. Her characterization of the situation was that the New York law effectively provided a cap on damages:

> Sensibly read, Rule 23 governs procedural aspects of class litigation, but allows state law to control the size of a monetary award a class plaintiff may pursue.... Rule 23 describes a method of enforcing a claim for relief, while [New York law] defines the dimensions of the claim itself.

She also argued that the Court should "interpret Federal Rules with awareness of, and sensitivity to, important state regulatory policies." It should avoid "immoderate interpretations of the Federal Rules that would trench on state prerogatives without serving any countervailing federal interest." She accused the majority of "veer[ing] away from that approach ... in favor of a mechanical reading of Federal Rules, insensitive to state interests and productive of discord." She read New York law as designed to "prevent the exorbitant inflation of penalties," and disagreed with the majority that Rule 23 should be construed to conflict with that effort. "Sensibly read," she concluded, "Rule 23 governs procedural aspects of class litigation, but allows state law to control the size of a monetary award a class plaintiff may pursue."

The Court responded at length. The purpose of the New York law, it said, "cannot override the statute's clear text." Even if this was the aim of the New York law, it "achieves that end by limiting a plaintiff's power to maintain a class action," and "[w]e cannot rewrite that to reflect our perception of legislative purpose." The Court also rejected consideration of the "subjective intentions of the state legislature" in determining whether there was a conflict between a state law and a Federal Rule:

> It would mean, to begin with, that one State's statute could survive preemption (and accordingly affect the procedures in federal court) while another State's identical law would not, merely because its authors had different aspirations. It would also mean that district courts would have to discern, in every diversity case, the purpose behind any putatively preempted state procedural rule, even if its text squarely conflicts with federal law. That task will often prove arduous. Many laws further more than one aim, and the aim of others may be impossible to discern. Moreover, to the extent the dissent's purpose-driven approach depends on its characterization of [the New York law] as substantive, it would apply to many state rules ostensibly addressed to procedure. Pleading standards, for example, often embody policy preferences about the types of claims that should succeed—as do rules governing summary judgment, pretrial discovery, and the admissibility of certain evidence. Hard cases will abound. It is not even clear that a state supreme court's pronouncement of the law's purpose would settle the issue, since existence of the factual predicate for avoiding federal pre-emption is ultimately a federal question. Predict-

ably, federal judges would be condemned to poring through state legislative history—which may be less easily obtained, less thorough, and less familiar than its federal counterpart.

The "central difficulty" of the dissent's focus on legislative intent, the Court continued, is that by their terms Rule 23 and New York law are in conflict:

> *Whatever* the policies they pursue, they flatly contradict each other. [It is argued that] we can (and must) interpret Rule 23 in a manner that avoids overstepping its authorizing statute. If the Rule were susceptible of two meanings—one that would violate [the Rules Enabling Act] and another that would not—we would agree. But it is not. Rule 23 unambiguously authorizes any plaintiff, in any federal civil proceeding, to maintain a class action if the Rule's prerequisites are met. We cannot contort its text, even to avert a collision with state law that might render it invalid.

A footnote to this passage added:

> If all the dissent means is that we should read an ambiguous Federal Rule to avoid "substantial variations [in outcomes] between state and federal litigation," Semtek Int'l Inc. v. Lockheed Martin Corp., 531 U.S. 497, 504 (2001), we entirely agree. We should do so not to avoid doubt as to the Rule's validity—since a Federal Rule that fails *Erie*'s forum-shopping test is not ipso facto invalid, see Hanna v. Plumer, 380 U.S. 460, 469–72 (1965)—but because it is reasonable to assume that "Congress is just as concerned as we have been to avoid significant differences between state and federal courts in adjudicating claims," Stewart Organization, Inc. v. Ricoh Corp., 487 U.S. 22, 37–38 (1988) (Scalia, J., dissenting). The assumption is irrelevant here, however, because there is only one reasonable reading of Rule 23.

(ii) Validity under Rules Enabling Act. Justice Scalia concluded his opinion for the Court with the observation that "[w]e must therefore confront head-on whether Rule 23 falls within the statutory authorization." His affirmative answer to this question was provided in an opinion joined only by Chief Justice Roberts and Justices Thomas and Sotomayor. He began with these observations:

> *Erie* involved the constitutional power of federal courts to supplant state law with judge-made rules. In that context, it made no difference whether the rule was technically one of substance or procedure; the touchstone was whether it "significantly affect[s] the result of a litigation." Guaranty Trust Co. v. York, 326 U.S. 99, 109 (1945). That is not the test for either the constitutionality or the statutory validity of a Federal Rule of Procedure. Congress has undoubted power to supplant state law, and undoubted power to prescribe rules for the courts it has created, so long as those rules regulate matters "rationally capable of classification" as procedure. *Hanna*, 380 U.S., at 472. In the Rules Enabling Act,

Congress authorized this Court to promulgate rules of procedure subject to its review, but with the limitation that those rules "shall not abridge, enlarge or modify any substantive right."

We have long held that this limitation means that the Rule must "really regulat[e] procedure,—the judicial process for enforcing rights and duties recognized by substantive law and for justly administering remedy and redress for disregard or infraction of them," Sibbach v. Wilson & Co., 312 U.S. 1, 14 (1941). The test is not whether the rule affects a litigant's substantive rights; most procedural rules do. What matters is what the rule itself regulates: If it governs only "the manner and the means" by which the litigants' rights are "enforced," it is valid; if it alters "the rules of decision by which [the] court will adjudicate [those] rights," it is not. Mississippi Publishing Corp. v. Murphree, 326 U.S. 438, 446 (1946). . . .

Applying that criterion, we think it obvious that rules allowing multiple claims (and claims by or against multiple parties) to be litigated together are also valid. Such rules neither change plaintiffs' separate entitlements to relief nor abridge defendants' rights; they alter only how the claims are processed. For the same reason, Rule 23—at least insofar as it allows willing plaintiffs to join their separate claims against the same defendants in a class action— falls within [the Rules Enabling Act's] authorization. A class action, no less than traditional joinder (of which it is a species), merely enables a federal court to adjudicate claims of multiple parties at once, instead of in separate suits. And like traditional joinder, it leaves the parties' legal rights and duties intact and the rules of decision unchanged.

It did not matter, Scalia continued, that the New York law may have had a substantive purpose:

The . . . substantive nature of New York's law, or its substantive purpose, *makes no difference*. A Federal Rule of Procedure is not valid in some jurisdictions and invalid in others—or valid in some cases and invalid in others—depending upon whether its effect is to frustrate a state substantive law (or a state procedural law enacted for substantive purposes). [I]t is not the substantive or procedural nature or purpose of the affected state law that matters, but the substantive or procedural nature of the Federal Rule. We have held since *Sibbach*, and reaffirmed repeatedly, that the validity of a Federal Rule depends entirely upon whether it regulates procedure. If it does, it is authorized by [the Rules Enabling Act] and is valid in all jurisdictions, with respect to all claims, regardless of its incidental effect upon state-created rights.

Scalia acknowledged that "keeping the federal-court door open to class actions that cannot proceed in state court will produce forum shopping." But, while such forum shopping "is unacceptable when it comes as the consequence of judge-made rules created to fill supposed 'gaps' in positive federal law," he concluded that "divergence from state law, with the attendant consequence of forum shopping, is the inevitable (indeed, one might say the intended) result of a uniform system of federal procedure."

Justice Stevens concurred in the result reached by Justice Scalia and his three colleagues. But he approached the case differently. He described his disagreement in the following terms:

> The New York law at issue is a procedural rule that is not part of New York's substantive law. Accordingly, I agree with Justice Scalia that Federal Rule of Civil Procedure 23 must apply in this case.... But I also agree with Justice Ginsburg that there are some state procedural rules that federal courts must apply in diversity cases because they function as a part of the State's definition of substantive rights and remedies.... Unlike Justice Scalia, I believe that an application of a federal rule that effectively abridges, enlarges, or modifies a state-created right or remedy violates [the command of the Rules Enabling Act]. Congress may have the constitutional power "to supplant state law" with rules that are "rationally capable of classification as procedure," but we should generally presume that it has not done so. Indeed, the mandate that federal rules "shall not abridge, enlarge or modify any substantive right" evinces the opposite intent, as does Congress' decision to delegate the creation of rules to this Court rather than to a political branch.

In response, Justice Scalia—on this point joined only by Chief Justice Roberts and Justice Thomas—argued that the approach that Justice Stevens was suggesting was ruled out by *Sibbach*. Scalia acknowledged that there is tension between *Sibbach* and the text of the Rules Enabling Act:

> In reality, the concurrence seeks not to apply *Sibbach*, but to overrule it (or, what is the same, to rewrite it). Its approach, the concurrence insists, gives short shrift to the statutory text forbidding the Federal Rules from "abridg[ing], enlarg[ing], or modify[ing] any substantive right." There is something to that. It is possible to understand how it can be determined whether a Federal Rule "enlarges" substantive rights without consulting State law: If the Rule creates a substantive right, even one that duplicates some state-created rights, it establishes a new *federal* right. But it is hard to understand how it can be determined whether a Federal Rule "abridges" or "modifies" substantive rights without knowing what state-created rights would obtain if the Federal Rule did not exist. *Sibbach*'s exclusive focus on the challenged Federal Rule—driven by the very real concern that Federal Rules which vary from State to State would be chaos—is hard to square with [the Rules Enabling Act's] terms.

But he noted that "*Sibbach* has been settled law ... for nearly seven decades."

6. Questions and Comments on *Shady Grove*. The specific holding in *Shady Grove* may be relatively inconsequential, in that the majority does not dispute that the outcome might have been different if the New York law had simply been framed as a limitation on remedies rather than as a limitation on the use of class actions. The opinions in the case nevertheless reveal fundamental disagreements over how to interpret the Federal Rules in the face of a potential conflict with state law and over how to assess their validity under the Rules Enabling Act. Does the majority opinion evidence a retreat by the Court from construing the Federal Rules with sensitivity to state interests? Was the majority correct in concluding that "there is only one reasonable reading of Rule 23"? In evaluating the validity of a Federal Rule under the Enabling Act, to what extent, if at all, should a court take account of either the nature of the state law that is being displaced by the Federal Rule, or the danger that application of the Federal Rule will promote forum shopping?

7. Bibliography. There is an extensive literature on the substance/procedure issues presented by both *Erie* and the Federal Rules. The most famous article is John Hart Ely, The Irrepressible Myth of *Erie*, 87 Harv. L. Rev. 693 (1974). In that article, Ely argued, consistent with the Court's decision in *Hanna*, that the validity of the Federal Rules should be evaluated solely under the Rules Enabling Act, not under the *Erie* jurisprudence. He also argued, however, that, contrary to the Court's suggestion in *Sibbach*, a Federal Rule should not be considered valid under the Enabling Act merely because it is procedural. The Rules Enabling Act makes clear, he contended, that the Rule must also not abridge or modify a substantive right. He proposed the following approach to the substance/procedure issue:

> When there is no Federal Rule, and as a result the Rules of Decision Act constitutes the controlling text, the court need ordinarily not concern itself with whether the federal rule urged by one party, or the state rule urged by the other, is most fairly designated substantive or procedural. The test is whether the choice between the two is material in the sense *Hanna* indicated, and that is not a function of the goals the rulemakers on either side were pursuing.... Where there is [a Federal] Rule, however, the designation substantive and procedural become important, for the Enabling Act has made them so. Its first sentence, tracking the constitutional requirement, demands that the Federal Rule be procedural. Its second sentence (the one the Court and the commentators have ignored) add to this checklist restriction the further, and considerably more significant, enclave-type proviso that the Rule not abridge, enlarge or modify any substantive right.

Id. at 722–23. Ely's article provoked two responses in the Harvard Law Review. See Abram Chayes, Some Further Last Words on *Erie*: The Bead Game, 87 Harv. L. Rev. 741 (1974); Paul J. Mishkin, Some Further Last Words on *Erie*: The Thread, 87 Harv. L. Rev. 1682 (1974). Ely responded to Chayes in The Necklace, 87 Harv. L. Rev. 753 (1974).

For additional scholarship on this topic, see Amy Coney Barrett, Procedural Common Law, 94 Va. L. Rev. 813 (2008); Joseph P. Bauer, The *Erie* Doctrine Revisited: How a Conflicts Perspective Can Aid the Analysis, 74 Notre Dame L. Rev. 1235 (1999); Paul D. Carrington, "Substance" and "Procedure" in the Rules Enabling Act, 1989 Duke L.J. 281; Donald L. Doernberg, The Unseen Track of Erie Railroad: Why History and Jurisprudence Suggest a More Straightforward Form of *Erie* Analysis, 109 W. Va. L. Rev. 611 (2007); Earl C. Dudley, Jr. & George Rutherglen, Deforming the Federal Rules: An Essay on What's Wrong with the Recent *Erie* Decisions, 92 Va. L. Rev. 707 (2006); Richard D. Freer, Some Thoughts on the State of *Erie* After *Gasperini*, 76 Tex. L. Rev. 1637 (1998); Leslie M. Kelleher, Taking "Substantive Rights" (in the Rules Enabling Act) More Seriously, 74 Notre Dame L. Rev. 47 (1998); John C. McCoid, II, *Hanna v. Plumer*: The *Erie* Doctrine Changes Shape, 51 Va. L. Rev. 884 (1965); Martin H. Redish & Carter G. Phillips, *Erie* and the Rules of Decision Act: In Search of the Appropriate Dilemma, 91 Harv. L. Rev. 356 (1977); Thomas D. Rowe, Jr., Not Bad for Government Work: Does Anyone Else Think the Supreme Court is Doing a Halfway Decent Job in its *Erie-Hanna* Jurisprudence?, 73 Notre Dame L. Rev. 963 (1998); Ralph Whitten, *Erie* and the Federal Rules: A Review and Reappraisal After *Burlington Northern Railroad Co. v. Woods*, 21 Creighton L. Rev. 1 (1987); Richard C. Worf, Jr., The Effect of State Law on the Judge–Jury Relationship in Federal Court, 30 N. Ill. U. L. Rev. 109 (2009).

Page 647, add a footnote at the end of the first paragraph of Note 1:

a. For a collection and categorization of data on GVRs and a proposed alternative to current GVR practice, see Aaron–Andrew P. Bruhl, The Supreme Court's Controversial GVRs—and an Alternative, 107 Mich. L. Rev. 711 (2009).

Page 658, add a footnote at the end of Note 5:

g. Joined by Justice Thomas, Justice Scalia returned to his "schoolboy" analogy in his dissent from a per curiam GVR in Wellons v. Hall, 558 U.S. ___ (2010): "Today the Court adds another beast to our growing menagerie: the SRIE, Summary Remand for Inconsequential Error—or, as the Court would have it, the SRTAEH, Summary Remand to Think About an Evidentiary Hearing. It disrespects the judges of the Courts of Appeals, who are appointed and confirmed as we are, to vacate and send back their authorized judgments for inconsequential imperfection of opinion—as though we were schoolmasters grading their homework." Justice Alito, joined by Chief Justice Roberts, also objected to the Court's disposition. As he read the decision below, the Circuit Court decision rested on two independent grounds: a procedural foreclosure and a merits decision that assumed the claim was not procedurally foreclosed. An intervening decision made clear that the procedural foreclosure dimension of the Circuit Court's opinion was wrong. Alito concluded: "What the Court has done—using a GVR as a vehicle for urging the Court of Appeals to reconsider its holding on a question that is entirely independent of the ground for the GVR—is extraordinary and, in my view, improper."

In Webster v. Cooper, 558 U.S. ___ (2009), the Court's per curiam GVR ordered reconsideration in light of a cited decision. In dissent, Justice Scalia pointed out that the case that formed the basis for the remand was decided more than two months before the Circuit Court acted in the case. Scalia concluded: "Since we review judgments rather than opinions, a lower court's failure to

discuss a pre-existing factor it should have
discussed is no basis for reversal.''

Page 675, add after Note 6 and renumber the remaining Notes:

7. ***Mohawk Industries, Inc. v. Carpenter.*** A former employee of
Mohawk Industries sued the company, alleging that his employment had
been unlawfully terminated. During discovery, the district judge ordered
Mohawk to turn over materials that were subject to the attorney-client
privilege, on the ground that Mohawk had implicitly waived the privilege.
Mohawk sought immediate review under the collateral order doctrine, but
the court of appeals held that doctrine inapplicable and the Supreme Court
affirmed. Mohawk Industries, Inc. v. Carpenter, 558 U.S. ___ (2009).

In an opinion by Justice Sotomayor, the Court concluded that Mohawk
had not satisfied the third requirement of the collateral order doctrine—
that the interlocutory decision be ''effectively unreviewable on appeal from
the final judgment.'' In response to Mohawk's argument that discovery
rulings implicating the attorney-client privilege ''differ in kind from run-of-
the-mill discovery orders because of the important institutional interests at
stake,'' the Court ''readily acknowledged the importance of the attorney-
client privilege.'' The Court explained, however, that ''[t]he crucial question ... is not whether an interest is important in the abstract; it is
whether deferring review until final judgment so imperils the interest as to
justify the cost of allowing immediate appeal of the entire class of relevant
orders.'' The Court found that this test was not met, because ''[a]ppellate
courts can remedy the improper disclosure of privileged material in the
same way they remedy a host of other erroneous evidentiary rulings: by
vacating an adverse judgment and remanding for a new trial in which the
protected material and its fruits are excluded from evidence.''

The Court also was unpersuaded by Mohawk's argument that forcing
litigants to wait until final judgment to appeal discovery orders like this
one would unduly chill attorney-client communications. The Court reasoned that, ''in deciding how freely to speak, clients and counsel are
unlikely to focus on the remote prospect of an erroneous disclosure order,
let alone on the timing of a possible appeal.'' Moreover, the Court said that
it is already the case that ''clients and counsel must account for the
possibility that they will later be required by law to disclose their communications for a variety of reasons—for example, because they misjudged the
scope of the privilege, because they waived the privilege, or because their
communications fell within the privilege's crime-fraud exception.'' The
Court further noted that litigants confronted with a potentially injurious
discovery order have other options for attempting to seek immediate
review, either by asking the district court to certify, and the court of
appeals to accept, an interlocutory appeal under 28 U.S.C. § 1292(b), or (in
extraordinary situations) through seeking a writ of mandamus.

Finally, the Court emphasized that ''the class of collaterally appealable
orders must remain 'narrow and selective in its membership' '' (quoting

Will v. Hallock, 546 U.S. 345, 350 (2006)). The Court said that this was particularly true in light of legislation enacted in 1990 and 1992 that authorizes the Court to promulgate rules that clarify which orders are final for purposes of § 1291 and that provide for interlocutory appeals not otherwise provided for by § 1292. The Court described this legislatively-authorized rulemaking process "as the preferred means for determining whether and when prejudgment orders should be immediately appealable."

Justice Thomas concurred in part and concurred in the judgment, arguing that the Court should not extend the collateral order doctrine any further and should instead rely solely on the rulemaking process specified by Congress. Further application of the collateral order doctrine, he argued, "needlessly perpetuates a judicial policy that we for many years have criticized and struggled to limit."

CHAPTER VI

ABSTENTION

Page 702, add at the end of footnote a:

The doctrine was revisited after *Exxon Mobil* and *Lance* in Dustin E. Buehler, Revisiting *Rooker-Feldman*: Extending the Doctrine to State Court Interlocutory Orders, 36 Fla. St. U. L. Rev. 373–414 (2009).

Page 802, add after Section 4:

SECTION 5: INTERNATIONAL COMITY ABSTENTION

Royal and Sun Alliance Ins. Co. of Canada v. Century International Arms, Inc.

U.S. Court of Appeals for the Second Circuit, 2006.
466 F.3d 88.

Before MCLAUGHLIN and CALABRESI, Circuit Judges, and LYNCH, District Judge [sitting by designation].

■ GERALD E. LYNCH, District Judge . . . .

Century America is in the business of manufacturing and distributing firearms and munitions. In connection with that business, Century America and its affiliate Century Canada obtained liability insurance policies from Royal and Sun Alliance Insurance Company of Canada ("RSA") for the time period between June 12, 1991, and March 25, 1994. During the policy period, Century America was sued by a number of individuals who alleged that they had suffered injuries caused by defects in Century America's products. RSA defended these lawsuits pursuant to the terms of the insurance policies, and eventually negotiated settlements with the various plaintiffs and paid the settlement amounts on behalf of Century America. At the conclusion of the actions, RSA requested reimbursement for defense expenses and deductibles it claimed to be owed under the policies. No payment was received.

RSA and Century Canada are both Canadian corporations, and under the insurance policies Century Canada is named as the first insured party while Century America is listed as an additional insured. Accordingly, when RSA did not receive the money it believed it was owed under the policies, RSA filed an action in Superior Court, Province of Quebec, District of

Montreal, Canada, against Century Canada, seeking payment for its expenses and deductibles. In its response to the Canadian action, Century Canada asserted that the expenses and deductibles for which RSA sought reimbursement "relate[d] to events which occurred in the United States and claims asserted against name[d] insureds other than . . . [Century Canada]," and that under the terms of the policies, the rights and obligations of RSA, Century Canada, and Century America apply "[s]eparately to each insured against whom claim is made or 'action' is brought."

Given Century Canada's averment that RSA had, in effect, sued the wrong insured party in the Canadian action, RSA filed the present complaint in the Southern District of New York against Century America. Soon after the case was filed, Century America moved to dismiss the complaint in favor of RSA's pending action against Century Canada. The district court granted Century America's motion to dismiss, stating that it had "the inherent power to stay or dismiss an action based on the pendency of a related proceeding in a foreign jurisdiction," but recognizing that its discretion was "limited by its obligation to exercise jurisdiction." In exercising its discretion, the district court concluded that the existence of a parallel proceeding in Canada involving Century America's affiliate, coupled with Century America's consent to jurisdiction in Canada, militated in favor of dismissal. This appeal followed. . . .

Century America argues that the district court's decision was supported by the doctrine of international comity abstention. International comity is "the recognition which one nation allows within its territory to the legislative, executive or judicial acts of another nation, having due regard both to international duty and convenience." Hilton v. Guyot, 159 U.S. 113, 163–64 (1895). While the doctrine can be stated clearly in the abstract, in practice we have described its boundaries as "amorphous" and "fuzzy." JP Morgan Chase Bank v. Altos Hornos de Mexico, 412 F.3d 418, 423 (2d Cir. 2005), quoting Harold G. Maier, Extraterritorial Jurisdiction at a Crossroads: An Intersection Between Public and Private International Law, 76 Am. J. Int'l L. 280, 281 (1982). In addition to its imprecise application, even where the doctrine clearly applies it "is not an imperative obligation of courts but rather is a discretionary rule of 'practice, convenience, and expediency.' " Id., quoting Pravin Banker Assocs., Ltd. v. Banco Popular Del Peru, 109 F.3d 850, 854 (2d Cir. 1997). . . .

Generally, concurrent jurisdiction in United States courts and the courts of a foreign sovereign does not result in conflict. China Trade & Dev. Corp. v. M.V. Choong Yong, 837 F.2d 33, 36 (2d Cir. 1987). Rather, " '[p]arallel proceedings in the same in personam claim should ordinarily be allowed to proceed simultaneously, at least until a judgment is reached in one which can be pled as res judicata in the other.' " Id., quoting Laker Airways, Ltd. v. Sabena, Belgian World Airlines, 731 F.2d 909, 926–27 (D.C. Cir. 1984), citing Colorado River Water Conservation Dist. v. United States, 424 U.S. 800, 817 (1976). The mere existence of parallel foreign proceedings does not negate the district courts' "virtually unflagging obligation ... to exercise the jurisdiction given them." *Colorado River*, 424 U.S., at 817.

We have recognized one discrete category of foreign litigation that generally requires the dismissal of parallel district court actions—foreign bankruptcy proceedings. A foreign nation's interest in the "equitable and orderly distribution of a debtor's property" is an interest deserving of particular respect and deference, and accordingly we have followed the general practice of American courts and regularly deferred to such actions. Outside the bankruptcy context, we have yet to articulate a list of factors a district court should consider when exercising its discretion to abstain in deference to pending litigation in a foreign court. However, whatever factors weigh in favor of abstention, "[o]nly the clearest of justifications will warrant dismissal." *Colorado River*, 424 U.S., at 819. The task of a district court evaluating a request for dismissal based on a parallel foreign proceeding is not to articulate a justification *for* the exercise of jurisdiction, but rather to determine whether exceptional circumstances exist that justify the surrender of that jurisdiction. Moses H. Cone Mem'l Hosp. v. Mercury Constr. Corp., 460 U.S. 1, 25–26 (1983). The exceptional circumstances that would support such a surrender must, of course, raise considerations which are not generally present as a result of parallel litigation, otherwise the routine would be considered exceptional, and a district court's unflagging obligation to exercise its jurisdiction would become merely a polite request.

Appellees contend that the above standards, articulated by the Supreme Court in *Colorado River* and *Moses H. Cone*, do not apply to the present matter because those cases involved abstention in favor of parallel state proceedings while the parallel action here at issue is pending in a foreign jurisdiction. Appellees' effort to distinguish these precedents is accurate, as far as it goes, but it does not go far. The factors a court must weigh in exercising its discretion to abstain in deference to parallel proceedings will indeed differ depending on the nature of the proceedings. For example, if the parallel proceeding is in a foreign jurisdiction, the district court need not consider the balance between state and federal power dictated by our Constitution. Conversely, if the parallel proceeding is in a state court, the district court need not concern itself with issues of international relations. However, while the relevant factors to be considered differ depending on the posture of the case, the starting point for the inquiry remains unchanged: a district court's "virtually unflagging obligation" to exercise its jurisdiction. In weighing the considerations for and against abstention, a court's "heavy obligation to exercise jurisdiction" exists regardless of what factors are present on the other side of the balance.

The Supreme Court has recognized that a decision to abstain from exercising jurisdiction based on the existence of parallel litigation "does not rest on a mechanical checklist, but on a careful balancing of the important factors ... as they apply in a given case, with the balance heavily weighted in favor of the exercise of jurisdiction." *Moses H. Cone*, 460 U.S. at 16. "No one factor is necessarily determinative; a carefully considered judgment taking into account both the obligation to exercise jurisdiction and the combination of factors counselling against that exercise is required." *Colorado River*, 424 U.S., at 818–19.

In the context of parallel proceedings in a foreign court, a district court should be guided by the principles upon which international comity is based: the proper respect for litigation in and the courts of a sovereign nation, fairness to litigants, and judicial efficiency. Proper consideration of these principles will no doubt require an evaluation of various factors, such as the similarity of the parties, the similarity of the issues, the order in which the actions were filed, the adequacy of the alternate forum, the potential prejudice to either party, the convenience of the parties, the connection between the litigation and the United States, and the connection between the litigation and the foreign jurisdiction. This list is not exhaustive, and a district court should examine the "totality of the circumstances," Finova Capital Corp. v. Ryan Helicopters U.S.A., Inc. 180 F.3d 896, 900 (7th Cir. 1999), to determine whether the specific facts before it are sufficiently exceptional to justify abstention.

In the present case, the district court did not identify any exceptional circumstances that would support abstention, and therefore the dismissal of the action was an abuse of discretion. The district court's decision to dismiss the action was based on four factors: the existence of the Canadian action against Century Canada, Century America's consent to jurisdiction in Canada, the affiliation between Century America and Century Canada, and the adequacy of Canadian judicial procedures. These factors led the district court to conclude that the action in Canada was a parallel action that provided an adequate forum for RSA's claims, and that therefore a dismissal of the case was warranted. ...

The existence of a parallel action in an adequate foreign jurisdiction must be the beginning, not the end, of a district court's determination of whether abstention is appropriate. As we explained above, circumstances that routinely exist in connection with parallel litigation cannot reasonably be considered exceptional circumstances, and therefore the mere existence of an adequate parallel action, by itself, does not justify the dismissal of a case on grounds of international comity abstention. Rather, additional circumstances must be present—such as a foreign nation's interest in uniform bankruptcy proceedings—that outweigh the district court's general obligation to exercise its jurisdiction. The district court did not identify any such special circumstances.

Finally, both parties address the question of whether, as an alternative to dismissing the action, the district court should have considered staying proceedings in deference to the Canadian litigation. Because the propriety of a temporary stay was not raised in the district court, we do not decide whether the entry of such a stay would have been appropriate. However, on remand the district court may consider the propriety of a stay based on the pending Canadian action.

In the context of abstention in deference to parallel state-court litigation, the Supreme Court has cautioned that "a stay is as much a refusal to exercise federal jurisdiction as a dismissal," because the decision to grant a stay "necessarily contemplates that the federal court will have nothing further to do in resolving any substantive part of the case." *Moses H. Cone*, 460 U.S. at 28. However, a measured temporary stay need not result in a complete forfeiture of jurisdiction. As a lesser intrusion on the principle of obligatory jurisdiction, which might permit the district court a window to determine whether the foreign action will in fact offer an efficient vehicle for fairly resolving all the rights of the parties, such a stay is an alternative that normally should be considered before a comity-based dismissal is entertained. . . .

Accordingly, on remand the district court may consider whether its obligation to exercise jurisdiction over this action could be satisfied despite the entry of a brief stay to allow the Canadian court to determine if, for example, Century Canada is liable for the money RSA claims to be owed under the policies. We do not now decide that such a stay would necessarily be appropriate, or that other bases for a temporary stay would not be proper. Those questions are left to the district court in the first instance. . . .

The judgment of the district court is vacated and remanded for further proceedings.

NOTES ON INTERNATIONAL COMITY ABSTENTION

1. International Comity. At its most general level, "international comity" refers to the respect that U.S. courts give to the laws, acts, and decisions of foreign countries. This respect is not mandated by international law, but it can help promote reciprocity and reduce friction in foreign relations. As the Supreme Court famously explained in a case involving an attempt to enforce a foreign judgment in a U.S. court:

> "Comity," in the legal sense, is neither a matter of absolute obligation, on the one hand, nor of mere courtesy and good will, upon the other. But it is the recognition which one nation allows within its territory to the legislative, executive, or judicial acts of another nation, having due regard both to international duty and convenience, and to the rights of its own citizens or of other persons who are under the protection of its laws.

Hilton v. Guyot, 159 U.S. 113, 163–64 (1895). The recognition and enforcement of foreign judgments by U.S. courts is discussed elsewhere in this

Supplement, specifically in Note 9 following *Medellin v. Texas*, which is to be added at page 350 of the Casebook.

2. Dismissal or Stay of U.S. Litigation. In some situations, U.S. courts will stay or dismiss litigation in the United States when similar or related litigation is pending in a foreign country. Courts disagree about the precise standards for this "international comity abstention," with some courts holding that it is appropriate only in exceptional circumstances and other courts holding that there is broad discretion to avoid duplicative litigation. See Turner Entertainment Co. v. Degeto Film GmbH, 25 F.3d 1512, 1518 (11th Cir. 1994) (describing the differing approaches). In the *Royal and Sun Alliance* decision excerpted above, the court applies the exceptional circumstances approach. In doing so, it relies heavily on *Colorado River* and related cases, which concern situations in which there are pending state court proceedings.

To what extent do the abstention considerations differ when the proceedings are pending instead in a foreign court? On the one hand, the federalism considerations applicable in the *Colorado River* situation, which might support federal court abstention, are absent in the international context. On the other hand, many of the international cases involve the application of state law or foreign law rather than federal law and thus there might be less of an interest in exercising federal jurisdiction. In *Royal and Sun Alliance*, for example, the relevant law was either state contract law or Canadian law. In addition, the international cases present foreign relations considerations that might also support abstention. In light of these differences, should the court in *Royal and Sun Alliance* have been more receptive to abstention? Cf. Posner v. Essex Ins. Co., 178 F.3d 1209, 1223 (11th Cir. 1999) ("[T]he Supreme Court's admonition that courts generally must exercise their non-discretionary authority in cases over which Congress has granted them jurisdiction can apply only to those abstention doctrines addressing the unique concerns of federalism. . . . The relationship between the federal courts and the states (grounded in federalism and the Constitution) is different from the relationship between federal courts and foreign nations (grounded in the historical notion of comity).").

Courts consider a variety of factors in deciding whether to apply international comity abstention. In *Royal and Sun Alliance*, the court refers to "the similarity of the parties, the similarity of the issues, the order in which the actions were filed, the adequacy of the alternate forum, the potential prejudice to either party, the convenience of the parties, the connection between the litigation and the United States, and the connection between the litigation and the foreign jurisdiction." Other circuits apply similar lists of factors. See, e.g., Finova Capital Corp. v. Ryan Helicopters U.S.A., Inc., 180 F.3d 896, 898–99 (7th Cir. 1999). What weight should courts give to these various factors? Are some more important than others? The court in *Royal and Sun Alliance* notes that international comity abstention is particularly appropriate when the parallel foreign proceedings involve bankruptcy. Why should this be so?

The court in *Royal and Sun Alliance* also suggests that district courts should have more discretion to issue a temporary stay rather than outright dismissal in the face of parallel foreign proceedings. The court agreed in Ingersoll Milling Machine Co. v. Granger, 833 F.2d 680, 686 (7th Cir. 1987):

> Moreover, it is not insignificant—indeed, it is very significant—that the district court's action in this case was a decidedly measured one. The court did not dismiss the action; it simply stayed further proceedings until the Belgian appeals were concluded. This approach protects the substantial rights of the parties while permitting the district court to manage its time effectively.

Under the *Colorado River* line of cases, by contrast, the Supreme Court has indicated that "a stay is as much a refusal to exercise federal jurisdiction as a dismissal" because "the decision to invoke *Colorado River* necessarily contemplates that the federal court will have nothing further to do in resolving any substantive part of the case, whether it stays or dismisses." Moses H. Cone Mem'l Hosp. v. Mercury Constr. Corp., 460 U.S. 1, 28 (1983). A stay of litigation is more common, however, under the *Pullman* abstention doctrine (see Section 2 of Chapter VI). If an international case involves the application of foreign law or implicates important policy interests of a foreign nation, might a stay be warranted based on considerations analogous to those underlying *Pullman*? Or does the lack of an underlying constitutional question in the international cases serve to distinguish *Pullman*? Is *Burford* abstention (see pp. 707–08 of the casebook) a better analogy in this situation? Note that the Supreme Court has held that a dismissal under *Burford* is warranted only if the relief being sought is equitable or otherwise discretionary in nature, and is not appropriate when the claim is for damages. See Quackenbush v. Allstate Ins. Co., 517 U.S. 706, 731 (1996). The Court has also noted, however, that "*Burford* might support a federal court's decision to postpone adjudication of a damages action pending the resolution by the state courts of a disputed question of state law." Id. at 730–31.

3. Anti–Suit Injunctions. Occasionally, U.S. courts will issue a so-called "anti-suit" injunction to prevent persons or entities subject to their personal jurisdiction from pursuing litigation in a foreign country. See, e.g., Laker Airways, Ltd. v. Sabena, Belgian World Airlines, 731 F.2d 909, 927–31 (D.C. Cir. 1984). In this context, international comity considerations provide a reason for caution before entering the injunction. As with international comity abstention, courts disagree about the precise standards for issuing anti-suit injunctions. Some courts hold that they are appropriate whenever there is a duplication of parties and issues and the prosecution of simultaneous proceedings would frustrate the speedy and efficient determination of the case. Others focus more narrowly on whether the foreign action imperils the jurisdiction of the forum court or threatens some strong national policy. See Quaak v. Klynveld Peat Marwick Goerdeler Bedrijfsrevisoren, 361 F.3d 11, 17–19 (1st Cir. 2004) (describing differing approaches). To what extent might the considerations underlying *Younger* abstention, which limits the issuance of injunctive relief directed at state court proceedings (see Section 3 of Chapter VI), apply to injunctions directed at foreign court proceedings?

   4. Respect for Foreign Laws. International comity abstention can involve respect not only for foreign judicial proceedings, but also for foreign laws. Consider, for example, Bi v. Union Carbide Chemical and Plastics Co., 984 F.2d 582 (2d Cir. 1993). In 1984, deadly gas escaped from a pesticide plant in Bhopal, India, killing thousands of people. The plant was operated by an Indian subsidiary of a U.S. company. India subsequently enacted a statute giving the Indian government exclusive standing to represent the victims of the disaster in India. Pursuant to this statute, the Indian government brought suit in Indian courts against the U.S. company and its subsidiary, and entered into a comprehensive settlement that was approved by the Indian Supreme Court. The suit in *Bi* was an attempt by plaintiffs who were unhappy with the Indian settlement to litigate their claims in the United States. In affirming a dismissal of the suit, the court of appeals described the case as raising "an issue of comity among nations." The court reasoned that "were we to pass on the validity of India's response to a disaster that occurred within its borders, it would disrupt our relations with the country and frustrate the efforts of the international community to develop methods to deal with problems of this magnitude in the future." As a result, the court concluded that "when a recognized democracy determines that the interests of the victims of a mass tort that occurred within its borders will be best served if the foreign government exclusively represents the victims in courts around the world, we will not pass judgment on that determination." Why should an Indian statute rather than U.S. law determine the exercise of jurisdiction by a U.S. federal court in a case involving the actions of a U.S. corporation and its subsidiary? Should it matter that India is a democracy?

   5. Respect for Alternative Dispute Resolution Effort. Considerations of comity can also arise when courts are asked to abstain not in the face of a foreign judicial proceeding or law, but rather in the face of some alternate foreign or international effort to resolve issues related to the litigation. For example, in Pravin Banker Assocs. v. Banco Popular Del Peru, 109 F.3d 850 (2d Cir. 1997), a Peruvian bank that had defaulted on loans from U.S. financial institutions sought to stay enforcement proceedings in U.S. courts while it attempted to restructure its commercial debt under a plan worked out by U.S. Treasury Secretary Nicholas Brady. In affirming the denial of a stay, the court noted that there were two competing U.S. government policy interests in the case: foreign debt resolution under the Brady plan and ensuring the enforceability of valid debts. The district court had previously granted a six-month stay, thus serving to some degree the first interest, and the court of appeals concluded that a further stay would unduly prejudice the second interest. "[C]ourts will not extend comity to foreign proceedings when doing so would be contrary to the policies or prejudicial to the interests of the United States," the court reasoned.

For a decision that was more receptive to granting international comity abstention based on the existence of an alternative dispute resolution effort, see Ungaro–Benages v. Dresdner Bank AG, 379 F.3d 1227 (11th Cir. 2004). In that case, the plaintiff sued two German banks, alleging that, during the 1930s and 1940s, they had stolen her family's interest in a company, pursuant to the Nazi program of "Aryanization" of Jewish assets. In upholding a dismissal of the suit, the court explained that international comity abstention can operate either retrospectively or prospectively:

> When applied retrospectively, domestic courts consider whether to respect the judgment of a foreign tribunal or to defer to parallel foreign proceedings. . . .

> When applied prospectively, domestic courts consider whether to dismiss or stay a domestic action based on the interests of our government, the foreign government and the international community in resolving the dispute in a foreign forum.

In concluding that abstention was proper in this case, the court noted that the United States and Germany had concluded an agreement in 2000 that established a private foundation to hear claims brought by victims of the Nazi regime. The court found that both the U.S. government and the German government had a strong interest in having the foundation operate as the exclusive basis for recovery, and that the foundation offered an adequate forum for resolving the claims. The court reached this conclusion even though nothing in the foundation agreement expressly precluded litigation in U.S. courts. But cf. Gross v. German Foundation Industrial Initiative, 456 F.3d 363, 394 (3d Cir. 2006) ("We remain skeptical of this broad application of the international comity doctrine [in *Ungaro-Benages*], noting our 'virtually unflagging obligation' to exercise the jurisdiction granted to us, Colorado River v. United States, 424 U.S. 800, 817 (1976), which is not diminished simply because foreign relations might be involved . . . .").

6. Comparison with Forum Non Conveniens. International comity abstention is similar in some ways to forum non conveniens. Under that doctrine, federal district courts have discretion to dismiss a case if they determine that various private and public interest factors weigh in favor of adjudicating the case in an alternate forum and that the forum is adequate. See Piper Aircraft Co. v. Reyno, 454 U.S. 235 (1981). The private interest factors to be considered include "the 'relative ease of access to sources of proof; availability of compulsory process for attendance of unwilling, and the cost of obtaining attendance of willing, witnesses; possibility of view of premises, if view would be appropriate to the action; and all other practical problems that make trial of a case easy, expeditious and inexpensive.' " Id. at 241 n. 6 (quoting Gulf Oil Corp. v. Gilbert, 330 U.S. 501, 508 (1947)). The public interest factors include "the administrative difficulties flowing from court congestion; the 'local interest in having localized controversies decided at home'; the interest in having the trial of a diversity case in a forum that is at home with the law that must govern the action; the avoidance of unnecessary problems in conflict of laws, or in the application of foreign law; and the unfairness of burdening citizens in an unrelated forum with jury duty." Id. (quoting *Gilbert*, 330 U.S. at 508, 509). In considering these factors, courts apply a presumption in favor of the plaintiff's choice of forum, although less of a presumption is given when the plaintiff is a foreign citizen. In determining whether an alternate forum is "adequate," courts look primarily at whether the forum would have jurisdiction to hear the dispute and the ability to provide a remedy. Ordinarily, an alternate forum will not be considered inadequate merely because its laws or procedures are less favorable to the plaintiff than those of the United States.

Because of statutory provisions allowing for transfer of venue between federal district courts, the forum non conveniens doctrine is applied by federal courts today only in international cases. How does international comity abstention differ from applying forum non conveniens? Is there a need to have both doctrines? Consider this observation by the Supreme Court about the differences between domestic abstention and forum non conveniens:

> [T]he abstention doctrines and the doctrine of forum non conveniens proceed from a similar premise: In rare circumstances, federal courts can relinquish their jurisdiction in favor of another forum. But our abstention doctrine is of a distinct historical pedigree, and the traditional considerations behind dismissal for forum non conveniens differ markedly from those informing the decision to abstain. . . . Federal courts abstain out of deference to the paramount interests of another sovereign, and the concern is with principles of comity and federalism. Dismissal for forum non conveniens, by contrast, has historically reflected a far broader range of considerations. . . .

Quackenbush v. Allstate Ins. Co., 517 U.S. 706, 723 (1996).

7. Bibliography. For general discussions of international comity, see, for example, Harold G. Maier, Extraterritorial Jurisdiction at a Crossroads: An Intersection Between Public and Private International Law, 76 Am. J. Int'l L. 280 (1982); Joel R. Paul, Comity in International Law, 32 Harv. Int'l L.J. 1 (1991); and Michael D. Ramsey, Escaping "International Comity," 83 Iowa L. Rev. 893 (1998). For specific discussions of international comity abstention and antisuit injunctions, see, for example, George A. Bermann, The Use of Anti–Suit Injunctions in International Litigation, 28 Colum. J. Transnat'l L. 589 (1990); N. Jansen Calamita, Rethinking

Comity: Towards a Coherent Treatment of International Parallel Proceedings, 27 U. Pa. J. Int'l Econ. L. 601 (2006); Austen L. Parrish, Duplicative Foreign Litigation, 78 Geo. Wash. L. Rev. 237 (2010); William L. Reynolds, The Proper Forum for a Suit: Transnational Forum Non Conveniens and Counter–Suit Injunctions in the Federal Courts, 70 Tex. L. Rev. 1663 (1992); and Steven R. Swanson, The Vexatiousness of a Vexation Rule: International Comity and Antisuit Injunctions, 30 Gw. J. Int'l & Econ. 1 (1996).

CHAPTER VII

HABEAS CORPUS

Page 838, add at the end of footnote c:

For consideration of how modern habeas corpus should be applied to claims that the petitioner is ineligible for the death penalty by reason, for example, of relation to a felony murder, age at the time of the offense, or mental condition at the time of offense or potential execution, see Lee Kovarsky, Death Ineligibility and Habeas Corpus, 95 Cornell L. Rev. 329 (2010).

Page 843, add at the end of Note 5:

In Holland v. Florida, 560 U.S. ___ (2010), the Court decided the question left open in *Pace* and *Lawrence*, holding that equitable tolling was available under AEDPA.[c] Over a dissent by Justice Scalia that was joined by Justice Thomas, Justice Breyer's opinion for the Court agreed that the circumstances must be "extraordinary," as *Pace* had said, and that the risk of attorney error normally remains on the client in situations where, as with state and federal habeas petitions, there is no constitutional right to counsel. But:

> In this case, the "extraordinary circumstances" at issue involve an attorney's failure to satisfy professional standards of care. The Court of Appeals held that, where that is so, even attorney conduct that is "grossly negligent" can never warrant tolling absent "bad faith, dishonesty, divided loyalty, mental impairment or so forth on the lawyer's part." [I]n our view, the Court of Appeals' standard is too rigid. [Its] rule is difficult to reconcile with more general equitable principles in that it fails to recognize that, at least sometimes, professional misconduct that fails to meet [its] standard could nonetheless amount to egregious behavior and create an extraordinary circumstance that warrants equitable tolling.

The Court did not, however, say much more about what the right standard should be. Lower courts should "exercise judgment in light of prior precedent," it said, "but with awareness of the fact that specific circumstances, often hard to predict in advance, could warrant special treatment in an appropriate case." In the end, the case was remanded because "no lower court has yet considered in detail the facts of this case to determine whether they indeed constitute extraordinary circumstances sufficient to

---

c. For a pre-*Holland* analysis of the issue concluding, as did the Court, that equitable tolling should apply in this context, see Anne R. Traum, Last Best Chance for the Great Writ: Equitable Tolling and Federal Habeas Corpus, 68 Md. L. Rev. 545 (2009).

warrant equitable relief." Justice Alito wrote separately, agreeing that equitable tolling was available and that the remand was appropriate but arguing for more clarity on the standard. There were allegations that the attorney had essentially abandoned the petitioner as a client, that communications had broken down, and that the petitioner had made reasonable efforts to terminate his appointed attorney but "that such efforts were successfully opposed by the State on the perverse ground that petitioner failed to act through [the] counsel [he was seeking to replace]." "If true," Alito concluded, "petitioner's allegations would suffice to establish extraordinary circumstances beyond his control. Common sense dictates that a litigant cannot be held . . . responsible for the conduct of an attorney who is not operating as his agent in any meaningful sense of that word."

Page 844, add at the end of footnote c:

For consideration of the tension between Rule 22 and the COA process, see Christopher Q. Cutler, Friendly Habeas Reform— Reconsidering a District Court's Threshold Role in the Appellate Habeas Process, 43 Willamette L. Rev. 281 (2007).

Page 866, insert a new Note 3 and renumber the remaining Notes:

3.   ***Renico v. Lett.*** The Court elaborated on the standard for judging whether a state court decision was an "unreasonable" application of clearly established federal law in Renico v. Lett, 559 U.S. ___ (2010). Lett's first trial for murder resulted in a mistrial on the ground that the jury was deadlocked. After conviction in a second trial, Lett sought review in the Michigan courts on the ground that the mistrial had been declared without a "manifest necessity" for doing so and therefore violated the Double Jeopardy Clause. The intermediate Michigan appeals court agreed with Lett, and reversed his conviction. But the Michigan Supreme Court reinstated the conviction, holding that the trial judge had not abused her discretion and that the applicable federal double jeopardy standard was not violated. A District Court set aside the conviction on federal habeas, and the Circuit Court affirmed. In an opinion by Chief Justice Roberts, the Supreme Court reversed. The Court's analysis began:

> It is important at the outset to define the question before us. That question is not whether the trial judge should have declared a mistrial. It is not even whether it was an abuse of discretion for her to have done so—the applicable standard on direct review. The question under AEDPA is instead whether the determination of the Michigan Supreme Court that there was no abuse of discretion was "an unreasonable application of . . . clearly established Federal law."

> We have explained that "an unreasonable application of federal law is different from an incorrect application of federal law." Williams v. Taylor, 529 U.S. 362, 410 (2000). Indeed, [we continued in *Williams*,] "a federal habeas court may not issue the writ simply because that court concludes in its independent judgment that the relevant state-court decision applied clearly established

federal law erroneously or incorrectly." Rather, that application must be "objectively unreasonable." This distinction creates "a substantially higher threshold" for obtaining relief than de novo review. Schriro v. Landrigan, 550 U.S. 465, 473 (2007). AEDPA thus imposes a "highly deferential standard for evaluating state-court rulings," Lindh v. Murphy, 521 U.S. 320, 333, n.7 (1997), and "demands that state-court decisions be given the benefit of the doubt," Woodford v. Visciotti, 537 U.S. 19, 24 (2002).

The Court then noted that the clearly established federal law in this area reserved to the trial judge a "broad discretion" and was entitled to "great deference" on review:

> The legal standard applied by the Michigan Supreme Court in this case was whether there was an abuse of the "broad discretion" reserved to the trial judge. This type of general standard triggers another consideration under AEDPA. When assessing whether a state court's application of federal law is unreasonable, "the range of reasonable judgment can depend in part on the nature of the relevant rule" that the state court must apply. Yarborough v. Alvarado, 541 U.S. 652, 664 (2004). Because AEDPA authorizes federal courts to grant relief only when state courts act unreasonably, it follows that "[t]he more general the rule" at issue—and thus the greater the potential for reasoned disagreement among fair-minded judges—"the more leeway [state] courts have in reaching outcomes in case-by-case determinations." Ibid.

Under this standard, the Court concluded, the Michigan Supreme Court decision was not an unreasonable application of federal law:

> [T]he Michigan Supreme Court's decision upholding the trial judge's exercise of discretion—while not necessarily correct—was not objectively unreasonable. Not only are there a number of plausible ways to interpret the record of Lett's trial, but the standard applied by the Michigan Supreme Court—whether the judge exercised sound discretion—is a general one, to which there is no "plainly correct or incorrect" answer in this case. The Court of Appeals' ruling in Lett's favor failed to grant the Michigan courts the dual layers of deference required by AEDPA and our double jeopardy precedents.
>
> The Court of Appeals also erred in a second respect. It relied upon [one of] its own decision[s] to buttress its conclusion that the Michigan Supreme Court erred in concluding that the trial judge had exercised sound discretion. [A Circuit Court decision], however, does not constitute "clearly established Federal law, as determined by the Supreme Court," § 2254(d)(1), so any failure to apply that decision cannot independently authorize habeas relief under AEDPA.

Joined by Justices Breyer and Sotomayer, Justice Stevens dissented. Stevens analyzed the record carefully, and concluded that the Michigan decision unreasonably applied federal law:

In this case, Reginald Lett's constitutional rights were violated when the trial court terminated his first trial without adequate justification and he was subsequently prosecuted for the same offense. The majority does not appear to dispute this point, but it nevertheless denies Lett relief by applying a level of deference to the state court's ruling that effectively effaces the role of the federal courts. Nothing one will find in the United States Code or the United States Reports requires us to turn a blind eye to this manifestly unlawful conviction.

In a part of his opinion joined only by Justice Breyer, he added:

The Court does not really try to vindicate the Michigan Supreme Court on the merits, but instead ascribes today's outcome to the Antiterrorism and Effective Death Penalty Act of 1996 (AEDPA). The foregoing analysis shows why the Michigan Supreme Court's ruling cannot be saved by 28 U. S. C. § 2254(d)(1), however construed. That ruling was not only incorrect but also unreasonable by any fair measure. Three particular facets of the Court's AEDPA analysis require a brief comment.

First, the fact that the substantive legal standard applied by the state court "is a general one" has no bearing on the standard of review. We have said that "[t]he more general the rule, the more leeway courts have in reaching outcomes in case-by-case determinations." Yarborough v. Alvarado, 541 U.S. 652, 664 (2004). But this statement stands only for the unremarkable proposition that more broadly framed rules will tend to encompass a broader set of conforming applications. Regardless of the nature of the legal principle at issue, the task of a federal court remains the same under § 2254(d)(1): to determine whether the state court's decision "was contrary to, or involved an unreasonable application of, clearly established Federal law." General standards are no less binding law than discrete rules.

Second, I do not agree that the Federal Court of Appeals"erred" by "rel[ying] upon its own decision." ... The Sixth Circuit ... panel examined its own precedents not as the relevant "clearly established Federal law" under AEDPA, but as a tool for illuminating the precise contours of that law. Lower courts routinely look to circuit cases to "provide evidence that Supreme Court precedents ha[ve] clearly established a rule as of a particular time or [to] shed light on the 'reasonableness' 'of the state courts' application of existing Supreme Court precedents." This is a healthy practice—indeed, a vital practice, considering how few cases this Court decides—and we have never disapproved it.

Finally, I do not agree that AEDPA authorizes "the dual layers of deference" the Court has utilized in this case. There is little doubt that AEDPA "directs federal courts to attend to every state-court judgment with utmost care." Williams v. Taylor, 529 U.S. 362, 389 (2000) (opinion of Stevens, J.). But the statute never uses the term "deference," and the legislative history makes clear that Congress meant to preserve robust federal-court review. Any attempt to prevent federal courts from exercising independent review of habeas applications would have been a radical reform of dubious constitutionality, and Congress "would have spoken with much greater clarity" if that had been its intent. *Williams*, 529 U. S., at 379 (opinion of Stevens, J.).

So on two levels, it is absolutely "necessary for us to decide whether the Michigan Supreme Court's decision ... was right or wrong." If a federal judge were firmly convinced that such a decision were wrong, then in my view not only would he have no statutory duty to uphold it, but he might also have a constitutional obligation to reverse it. And regardless of how one conceptualizes the distinction between an incorrect and an "unreasonable" state-court ruling under § 2254(d)(1), one must always determine whether the ruling was wrong to be able to test the magnitude of any error. Substantive and methodological considerations compel federal courts to give habeas claims a full, independent review—and then to decide for themselves. Even under AEDPA, there is no escaping the burden of judgment.

Page 868, add a footnote after the words "defy generalization" in the sentence at the top of the page:

g. The Court granted certiorari in Wood v. Allen, 558 U.S. __ (2010), "to resolve the question of how §§ 2254(d)(2) and (e)(1) fit together," but in the end decided that it did not have to face that issue. The Court denied relief under the standard stated in subsection (d)(2), and hence did not need to decide what would have happened "under the arguably more deferential standard" in subsection (e)(1). Justice Stevens dissented, joined by Justice Kennedy. They would have granted relief under either standard.

Page 869, add to citations in Note 6:

Lee Kovarsky, AEDPA's Wrecks: Comity, Finality, and Federalism, 82 Tul. L. Rev. 443 (2007); Justin F. Marceau, Deference and Doubt: The Interaction of AEDPA Section 2254(d)(2) and (e)(1), 82 Tul. L. Rev. 385 (2007).

Page 869, add at the end of Note 6:

Finally, for extensive consideration of *Bell v. Cone*, see William B. Rubenstein, Finality in Class Action Litigation: Lessons from Habeas, 82 N.Y.U. L. Rev. 790 (2007).

Page 899, add a footnote at the end of Note 1:

c. In Beard v. Kindler, 558 U.S. __ (2009), a unanimous Court answered "no" to the following question: "Is a state procedural rule automatically 'inadequate' under the ad-equate-state-grounds doctrine—and therefore unenforceable on federal habeas review—because the state rule is discretionary rather than mandatory?"

Page 907, add to Note 2:

Steven W. Allen, Toward a Unified Theory of Retroactivity, 54 N.Y. L. Sch. L. Rev. 105 (2009/10); Kermit Roosevelt III, A Retroactivity Retrospective, With Thoughts for the Future: What the Supreme Court Learned from Paul Mishkin, and What it Might, 95 Cal. L. Rev. 1677 (2007);

Page 909, add a new Note 4 and renumber the remaining Notes

4. Applicability of *Teague* to State Courts. In Danforth v. Minnesota, 552 U.S. 264 (2008), the Court held that *Teague* does not restrain the ability of state courts to give broader effect to new rules of criminal procedure than is allowed in a federal habeas corpus proceeding. In that case, the defendant was convicted of sexual conduct with a minor, based in part on the videotaped testimony of the six-year-old victim. Some years later, after the defendant's conviction had become final, the Court decided Crawford v. Washington, 541 U.S. 36 (2004), which held that testimonial evidence is constitutionally admissible only if there is an opportunity to cross-examine the witness. As noted above, the Court subsequently concluded that *Crawford* established a "new rule" under *Teague* that therefore did not apply retroactively. The defendant nevertheless sought relief in state court. The question was whether the state court was precluded from giving broader retroactive effect to *Crawford* than *Teague* would allow in a federal habeas proceeding. The Court concluded that it was not.[a]

As an initial matter, the Court noted that:

> [T]he very word "retroactivity" is misleading because it speaks in temporal terms. "Retroactivity" suggests that when we declare that a new constitutional rule of criminal procedure is "nonretroactive," we are implying that the right at issue was not in existence prior to the date the "new rule" was announced. But this is incorrect. . . . [T]he source of a "new rule" is the Constitution itself, not any judicial power to create new rules of law. Accordingly, the underlying right necessarily pre-exists our articulation of the new rule. What we are actually determining when we assess the "retroactivity" of a new rule is not the temporal scope of a newly announced right, but whether a violation of the right that occurred prior to the announcement of the new rule will entitle a criminal defendant to the relief sought.

The Court then observed that the *Teague* rule is based in part on considerations of "comity and respect for the finality of state convictions," considerations that are "unique to *federal* habeas review of state convictions." While acknowledging that the rule is also based on a concern about disuniformity, the Court said that "[the] interest in uniformity . . . does not outweigh the general principle that States are independent sovereigns with plenary authority to make and enforce their own laws as long as they do not infringe on federal constitutional guarantees." "In sum," said the Court, "the *Teague* decision limits the kinds of constitutional violations

---

a. The Court added an early footnote explaining what it was not deciding: "We note at the outset that this case does not present the questions whether States are required to apply 'watershed' rules in state post-conviction proceedings, whether the *Teague* rule applies to cases brought under 28 U.S.C. § 2255, or whether Congress can alter the rules of retroactivity by statute. Accordingly, we express no opinion on these issues."

that will entitle an individual to relief on federal habeas, but does not in any way limit the authority of a state court, when reviewing its own state criminal convictions, to provide a remedy for a violation that is deemed 'nonretroactive' under *Teague*."

The Court also believed that its conclusion was "confirmed by several additional considerations":

First, if there is such a federal rule of law, presumably the Supremacy Clause in Article [VI] of the Federal Constitution would require all state entities—not just state judges—to comply with it. We have held that States can waive a *Teague* defense, during the course of litigation, by expressly choosing not to rely on it, or by failing to raise it in a timely manner. It would indeed be anomalous to hold that state legislatures and executives are not bound by *Teague*, but that state courts are.

Second, the State has not identified, and we cannot discern, the source of our authority to promulgate such a novel rule of federal law. While we have ample authority to control the administration of justice in the federal courts—particularly in their enforcement of federal legislation—we have no comparable supervisory authority over the work of state judges. And while there are federal interests that occasionally justify this Court's development of common-law rules of federal law, our normal role is to interpret law created by others and "not to prescribe what it shall be." Just as constitutional doubt may tip the scales in favor of one construction of a statute rather than another, so does uncertainty about the source of authority to impose a federal limit on the power of state judges to remedy wrongful state convictions outweigh any possible policy arguments favoring the rule that respondent espouses.

Finally, the dissent contends that the "end result [of this opinion] is startling" because "two criminal defendants, each of whom committed the same crime, at the same time, whose convictions became final on the same day, and each of whom raised an identical claim at the same time under the Federal Constitution" could obtain different results. This assertion ignores the fact that the two hypothetical criminal defendants did not actually commit the "same crime." They violated different state laws, were tried in and by different state sovereigns, and may—for many reasons—be subject to different penalties. As previously noted, such nonuniformity is a necessary consequence of a federalist system of government.

Chief Justice Roberts, joined by Justice Kennedy, dissented. He argued:

Some of our new rulings on the meaning of the United States Constitution apply retroactively—to cases already concluded—and some do not. This Court has held that the question whether a particular ruling is retroactive is itself a question of federal law. It is basic that when it comes to any such question of federal law, it is "the province and duty" of this Court "to say what the law is." Marbury v. Madison, 1 Cranch 137, 177 (1803). State courts are the final arbiters of their own state law; this Court is the final arbiter of federal law. State courts are therefore bound by our rulings on whether our cases construing federal law are retroactive.

The majority contravenes these bedrock propositions. The end result is startling: Of two criminal defendants, each of whom committed the same crime, at the same time, whose convictions became final on the same day, and each of whom raised an identical claim at the same time under the Federal Constitution, one may be executed while the other is set free—the first despite being correct on his claim, and the second because of it. That result is contrary to the Supremacy Clause and the Framers' decision to vest in "one supreme Court" the responsibility and authority to ensure the uniformity of federal law.[b]

b. For extensive consideration of *Danforth*, see Christopher N. Lasch, The Future of *Teague* Retroactivity, or "Redressability," After *Danforth v. Minnesota*: Why Lower Courts Should Give Retroactive Effect to New Constitutional Rules of Criminal Procedure, 46 Am. Crim. L. Rev. 1 (2009).

Page 926, add a new Note 4 and renumber the remaining Notes:

4. Error Repeated in a Second Judgment: *Magwood v. Patterson*. Magwood v. Patterson, 561 U.S. ___ (2010), involved successive federal habeas petitions challenging Magwood's death sentence. In the first, he was successful in getting the sentence set aside, but not the conviction. He was then resentenced to death. His second federal habeas petition challenged the sentence on a ground he could have raised in his first petition but did not. The question was whether this was a "claim presented in a second or successive habeas corpus application . . . that was not presented in a prior application." If it was, dismissal was required because prior Circuit Court approval had not been obtained under § 2244(b)(3)(A) and in any event the claim would not have satisfied the criteria stated in § 2244(b)(2). The District Court granted relief, but the Circuit Court reversed. The Supreme Court held five to four that the District Court correctly refused to apply the barrier contained in § 2244(b).

Justice Thomas wrote for the majority. "Because Magwood's habeas application challenges a new judgment for the first time," he wrote, "it is not 'second or successive' under § 2244(b)." The opinion continued:

This is Magwood's *first* application challenging [the resentencing] judgment. The errors he alleges are *new*. . . . An error made a second time is still a new error. That is especially clear here, where the state court conducted a full resentencing and reviewed the ... evidence afresh. ...AEDPA's text commands a ... straightforward rule: where ... there is a "new judgment intervening between the two habeas petitions," an application challenging the resulting new judgment is not "second or successive" at all.

Joined by Chief Justice Roberts and by Justices Ginsburg and Alito, Justice Kennedy dissented.[a] The dissenters concluded:

Had Magwood been unsuccessful in his first petition, all agree that claims then available, but not raised, would be barred. But because he prevailed in his attack on one part of his sentencing proceeding the first time around, the Court rules that he is free, postsentencing, to pursue claims on federal habeas review that might have been raised earlier. The Court is mistaken in concluding that Congress, in enacting a statute aimed at placing new restrictions on successive petitions, would have intended this irrational result.

Magwood had every chance to raise his death-eligibility claim in his first habeas petition. He has abused the writ by raising this claim for the first time in his second petition. His application is therefore "second or successive."

Page 946, add a footnote at the end of Note 1:

b. District Attorney's Office v. Osborne, 557 U.S. ___ (2009), involved a § 1983 suit seeking access to DNA evidence that would, if tested at the claimant's own expense he asserted, prove his innocence. As in *House* and *Herrera*, the Court declined to decide whether there is a federal constitutional right to be released upon proof of "actual innocence." Excerpts from the *Osborne* opinion on this point and on whether § 1983 or habeas was the appropriate remedy appear in the Notes following *Heck v. Humphrey* in Chapter VII, Section 4, infra.

Page 947, add to the citations in Note 3:

David Dow, Jared Tyler, Frances Bourliot & Jennifer Jeans, Is it Constitutional to Execute Someone Who Is Innocent (And If it Isn't, How Can it Be Stopped Following *House v. Bell*)?, 42 Tulsa L. Rev. 277 (2006) (identifying questions that remain open after *House* and containing detailed appendices covering state habeas and clemency procedures).

Page 982, add at the end of footnote a:

The administration of the *Preiser* holding after the Antiterrorism and Effective Death Penalty Act (AEDPA) is explored and proposed reforms suggested in Nancy J. King & Suzanna Sherry, Habeas Corpus and State Sentencing Reform: A Story of Unintended Consequences, 58 Duke L.J. 1 (2008).

Page 1000, add a new Note 3 and renumber the remaining Notes:

3. ***District Attorney's Office v. Osborne.*** Osborne was convicted in state court of kidnaping, assault, and sexual assault. He unsuccessfully

a. Joined by Justices Stevens and Sotomayor, Justice Breyer wrote a short concurrence in which he joined the Court's opinion except for a small part of its reasoning.

pursued appeals and postconviction relief in state courts. He was released on mandatory parole, but was later arrested for another offense and the state sought to revoke his parole. The present litigation involved a § 1983 proceeding in federal court in which he claimed a constitutional right of access to DNA evidence that would, if tested at his own expense he asserted, prove his innocence of the offenses on which he had been paroled.[a] In District Attorney's Office v. Osborne, 557 U.S. ___ (2009), the Court denied relief.

The first question was whether habeas corpus was the appropriate remedy. Relying on *Wilkinson v. Dotson*, Osborne argued "that his claim does not sound in habeas at all." For the Court, Chief Justice Roberts summarized his argument:

> Although invalidating his conviction is of course his ultimate goal, giving him the evidence he seeks "would not necessarily imply the invalidity of [his] confinement." If he prevails, he would receive only *access* to the DNA, and even if DNA testing exonerates him, his conviction is not automatically invalidated. He must bring an entirely separate suit or a petition for clemency to invalidate his conviction. If he were proved innocent, the State might also release him on its own initiative, avoiding any need to pursue habeas at all.

Roberts noted that "[e]very Court of Appeals to consider the question since *Dotson* has decided that because access to DNA evidence ... does not 'necessarily spell speedier release,' it can be sought under § 1983." In the end, the Court demurred:

> While we granted certiorari on this question, our resolution of Osborne's claims does not require us to resolve this difficult issue. Accordingly, we will assume without deciding that the Court of Appeals was correct that *Heck v. Humphrey* does not bar Osborne's § 1983 claim. Even under this assumption, it was wrong to find a due process violation.

Roberts then explained why Osborne had no procedural and substantive due process right to the evidence he sought. On the procedural due process claim, he observed:

> We see nothing inadequate about the procedures Alaska has provided to vindicate its state right to postconviction relief in general, and nothing inadequate about how those procedures apply to those who seek access to DNA evidence. Alaska provides a substantive right to be released on a sufficiently compelling showing of new evidence that establishes innocence. It exempts such claims from otherwise applicable time limits. The State provides

---

a. On several occasions in his efforts to obtain parole, he confessed in some detail to the crimes for which he had been convicted.

for discovery in postconviction proceedings, and has—through judicial decision—specified that this discovery procedure is available to those seeking access to DNA evidence. These procedures are not without limits. The evidence must indeed be newly available to qualify under Alaska's statute, must have been diligently pursued, and must also be sufficiently material. These procedures are similar to those provided for DNA evidence by federal law and the law of other States. . . .

To the degree there is some uncertainty in the details of Alaska's newly developing procedures for obtaining postconviction access to DNA, we can hardly fault the State for that. Osborne has brought this § 1983 action without ever using these procedures in filing a state or federal habeas claim relying on actual innocence. In other words, he has not tried to use the process provided to him by the State or attempted to vindicate the liberty interest that is now the centerpiece of his claim. . . . His attempt to sidestep state process through a new federal lawsuit puts Osborne in a very awkward position. If he simply seeks the DNA through the State's discovery procedures, he might well get it. If he does not, it may be for a perfectly adequate reason, just as the federal statute and all state statutes impose conditions and limits on access to DNA evidence. It is difficult to criticize the State's procedures when Osborne has not invoked them. This is not to say that Osborne must exhaust state-law remedies. See Patsy v. Board of Regents of Fla., 457 U.S. 496, 500–01 (1982). But it is Osborne's burden to demonstrate the inadequacy of the state-law procedures available to him in state postconviction relief. These procedures are adequate on their face, and without trying them, Osborne can hardly complain that they do not work in practice.

As a fallback, Osborne also obliquely relies on an asserted federal constitutional right to be released upon proof of "actual innocence." Whether such a federal right exists is an open question. We have struggled with it over the years, in some cases assuming, arguendo, that it exists while also noting the difficult questions such a right would pose and the high standard any claimant would have to meet. In this case too we can assume without deciding that such a claim exists, because even if so there is no due process problem. Osborne does not dispute that a federal actual innocence claim (as opposed to a DNA access claim) would be brought in habeas. If such a habeas claim is viable, federal procedural rules permit discovery. . . . Just as with state law, Osborne cannot show that available discovery is facially inadequate, and cannot show that it would be arbitrarily denied to him.[b]

---

b. Justice Stevens dissented. He was joined by Justices Ginsburg, Breyer, and Souter on Osborne's procedural due process argument, and by Justices Ginsburg and

Justice Alito wrote a separate concurrence. He was joined by Justice Kennedy in the conclusion that Osborne had sought the wrong remedy:

> It is no answer to say, as respondent does, that he simply wants to use § 1983 as a discovery tool to lay the foundation for a future state postconviction application, a state clemency petition, or a request for relief by means of "prosecutorial consent." Such tactics implicate precisely the same federalism and comity concerns that motivated our decisions (and Congress') to impose exhaustion requirements and discovery limits in federal habeas proceedings. If a petitioner can evade the habeas statute's exhaustion requirements in this way, I see no reason why a state prisoner asserting an ordinary *Brady* claim—i.e., a state prisoner who claims that the prosecution failed to turn over exculpatory evidence prior to trial—could not follow the same course.

> What respondent seeks was accurately described in his complaint—the discovery of evidence that has a material bearing on his conviction. Such a claim falls within "the core" of habeas. Preiser v. Rodriguez, 411 U.S. 475, 489 (1973). Recognition of a constitutional right to postconviction scientific testing of evidence in the possession of the prosecution would represent an expansion of *Brady* and a broadening of the discovery rights now available to habeas petitioners. We have never previously held that a state prisoner may seek discovery by means of a § 1983 action, and we should not take that step here. I would hold that respondent's claim (like all other *Brady* claims) should be brought in habeas.[c]

Justice Alito made a second argument for denial of relief, in this instance joined by Justices Kennedy and Thomas. Osborne's attorney had declined to pursue DNA testing at trial on the ground, as she testified, that doing so would merely confirm Osborne's guilt. Osborne claimed that he objected to this manner of proceeding, an objection that his attorney did not recall. Alito concluded:

> When a criminal defendant, for tactical purposes, passes up the opportunity for DNA testing at trial, that defendant, in my judgment, has no constitutional right to demand to perform DNA testing after conviction. Recognition of such a right would allow

Breyer on Osborne's substantive due process claim. Justice Souter wrote a separate dissent.—[Footnote by eds.]

    c. In a prior footnote, Alito said: "This case is quite different from *Dotson*. In that case, two state prisoners filed § 1983 actions challenging the constitutionality of Ohio's parole procedures and seeking 'a new parole hearing that may or may not result in release, prescription of the composition of the hearing panel, and specification of the procedures to be followed.' Regardless of whether such remedies fall outside the authority of federal habeas judges, there is no question that the relief respondent seeks in this case—'exculpatory' evidence that tends to prove his innocence—lies 'within the core of habeas corpus.' "—[Footnote by eds.]

defendants to play games with the criminal justice system. A guilty defendant could forgo DNA testing at trial for fear that the results would confirm his guilt, and in the hope that the other evidence would be insufficient to persuade the jury to find him guilty. Then, after conviction, with nothing to lose, the defendant could demand DNA testing in the hope that some happy accident—for example, degradation or contamination of the evidence—would provide the basis for seeking postconviction relief. ... There is ample evidence in this case that respondent attempted to game the system.[d]

Page 1009, add a new Section 5:

SECTION 5: HABEAS CORPUS AND THE WAR ON TERROR

Boumediene v. Bush

Supreme Court of the United States, 2008.
553 U.S. 723.

■ JUSTICE KENNEDY delivered the opinion of the Court.

Petitioners are aliens designated as enemy combatants and detained at the United States Naval Station at Guantanamo Bay, Cuba. There are others detained there, also aliens, who are not parties to this suit.

Petitioners present a question not resolved by our earlier cases relating to the detention of aliens at Guantanamo: whether they have the constitutional privilege of habeas corpus, a privilege not to be withdrawn except in conformance with the Suspension Clause, Art. I, § 9, cl. 2. We hold these petitioners do have the habeas corpus privilege. Congress has enacted a statute, the Detainee Treatment Act of 2005 (DTA), that provides certain procedures for review of the detainees' status. We hold that those procedures are not an adequate and effective substitute for habeas corpus. Therefore § 7 of the Military Commissions Act of 2006 (MCA), operates as an unconstitutional suspension of the writ. ...

I

Under the Authorization for Use of Military Force (AUMF) [enacted on September 18, 2001], the President is authorized "to use all necessary and appropriate force against those nations, organizations, or persons he deter-

---

d. DNA technology had advanced in the time between Osborne's trial and his § 1983 claim, and his § 1983 claim was for the more advanced test. On this point, Alito said: "It is true that the ... testing respondent now seeks is even more advanced than the ... testing he declined—but his counsel did not decline [the] testing [available at the time] because she thought it was not good enough; she declined because she thought it was too good."—[Footnote by eds.]

mines planned, authorized, committed, or aided the terrorist attacks that occurred on September 11, 2001, or harbored such organizations or persons, in order to prevent any future acts of international terrorism against the United States by such nations, organizations or persons."

In Hamdi v. Rumsfeld, 542 U.S. 507 (2004), five Members of the Court recognized that detention of individuals who fought against the United States in Afghanistan "for the duration of the particular conflict in which they were captured, is so fundamental and accepted an incident to war as to be an exercise of the 'necessary and appropriate force' Congress has authorized the President to use." After *Hamdi*, the Deputy Secretary of Defense established Combatant Status Review Tribunals (CSRTs) to determine whether individuals detained at Guantanamo were "enemy combatants," as the Department defines that term. A later memorandum established procedures to implement the CSRTs. The Government maintains these procedures were designed to comply with the due process requirements identified by the plurality in *Hamdi*.

Interpreting the AUMF, the Department of Defense ordered the detention of these petitioners, and they were transferred to Guantanamo. Some of these individuals were apprehended on the battlefield in Afghanistan, others in places as far away from there as Bosnia and Gambia. All are foreign nationals, but none is a citizen of a nation now at war with the United States. Each denies he is a member of the al Qaeda terrorist network that carried out the September 11 attacks or of the Taliban regime that provided sanctuary for al Qaeda. Each petitioner appeared before a separate CSRT; was determined to be an enemy combatant; and has sought a writ of habeas corpus in the United States District Court for the District of Columbia. . . .

The first actions commenced in February 2002. The District Court ordered the cases dismissed for lack of jurisdiction because the naval station is outside the sovereign territory of the United States. The Court of Appeals for the District of Columbia Circuit affirmed. We granted certiorari and reversed, holding that 28 U.S.C. § 2241 extended statutory habeas corpus jurisdiction to Guantanamo. See Rasul v. Bush, 542 U.S. 466, 473 (2004). The constitutional issue presented in the instant cases was not reached in *Rasul*.

After *Rasul*, petitioners' cases were consolidated and entertained in two separate proceedings. In the first set of cases, Judge Richard J. Leon granted the Government's motion to dismiss, holding that the detainees had no rights that could be vindicated in a habeas corpus action. In the second set of cases Judge Joyce Hens Green reached the opposite conclusion, holding the detainees had rights under the Due Process Clause of the Fifth Amendment.

While appeals were pending from the District Court decisions, Congress passed the DTA. Subsection (e) of § 1005 of the DTA amended 28 U.S.C. § 2241 to provide that "no court, justice, or judge shall have jurisdiction to hear or consider ... an application for a writ of habeas corpus filed by or on behalf of an alien detained by the Department of Defense at Guantanamo Bay, Cuba." Section 1005 further provides that the Court of Appeals for the District of Columbia Circuit shall have "exclusive" jurisdiction to review decisions of the CSRTs.

In Hamdan v. Rumsfeld, 548 U.S. 557, 576–77 (2006), the Court held this provision did not apply to cases (like petitioners') pending when the DTA was enacted. Congress responded by passing the MCA, which again amended § 2241. The text of the statutory amendment is discussed below. . . .

The Court of Appeals concluded that MCA § 7 must be read to strip from it, and all federal courts, jurisdiction to consider petitioners' habeas corpus applications; that petitioners are not entitled to the privilege of the writ or the protections of the Suspension Clause; and, as a result, that it was unnecessary to consider whether Congress provided an adequate and effective substitute for habeas corpus in the DTA. . . .

II

[In Part II, the Court concluded that Section 7 of the MCA denied the federal courts jurisdiction to hear habeas corpus actions brought by aliens designated by the government as enemy combatants, including habeas actions, like those of the petitioners, pending at the time of the MCA's enactment. Section 7(a) provides that "[n]o court, justice, or judge shall have jurisdiction to hear or consider an application for a writ of habeas corpus filed by or on behalf of an alien detained by the United States who has been determined by the United States to have been properly detained as an enemy combatant or is awaiting such determination." Section 7(b) provides that "[t]he amendment made by [Section 7(a) of the MCA] shall take effect on the date of the enactment of this Act, and shall apply to all cases, without exception, pending on or after the date of the enactment of this Act which relate to any aspect of the detention, transfer, treatment, trial, or conditions of detention of an alien detained by the United States since September 11, 2001."]

III

In deciding the constitutional questions now presented we must determine whether petitioners are barred from seeking the writ or invoking the protections of the Suspension Clause either because of their status, i.e., petitioners' designation by the Executive Branch as enemy combatants, or their physical location, i.e., their presence at Guantanamo Bay. The Government contends that noncitizens designated as enemy combatants and detained in territory located outside our Nation's borders have no constitutional rights and no privilege of habeas corpus. Petitioners contend they do have cognizable constitutional rights and that Congress, in seeking to eliminate recourse to habeas corpus as a means to assert those rights, acted in violation of the Suspension Clause. . . .

A

[The Court here examined the history of the writ of habeas corpus as it evolved in England and noted that "the writ proved to be an imperfect check" because "[d]enial or suspension [of the writ] occurred in times of political unrest, to the anguish of the imprisoned and the outrage of those in sympathy with them." The Court observed that "[t]his history was known to the Framers" and that it "no doubt confirmed their view that pendular swings to and away from individual liberty were endemic to undivided, uncontrolled power." It concluded:]

In our own system the Suspension Clause is designed to protect against these cyclical abuses. The Clause protects the rights of the detained by a means consistent with the essential design of the Constitution. It ensures that, except during periods of formal suspension, the Judiciary will have a time-tested device, the writ, to maintain the "delicate balance of governance" that is itself the surest safeguard of liberty. The Clause protects the rights of the detained by affirming the duty and authority of the Judiciary to call the jailer to account. The separation-of-powers doctrine, and the history that influenced its design, therefore must inform the reach and purpose of the Suspension Clause.

B

. . . The Court has been careful not to foreclose the possibility that the protections of the Suspension Clause have expanded along with post–1789 developments that define the present scope of the writ. See INS v. St. Cyr, 533 U.S. 289, 300–01 (2001). But the analysis may begin with precedents as of 1789, for the Court has said that "at the absolute minimum" the Clause protects the writ as it existed when the Constitution was drafted and ratified. Id. at 301. . . .

[The Court considered English common law cases concerning the extraterritorial reach of the writ of habeas corpus and found them inconclusive: "In none of the cases cited do we find that a common-law court would or would not have granted, or refused to hear for lack of jurisdiction, a petition for a writ of habeas corpus brought by a prisoner deemed an enemy combatant, under a standard like the one the Department of Defense has used in these cases, and when held in a territory, like Guantanamo, over which the Government has total military and civil control." Although the Court acknowledged that the writ did not extend to Scotland and Hanover, territories formally separate from England but over which the English monarch exercised control, the Court noted that:

> The prudential barriers that may have prevented the English courts from issuing the writ to Scotland and Hanover are not relevant here. We have no reason to believe an order from a

federal court would be disobeyed at Guantanamo. No Cuban court has jurisdiction to hear these petitioners' claims, and no law other than the laws of the United States applies at the naval station. The modern-day relations between the United States and Guantanamo thus differ in important respects from the 18th-century relations between England and the kingdoms of Scotland and Hanover.

Finally, the Court observed that, "given the unique status of Guantanamo Bay and the particular dangers of terrorism in the modern age, the common-law courts simply may not have confronted cases with close parallels to this one."]

IV

Drawing from its position that at common law the writ ran only to territories over which the Crown was sovereign, the Government says the Suspension Clause affords petitioners no rights because the United States does not claim sovereignty over the place of detention.

Guantanamo Bay is not formally part of the United States. And under the terms of the lease between the United States and Cuba [concluded in 1903], Cuba retains "ultimate sovereignty" over the territory while the United States exercises "complete jurisdiction and control." Under the terms of [a 1934 treaty between the United States and Cuba], however, Cuba effectively has no rights as a sovereign until the parties agree to modification of the 1903 Lease Agreement or the United States abandons the base.

The United States contends, nevertheless, that Guantanamo is not within its sovereign control. This was the Government's position well before the events of September 11, 2001. And in other contexts the Court has held that questions of sovereignty are for the political branches to decide. Even if this were a treaty interpretation case that did not involve a political question, the President's construction of the lease agreement would be entitled to great respect.

We therefore do not question the Government's position that Cuba, not the United States, maintains sovereignty, in the legal and technical sense of the term, over Guantanamo Bay. But this does not end the analysis. ...

A

[The Court reviewed its past decisions concerning the extraterritorial reach of the Constitution and concluded that they "undermine the Government's argument that, at least as applied to noncitizens, the Constitution necessarily stops where de jure sovereignty ends." Among the cases discussed by the Court was Johnson v. Eisentrager, 339 U.S. 763 (1950), in which a group of German nationals captured in China near the end of World War II and then imprisoned in occupied Germany were held not to have a right to seek habeas corpus review in a U.S. court. The disallowance of habeas jurisdiction in *Eisentrager*, the Court explained, was based in part on practical considerations:]

The prisoners were detained at Landsberg Prison in Germany during the Allied Powers' postwar occupation. The Court stressed the difficulties of ordering the Government to produce the prisoners in a habeas corpus proceeding. It "would require allocation of shipping space, guarding personnel, billeting and rations" and would damage the prestige of military commanders at a sensitive time. In considering these factors the Court sought to balance the constraints of military occupation with constitutional necessities. . . .

B

The Government's formal sovereignty-based test [for application of the Constitution] raises troubling separation-of-powers concerns as well. The political history of Guantanamo illustrates the deficiencies of this approach. The United States has maintained complete and uninterrupted control of the bay for over 100 years. At the close of the Spanish–American War, Spain ceded control over the entire island of Cuba to the United States and specifically "relinquishe[d] all claim[s] of sovereignty . . . and title." See Treaty of Paris, Dec. 10, 1898, U.S.-Spain, Art. I. From the date the treaty with Spain was signed until the Cuban Republic was established on May 20, 1902, the United States governed the territory "in trust" for the benefit of the Cuban people. And although it recognized, by entering into the 1903 Lease Agreement, that Cuba retained "ultimate sovereignty" over Guantanamo, the United States continued to maintain the same plenary control it had enjoyed since 1898. Yet the Government's view is that the Constitution had no effect there, at least as to noncitizens, because the United States disclaimed sovereignty in the formal sense of the term. The necessary implication of the argument is that by surrendering formal sovereignty over any unincorporated territory to a third party, while at the same time entering into a lease that grants total control over the territory back to the United States, it would be possible for the political branches to govern without legal constraint.

Our basic charter cannot be contracted away like this. The Constitution grants Congress and the President the power to acquire, dispose of, and govern territory, not the power to decide when and where its terms apply. Even when the United States acts outside its borders, its powers are not "absolute and unlimited" but are subject "to such restrictions as are expressed in the Constitution." Murphy v. Ramsey, 114 U.S. 15, 44 (1885). Abstaining from questions involving formal sovereignty and territorial governance is one thing. To hold the political branches have the power to switch the Constitution on or off at will is quite another. The former position reflects this Court's recognition that certain matters requiring political judgments are best left to the political branches. The latter would permit a striking anomaly in our tripartite system of government, leading to a regime in which Congress and the President, not this Court, say "what the law is." Marbury v. Madison, 5 U.S. (1 Cranch) 137, 177 (1803).

These concerns have particular bearing upon the Suspension Clause question in the cases now before us, for the writ of habeas corpus is itself an indispensable mechanism for monitoring the separation of powers. The test for determining the scope of this provision must not be subject to manipulation by those whose power it is designed to restrain.

C

As we recognized in *Rasul*, the outlines of a framework for determining the reach of the Suspension Clause are suggested by the factors the Court relied upon in *Eisentrager*. In addition to the practical concerns discussed above, the *Eisentrager* Court found relevant that each petitioner:

> (a) is an enemy alien; (b) has never been or resided in the United States; (c) was captured outside of our territory and there held in military custody as a prisoner of war; (d) was tried and convicted by a Military Commission sitting outside the United States; (e) for offenses against laws of war committed outside the United States; (f) and is at all times imprisoned outside the United States.

Based on this language from *Eisentrager*, and the reasoning in our other extraterritoriality opinions, we conclude that at least three factors are relevant in determining the reach of the Suspension Clause: (1) the citizenship and status of the detainee and the adequacy of the process through which that status determination was made; (2) the nature of the sites where apprehension and then detention took place; and (3) the practical obstacles inherent in resolving the prisoner's entitlement to the writ.

Applying this framework, we note at the onset that the status of these detainees is a matter of dispute. The petitioners, like those in *Eisentrager*, are not American citizens. But the petitioners in *Eisentrager* did not contest, it seems, the Court's assertion that they were "enemy alien[s]." In the instant cases, by contrast, the detainees deny they are enemy combatants. They have been afforded some process in CSRT proceedings to determine their status; but, unlike in *Eisentrager,* there has been no trial by military commission for violations of the laws of war. The difference is not trivial. The records from the *Eisentrager* trials suggest that, well before the petitioners brought their case to this Court, there had been a rigorous adversarial process to test the legality of their detention. The *Eisentrager* petitioners were charged by a bill of particulars that made detailed factual allegations against them. To rebut the accusations, they were entitled to representation by counsel, allowed to introduce evidence on their own behalf, and permitted to cross-examine the prosecution's witnesses.

In comparison the procedural protections afforded to the detainees in the CSRT hearings are far more limited, and, we conclude, fall well short of the procedures and adversarial mechanisms that would eliminate the need for habeas corpus review. Although the detainee is assigned a "Personal Representative" to assist him during CSRT proceedings, the Secretary of the Navy's memorandum makes clear that person is not the detainee's lawyer or even his "advocate." The Government's evidence is accorded a presumption of validity. The detainee is allowed to present "reasonably available" evidence, but his ability to rebut the Government's evidence against him is limited by the circumstances of his confinement and his lack of counsel at this stage. And although the detainee can seek review of his status determination in the Court of Appeals, that review process cannot cure all defects in the earlier proceedings.

As to the second factor relevant to this analysis, the detainees here are similarly situated to the *Eisentrager* petitioners in that the sites of their apprehension and detention are technically outside the sovereign territory of the United States. As noted earlier, this is a factor that weighs against finding they have rights under the Suspension Clause. But there are critical differences between Landsberg Prison, circa 1950, and the United States Naval Station at Guantanamo Bay in 2008. Unlike its present control over the naval station, the United States' control over the prison in Germany was neither absolute nor indefinite. Like all parts of occupied Germany, the prison was under the jurisdiction of the combined Allied Forces. The United States was therefore answerable to its Allies for all activities occurring there. The Allies had not planned a long-term occupation of Germany, nor did they intend to displace all German institutions even during the period of occupation. . . . In every practical sense Guantanamo is not abroad; it is within the constant jurisdiction of the United States.

As to the third factor, we recognize, as the Court did in *Eisentrager*, that there are costs to holding the Suspension Clause applicable in a case of military detention abroad. Habeas corpus proceedings may require expenditure of funds by the Government and may divert the attention of military personnel from other pressing tasks. While we are sensitive to these concerns, we do not find them dispositive. Compliance with any judicial process requires some incremental expenditure of resources. Yet civilian courts and the Armed Forces have functioned along side each other at various points in our history. The Government presents no credible arguments that the military mission at Guantanamo would be compromised if habeas corpus courts had jurisdiction to hear the detainees' claims. And in light of the plenary control the United States asserts over the base, none are apparent to us.

The situation in *Eisentrager* was far different, given the historical context and nature of the military's mission in post-War Germany. When hostilities in the European Theater came to an end, the United States became responsible for an occupation zone encompassing over 57,000 square miles with a population of 18 million. In addition to supervising massive reconstruction and aid efforts the American forces stationed in Germany faced potential security threats from a defeated enemy. In retrospect the post-War occupation may seem uneventful. But at the time *Eisentrager* was decided, the Court was right to be concerned about judicial interference with the military's efforts to contain "enemy elements, guerilla fighters, and 'were-wolves.'"

Similar threats are not apparent here; nor does the Government argue that they are. The United States Naval Station at Guantanamo Bay consists of 45 square miles of land and water. The base has been used, at various points, to house migrants and refugees temporarily. At present, however, other than the detainees themselves, the only long-term residents are American military personnel, their families, and a small number of workers. The detainees have been deemed enemies of the United States. At present, dangerous as they may be if released, they are contained in a secure prison facility located on an isolated and heavily fortified military base.

There is no indication, furthermore, that adjudicating a habeas corpus petition would cause friction with the host government. No Cuban court has jurisdiction over American military personnel at Guantanamo or the enemy combatants detained there. While obligated to abide by the terms of the lease, the United States is, for all practical purposes, answerable to no other sovereign for its acts on the base. Were that not the case, or if the detention facility were located in an active theater of war, arguments that issuing the writ would be "impracticable or anomalous" would have more weight. Under the facts presented here, however, there are few practical barriers to the running of the writ. To the extent barriers arise, habeas corpus procedures likely can be modified to address them. . . .

V

In light of this holding [that the petitioners here have a right under the Suspension Clause to habeas corpus review] the question becomes whether the statute stripping jurisdiction to issue the writ avoids the Suspension Clause mandate because Congress has provided adequate substitute procedures for habeas corpus. The Government submits there has been compliance with the Suspension Clause because the DTA review process in the Court of Appeals provides an adequate substitute. Congress has granted that court jurisdiction to consider

> (i) whether the status determination of the [CSRT] . . . was consistent with the standards and procedures specified by the Secretary of Defense . . . and (ii) to the extent the Constitution and laws of the United States are applicable, whether the use of such standards and procedures to make the determination is consistent with the Constitution and laws of the United States.

The Court of Appeals, having decided that the writ does not run to the detainees in any event, found it unnecessary to consider whether an adequate substitute has been provided. In the ordinary course we would remand to the Court of Appeals to consider this question in the first instance. It is well settled, however, that the Court's practice of declining to address issues left unresolved in earlier proceedings is not an inflexible rule. Departure from the rule is appropriate in "exceptional" circumstances.

The gravity of the separation-of-powers issues raised by these cases and the fact that these detainees have been denied meaningful access to a judicial forum for a period of years render these cases exceptional. The parties before us have addressed the adequacy issue. While we would have found it informative to consider the reasoning of the Court of Appeals on this point, we must weigh that against the harms petitioners may endure from additional delay. And, given there are few precedents addressing what features an adequate substitute for habeas corpus must contain, in all likelihood a remand simply would delay ultimate resolution of the issue by this Court. . . .

Under the circumstances we believe the costs of further delay substantially outweigh any benefits of remanding to the Court of Appeals to consider the issue it did not address in these cases.

A

Our case law does not contain extensive discussion of standards defining suspension of the writ or of circumstances under which suspension has occurred. This simply confirms the care Congress has taken throughout our Nation's history to preserve the writ and its function. . . . [After examining past legislation and the DTA, the Court concluded, that "[i]n passing the DTA Congress did not intend to create a process that differs from traditional habeas corpus process in name only. It intended to create a more limited procedure."]

B

We do not endeavor to offer a comprehensive summary of the requisites for an adequate substitute for habeas corpus. We do consider it uncontroversial, however, that the privilege of habeas corpus entitles the prisoner to a meaningful opportunity to demonstrate that he is being held pursuant to "the erroneous application or interpretation" of relevant law. *St. Cyr*, 533 U.S. at 302. And the habeas court must have the power to order the conditional release of an individual unlawfully detained—though release need not be the exclusive remedy and is not the appropriate one in every case in which the writ is granted. These are the easily identified attributes of any constitutionally adequate habeas corpus proceeding. But, depending on the circumstances, more may be required. . . .

The idea that the necessary scope of habeas review in part depends upon the rigor of any earlier proceedings accords with our test for procedural adequacy in the due process context. See Mathews v. Eldridge, 424 U.S. 319, 335 (1976) (noting that the Due Process Clause requires an assessment of, inter alia, "the risk of an erroneous deprivation of [a liberty interest;] and the probable value, if any, of additional or substitute procedural safeguards"). This principle has an established foundation in habeas corpus jurisprudence as well. . . .

Accordingly, where relief is sought from a sentence that resulted from the judgment of a court of record . . . considerable deference is owed to the court that ordered confinement. Likewise in those cases the prisoner should exhaust adequate alternative remedies before filing for the writ in federal court. Both aspects of federal habeas corpus review are justified because it can be assumed that, in the usual course, a court of record provides defendants with a fair, adversary proceeding. In cases involving state convictions this framework also respects federalism; and in federal cases it has added justification because the prisoner already has had a chance to seek review of his conviction in a federal forum through a direct appeal. The present cases fall outside these categories, however; for here the detention is by executive order.

Where a person is detained by executive order, rather than, say, after being tried and convicted in a court, the need for collateral review is most pressing. A criminal conviction in the usual course occurs after a judicial hearing before a tribunal disinterested in the outcome and committed to procedures designed to ensure its own independence. These dynamics are not inherent in executive detention orders or executive review procedures. In this context the need for habeas corpus is more urgent. The intended duration of the detention and the reasons for it bear upon the precise scope of the inquiry. Habeas corpus proceedings need not resemble a criminal trial, even when the detention is by executive order. But the writ must be effective. The habeas court must have sufficient authority to conduct a meaningful review of both the cause for detention and the Executive's power to detain.

To determine the necessary scope of habeas corpus review, therefore, we must assess the CSRT process, the mechanism through which petitioners' designation as enemy combatants became final. Whether one characterizes the CSRT process as direct review of the Executive's battlefield determination that the detainee is an enemy combatant—as the parties have and as we do—or as the first step in the collateral review of a battlefield determination makes no difference in a proper analysis of whether the procedures Congress put in place are an adequate substitute for habeas corpus. What matters is the sum total of procedural protections afforded to the detainee at all stages, direct and collateral.

[The Court described potential procedural deficiencies in the CSRT process, including the lack of assistance of counsel, allowance of hearsay evidence, and practical limitations on the ability of detainees to find and present evidence to rebut the government's case. Although the Court "[made] no judgment as to whether the CSRTs, as currently constituted, satisfy due process standards," it "agree[d] with petitioners that, even when all the parties involved in this process act with diligence and in good faith, there is considerable risk of error in the tribunal's findings of fact." It concluded by stating:]

... For the writ of habeas corpus, or its substitute, to function as an effective and proper remedy in this context, the court that conducts the habeas proceeding must have the means to correct errors that occurred during the CSRT proceedings. This includes some authority to assess the sufficiency of the Government's evidence against the detainee. It also must have the authority to admit and consider relevant exculpatory evidence that was not introduced during the earlier proceeding. Federal habeas petitioners long have had the means to supplement the record on review, even in the postconviction habeas setting. Here that opportunity is constitutionally required. ...

C

We now consider whether the DTA allows the Court of Appeals to conduct a proceeding meeting these standards. "[W]e are obligated to construe the statute to avoid [constitutional] problems" if it is " 'fairly possible' " to do so. *St. Cyr*, 533 U.S. at 299–300. There are limits to this principle, however. The canon of constitutional avoidance does not supplant traditional modes of statutory interpretation. We cannot ignore the text and purpose of a statute in order to save it.

The DTA does not explicitly empower the Court of Appeals to order the applicant in a DTA review proceeding released should the court find that the standards and procedures used at his CSRT hearing were insufficient to justify detention. This is troubling. Yet, for present purposes, we can assume congressional silence permits a constitutionally required remedy. In that case it would be possible to hold that a remedy of release is impliedly provided for. The DTA might be read, furthermore, to allow the petitioners to assert most, if not all, of the legal claims they seek to advance, including their most basic claim: that the President has no authority under the AUMF to detain them indefinitely. ... At oral argument, the Solicitor General urged us to adopt both these constructions, if doing so would allow MCA § 7 to remain intact.

The absence of a release remedy and specific language allowing AUMF challenges are not the only constitutional infirmities from which the statute potentially suffers, however. The more difficult question is whether the DTA permits the Court of Appeals to make requisite findings of fact. The DTA enables petitioners to request "review" of their CSRT determination in the Court of Appeals; but the "Scope of Review" provision confines the Court of Appeals' role to reviewing whether the CSRT followed the "standards and procedures" issued by the Department of Defense and assessing whether those "standards and procedures" are lawful. Among these standards is "the requirement that the conclusion of the Tribunal be supported by a preponderance of the evidence ... allowing a rebuttable presumption in favor of the Government's evidence."

Assuming the DTA can be construed to allow the Court of Appeals to review or correct the CSRT's factual determinations, as opposed to merely certifying that the tribunal applied the correct standard of proof, we see no way to construe the statute to allow what is also constitutionally required in this context: an opportunity for the detainee to present relevant exculpatory evidence that was not made part of the record in the earlier proceedings.

On its face the statute allows the Court of Appeals to consider no evidence outside the CSRT record. In the parallel litigation, however, the Court of Appeals determined that the DTA allows it to order the production of all "reasonably available information in the possession of the U.S. Government bearing on the issue of whether the detainee meets the criteria to be designated as an enemy combatant," regardless of whether this evidence was put before the CSRT. The Government, with support from five members of the Court of Appeals, disagrees with this interpretation. For present purposes, however, we can assume that the Court of Appeals was correct that the DTA allows introduction and consideration of relevant exculpatory evidence that was "reasonably available" to the Government at the time of the CSRT but not made part of the record. Even so, the DTA review proceeding falls short of being a constitutionally adequate substitute, for the detainee still would have no opportunity to present evidence discovered after the CSRT proceedings concluded.

Under the DTA the Court of Appeals has the power to review CSRT determinations by assessing the legality of standards and procedures. This implies the power to inquire into what happened at the CSRT hearing and, perhaps, to remedy certain deficiencies in that proceeding. But should the Court of Appeals determine that the CSRT followed appropriate and lawful standards and procedures, it will have reached the limits of its jurisdiction. There is no language in the DTA that can be construed to allow the Court of Appeals to admit and consider newly discovered evidence that could not have been made part of the CSRT record because it was unavailable to either the Government or the detainee when the CSRT made its findings. This evidence, however, may be critical to the detainee's argument that he is not an enemy combatant and there is no cause to detain him. ...

By foreclosing consideration of evidence not presented or reasonably available to the detainee at the CSRT proceedings, the DTA disadvantages the detainee by limiting the scope of collateral review to a record that may not be accurate or complete. In other contexts, e.g., in post-trial habeas cases where the prisoner already has had a full and fair opportunity to develop the factual predicate of his claims, similar limitations on the scope of habeas review may be appropriate. In this context, however, where the underlying detention proceedings lack the necessary adversarial character, the detainee cannot be held responsible for all deficiencies in the record.

The Government does not make the alternative argument that the DTA allows for the introduction of previously unavailable exculpatory evidence on appeal. It does point out, however, that if a detainee obtains such evidence, he can request that the Deputy Secretary of Defense convene a new CSRT. Whatever the merits of this procedure, it is an insufficient replacement for the factual review these detainees are entitled to receive through habeas corpus. The Deputy Secretary's determination whether to initiate new proceedings is wholly a discretionary one. And we see no way to construe the DTA to allow a detainee to challenge the Deputy Secretary's decision not to open a new CSRT.... Congress directed the Secretary of Defense to devise procedures for considering new evidence, but the detainee has no mechanism for ensuring that those procedures are followed. ...

We do not imply DTA review would be a constitutionally sufficient replacement for habeas corpus but for these limitations on the detainee's ability to present exculpatory evidence. For even if it were possible, as a textual matter, to read into the statute each of the necessary procedures we have identified, we could not overlook the cumulative effect of our doing so. To hold that the detainees at Guantanamo may, under the DTA, challenge the President's legal authority to detain them, contest the CSRT's findings of fact, supplement the record on review with exculpatory evidence, and request an order of release would come close to reinstating the § 2241 habeas corpus process Congress sought to deny them. The language of the statute, read in light of Congress' reasons for enacting it, cannot bear this interpretation. Petitioners have met their burden of establishing that the DTA review process is, on its face, an inadequate substitute for habeas corpus. ...

* * *

... [O]ur opinion does not address the content of the law that governs petitioners' detention. That is a matter yet to be determined. We hold that petitioners may invoke the fundamental procedural protections of habeas corpus. The laws and Constitution are designed to survive, and remain in force, in extraordinary times. Liberty and security can be reconciled; and in our system they are reconciled within the framework of the law. The Framers decided that habeas corpus, a right of first importance, must be a part of that framework, a part of that law.

The determination by the Court of Appeals that the Suspension Clause and its protections are inapplicable to petitioners was in error. The judgment of the Court of Appeals is reversed. The cases are remanded to the Court of Appeals with instructions that it remand the cases to the District Court for proceedings consistent with this opinion.

It is so ordered.

■ CHIEF JUSTICE ROBERTS, with whom JUSTICE SCALIA, JUSTICE THOMAS, and JUSTICE ALITO join, dissenting.

Today the Court strikes down as inadequate the most generous set of procedural protections ever afforded aliens detained by this country as enemy combatants. The political branches crafted these procedures amidst an ongoing military conflict, after much careful investigation and thorough debate. The Court rejects them today out of hand, without bothering to say what due process rights the detainees possess, without explaining how the statute fails to vindicate those rights, and before a single petitioner has even attempted to avail himself of the law's operation. And to what effect? The majority merely replaces a review system designed by the people's representatives with a set of shapeless procedures to be defined by federal courts at some future date. One cannot help but think, after surveying the modest practical results of the majority's ambitious opinion, that this decision is not really about the detainees at all, but about control of federal policy regarding enemy combatants. . . .

Congress entrusted that threshold question in the first instance to the Court of Appeals for the District of Columbia Circuit, as the Constitution surely allows Congress to do. But before the D.C. Circuit has addressed the issue, the Court cashiers the statute, and without answering this critical threshold question itself. The Court does eventually get around to asking whether review under the DTA is, as the Court frames it, an "adequate substitute" for habeas, but even then its opinion fails to determine what rights the detainees possess and whether the DTA system satisfies them. The majority instead compares the undefined DTA process to an equally undefined habeas right—one that is to be given shape only in the future by district courts on a case-by-case basis. This whole approach is misguided.

It is also fruitless. How the detainees' claims will be decided now that the DTA is gone is anybody's guess. But the habeas process the Court mandates will most likely end up looking a lot like the DTA system it replaces, as the district court judges shaping it will have to reconcile review of the prisoners' detention with the undoubted need to protect the American people from the terrorist threat—precisely the challenge Congress undertook in drafting the DTA. All that today's opinion has done is shift responsibility for those sensitive foreign policy and national security decisions from the elected branches to the Federal Judiciary. . . .

The Court acknowledges that "the ordinary course" would be not to decide the constitutionality of the DTA at this stage, but abandons that "ordinary course" in light of the "gravity" of the constitutional issues presented and the prospect of additional delay. It is, however, precisely when the issues presented are grave that adherence to the ordinary course is most important. A principle applied only when unimportant is not much of a principle at all, and charges of judicial activism are most effectively rebutted when courts can fairly argue they are following normal practices.

The Court is also concerned that requiring petitioners to pursue "DTA review before proceeding with their habeas corpus actions" could involve additional delay. The nature of the habeas remedy the Court instructs lower courts to craft on remand, however, is far more unsettled than the process Congress provided in the DTA. There is no reason to suppose that review according to procedures the Federal Judiciary will design, case by case, will proceed any faster than the DTA process petitioners disdained.

On the contrary, the system the Court has launched (and directs lower courts to elaborate) promises to take longer. The Court assures us that before bringing their habeas petitions, detainees must usually complete the CSRT process. Then they may seek review in federal district court. Either success or failure there will surely result in an appeal to the D.C. Circuit—exactly where judicial review *starts* under Congress's system. The effect of the Court's decision is to add additional layers of quite possibly redundant review. And because nobody knows how these new layers of "habeas" review will operate, or what new procedures they will require, their contours will undoubtedly be subject to fresh bouts of litigation. If the majority were truly concerned about delay, it would have required petitioners to use the DTA process that has been available to them for 2½ years, with its Article III review in the D.C. Circuit. That system might well have provided petitioners all the relief to which they are entitled long before the Court's newly installed habeas review could hope to do so. . . .

The majority's overreaching is particularly egregious given the weakness of its objections to the DTA. Simply put, the Court's opinion fails on its own terms. The majority strikes down the statute because it is not an "adequate substitute" for habeas review, but fails to show what rights the detainees have that cannot be vindicated by the DTA system.

Because the central purpose of habeas corpus is to test the legality of executive detention, the writ requires most fundamentally an Article III court able to hear the prisoner's claims and, when necessary, order release. Beyond that, the process a given prisoner is entitled to receive depends on the circumstances and the rights of the prisoner. After much hemming and hawing, the majority appears to concede that the DTA provides an Article III court competent to order release. The only issue in dispute is the process the Guantanamo prisoners are entitled to use to test the legality of their detention. *Hamdi* concluded that American citizens detained as enemy combatants are entitled to only limited process, and that much of that process could be supplied by a military tribunal, with review to follow in an Article III court. That is precisely the system we have here. It is adequate to vindicate whatever due process rights petitioners may have.
. . .

[Chief Justice Roberts reviewed the procedures in the CSRTs, and the provisions in the DTA for appeal to the D.C. Circuit. He concluded that "[a]ll told the DTA provides the prisoners held at Guantanamo Bay adequate opportunity to contest the bases of their detentions, which is all habeas corpus need allow. The DTA provides more opportunity and more process, in fact, than that afforded prisoners of war or any other alleged enemy combatants in history."]

Despite these guarantees, the Court finds the DTA system an inadequate habeas substitute, for one central reason: Detainees are unable to introduce at the appeal stage exculpatory evidence discovered after the conclusion of their CSRT proceedings. The Court hints darkly that the DTA may suffer from other infirmities, but it does not bother to name them, making a response a bit difficult. As it stands, I can only assume the Court regards the supposed defect it did identify as the gravest of the lot.

If this is the most the Court can muster, the ice beneath its feet is thin indeed. As noted, the CSRT procedures provide ample opportunity for detainees to introduce exculpatory evidence—whether documentary in nature or from live witnesses—before the military tribunals. And if their ability to introduce such evidence is denied contrary to the Constitution or laws of the United States, the D.C. Circuit has the authority to say so on review.

Nevertheless, the Court asks us to imagine an instance in which evidence is discovered *after* the CSRT panel renders its decision, but *before* the Court of Appeals reviews the detainee's case. This scenario, which of course has not yet come to pass as no review in the D.C. Circuit has occurred, provides no basis for rejecting the DTA as a habeas substitute. While the majority is correct that the DTA does not contemplate the introduction of "newly discovered" evidence before the Court of Appeals, petitioners and the Solicitor General agree that the DTA *does* permit the D.C. Circuit to remand a detainee's case for a new CSRT determination. In the event a detainee alleges that he has obtained new and persuasive exculpatory evidence that would have been considered by the tribunal below had it only been available, the D.C. Circuit could readily remand the case to the tribunal to allow that body to consider the evidence in the first instance. The Court of Appeals could later review any new or reinstated decision in light of the supplemented record. . . .

The Court's hand wringing over the DTA's treatment of later-discovered exculpatory evidence is the most it has to show after a roving search for constitutionally problematic scenarios. But "[t]he delicate power of pronouncing an Act of Congress unconstitutional," we have said, "is not to be exercised with reference to hypothetical cases thus imagined." United States v. Raines, 362 U.S. 17, 22 (1960). The Court today invents a sort of reverse facial challenge and applies it with gusto: If there is *any* scenario in which the statute *might* be constitutionally infirm, the law must be struck down. The Court's new method of constitutional adjudication only underscores its failure to follow our usual procedures and require petitioners to demonstrate that *they* have been harmed by the statute they challenge. In the absence of such a concrete showing, the Court is unable to imagine a plausible hypothetical in which the DTA is unconstitutional.

The Court's second criterion for an adequate substitute is the "power to order the conditional release of an individual unlawfully detained." As the Court basically admits, the DTA can be read to permit the D.C. Circuit to order release in light of our traditional principles of construing statutes to avoid difficult constitutional issues, when reasonably possible. ...

The basis for the Court's [conclusion that the DTA does not provide an adequate substitute for habeas] is summed up in the following sentence near the end of its opinion: "To hold that the detainees at Guantanamo may, under the DTA, challenge the President's legal authority to detain them, contest the CSRT's findings of fact, supplement the record on review with newly discovered or previously unavailable evidence, and request an order of release would come close to reinstating the § 2241 habeas corpus process Congress sought to deny them." In other words, any interpretation of the statute that would make it an adequate substitute for habeas must be rejected, because Congress could not possibly have intended to enact an adequate substitute for habeas. The Court could have saved itself a lot of trouble if it had simply announced this Catch–22 approach at the beginning rather than the end of its opinion. ...

■ JUSTICE SCALIA, with whom THE CHIEF JUSTICE, JUSTICE THOMAS, and JUSTICE ALITO join, dissenting.

Today, for the first time in our Nation's history, the Court confers a constitutional right to habeas corpus on alien enemies detained abroad by our military forces in the course of an ongoing war. The Chief Justice's dissent, which I join, shows that the procedures prescribed by Congress in the Detainee Treatment Act provide the essential protections that habeas corpus guarantees; there has thus been no suspension of the writ, and no basis exists for judicial intervention beyond what the Act allows. My problem with today's opinion is more fundamental still: The writ of habeas corpus does not, and never has, run in favor of aliens abroad; the Suspension Clause thus has no application, and the Court's intervention in this military matter is entirely ultra vires. ...

America is at war with radical Islamists. The enemy began by killing Americans and American allies abroad: 241 at the Marine barracks in Lebanon, 19 at the Khobar Towers in Dhahran, 224 at our embassies in Dar es Salaam and Nairobi, and 17 on the USS Cole in Yemen. On September 11, 2001, the enemy brought the battle to American soil, killing 2,749 at the Twin Towers in New York City, 184 at the Pentagon in Washington, D.C., and 40 in Pennsylvania. It has threatened further attacks against our homeland; one need only walk about buttressed and barricaded Washington, or board a plane anywhere in the country, to know that the threat is a serious one. Our Armed Forces are now in the field against the enemy, in Afghanistan and Iraq. Last week, 13 of our countrymen in arms were killed.

The game of bait-and-switch that today's opinion plays upon the Nation's Commander in Chief will make the war harder on us. It will almost certainly cause more Americans to be killed. That consequence would be tolerable if necessary to preserve a time-honored legal principle vital to our constitutional Republic. But it is this Court's blatant *abandonment* of such a principle that produces the decision today. The President relied on our settled precedent in Johnson v. Eisentrager, 339 U.S. 763 (1950), when he established the prison at Guantanamo Bay for enemy aliens. ... Had the law been otherwise, the military surely would not have transported prisoners there, but would have kept them in Afghanistan, transferred them to another of our foreign military bases, or turned them over to allies for detention. Those other facilities might well have been worse for the detainees themselves.

In the long term, then, the Court's decision today accomplishes little, except perhaps to reduce the well-being of enemy combatants that the Court ostensibly seeks to protect. In the short term, however, the decision is devastating. At least 30 of those prisoners hitherto released from Guantanamo Bay have returned to the battlefield. Some have been captured or killed. But others have succeeded in carrying on their atrocities against innocent civilians. In one case, a detainee released from Guantanamo Bay masterminded the kidnapping of two Chinese dam workers, one of whom was later shot to death when used as a human shield against Pakistani commandoes. Another former detainee promptly resumed his post as a senior Taliban commander and murdered a United Nations engineer and three Afghan soldiers. It was reported only last month that a released detainee carried out a suicide bombing against Iraqi soldiers in Mosul, Iraq.

These, mind you, were detainees whom *the military* had concluded were not enemy combatants. Their return to the kill illustrates the incredible difficulty of assessing who is and who is not an enemy combatant in a foreign theater of operations where the environment does not lend itself to rigorous evidence collection. Astoundingly, the Court today raises the bar, requiring military officials to appear before civilian courts and defend their decisions under procedural and evidentiary rules that go beyond what Congress has specified. As the Chief Justice's dissent makes clear, we have no idea what those procedural and evidentiary rules are, but they will be determined by civil courts and (in the Court's contemplation at least) will be more detainee-friendly than those now applied, since otherwise there would no reason to hold the congressionally prescribed procedures unconstitutional. If they impose a higher standard of proof (from foreign battlefields) than the current procedures require, the number of the enemy returned to combat will obviously increase.

But even when the military has evidence that it can bring forward, it is often foolhardy to release that evidence to the attorneys representing our enemies. And one escalation of procedures that the Court *is* clear about is affording the detainees increased access to witnesses (perhaps troops serving in Afghanistan?) and to classified information. During the 1995 prosecution of Omar Abdel Rahman, federal prosecutors gave the names of 200 unindicted co-conspirators to the "Blind Sheik's" defense lawyers; that information was in the hands of Osama Bin Laden within two weeks. In another case, trial testimony revealed to the enemy that the United States had been monitoring their cellular network, whereupon they promptly stopped using it, enabling more of them to evade capture and continue their atrocities. . . .

The Court today decrees that no good reason to accept the judgment of the other two branches is "apparent." "The Government," it declares, "presents no credible arguments that the military mission at Guantanamo would be compromised if habeas corpus courts had jurisdiction to hear the detainees' claims." What competence does the Court have to second-guess the judgment of Congress and the President on such a point? None whatever. But the Court blunders in nonetheless. Henceforth, as today's opinion makes unnervingly clear, how to handle enemy prisoners in this war will ultimately lie with the branch that knows least about the national security concerns that the subject entails. . . .

There is simply no support for the Court's assertion that constitutional rights extend to aliens held outside U.S. sovereign territory, and *Eisentrager* could not be clearer that the privilege of habeas corpus does not extend to aliens abroad. By blatantly distorting *Eisentrager*, the Court avoids the difficulty of explaining why it should be overruled. The rule that aliens abroad are not constitutionally entitled to habeas corpus has not proved unworkable in practice; if anything, it is the Court's "functional" test that does not (and never will) provide clear guidance for the future. *Eisentrager* forms a coherent whole with the accepted proposition that aliens abroad have no substantive rights under our Constitution. Since it was announced, no relevant factual premises have changed. It has engendered considerable reliance on the part of our military. And, as the Court acknowledges, text and history do not clearly compel a contrary ruling. It is a sad day for the rule of law when such an important constitutional precedent is discarded without an apologia, much less an apology.

What drives today's decision is neither the meaning of the Suspension Clause, nor the principles of our precedents, but rather an inflated notion of judicial supremacy. The Court says that if the extraterritorial applicability of the Suspension Clause turned on formal notions of sovereignty, "it would be possible for the political branches to govern without legal constraint" in areas beyond the sovereign territory of the United States. That cannot be, the Court says, because it is the duty of this Court to say what the law is. It would be difficult to imagine a more question-begging analysis. . . . Our power "to say what the law is" is circumscribed by the limits of our statutorily and constitutionally conferred jurisdiction. And that is precisely the question in these cases: whether the Constitution confers habeas jurisdiction on federal courts to decide petitioners' claims. It is both irrational and arrogant to say that the answer must be yes, because otherwise we would not be supreme.

But so long as there are *some* places to which habeas does not run—so long as the Court's new "functional" test will not be satisfied *in every case*—then there will be circumstances in which "it would be possible for the political branches to govern without legal constraint." Or, to put it more impartially, areas in which the legal determinations of the *other* branches will be (shudder!) *supreme*. In other words, judicial supremacy is not really assured by the constitutional rule that the Court creates. The gap between rationale and rule leads me to conclude that the Court's ultimate, unexpressed goal is to preserve the power to review the confinement of enemy prisoners held by the Executive anywhere in the world. The "functional" test usefully evades the precedential landmine of *Eisentrager* but is so inherently subjective that it clears a wide path for the Court to traverse in the years to come. . . .

NOTES ON HABEAS CORPUS AND THE WAR ON TERROR

    1. The September 11 Attacks and the AUMF. On September 11, 2001, members of the Al Qaeda terrorist network hijacked four commercial airplanes in the United States, crashing two into the World Trade Center in New York and one into the Pentagon. The fourth crashed in a field in Pennsylvania. The attacks killed several thousand people and resulted in billions of dollars in property damage. A week later, Congress enacted an Authorization for the Use of Military Force (AUMF), which provides in relevant part that:

> [T]he President is authorized to use all necessary and appropriate force against those nations, organizations, or persons he determines planned, authorized, committed, or aided the terrorist attacks that occurred on September 11, 2001, or harbored such organizations or persons, in order to prevent any future acts of international terrorism against the United States by such nations, organizations or persons.

A few weeks later, the United States began combat operations in Afghanistan against both the military forces of the Taliban (the Sunni Islamist group that ruled most of Afghanistan at the time) and Al Qaeda. As part of this conflict, and as part of a broader global war on terrorism, the United States began capturing and detaining a variety of individuals.

    In November 2001, citing the AUMF and his authority as Commander in Chief, President Bush issued a Military Order on the "Detention, Treatment, and Trial of Certain Non–Citizens in the War Against Terrorism." This Order authorized the detention and trial by military commission of several classes of non-citizens: past or present members of Al Qaeda;

individuals who have "engaged in, aided or abetted, or conspired to commit, acts of international terrorism, or acts in preparation therefor, that have caused, threaten to cause, or have as their aim to cause, injury to or adverse effects on the United States, its citizens, national security, foreign policy, or economy"; and individuals who have "knowingly harbored" one or more individuals in the first two categories.

2. The Guantanamo Bay Naval Base. The United States has had a naval base at Guantanamo Bay since the early 1900s. In 1903, the United States entered into a lease arrangement with Cuba, pursuant to which the United States was given "complete jurisdiction and control" over the Guantanamo Bay area while Cuba retained "ultimate sovereignty." In a 1934 treaty, Cuba and the United States agreed that the area would revert to Cuban control only by mutual consent or if the United States abandoned it. Since the September 11 attacks, the U.S. military has detained a variety of foreign citizens at the naval base as "enemy combatants." Many of these detainees were apprehended in Afghanistan, but some were apprehended in other locations, such as Bosnia. At times, there have been over 600 detainees at the base, but as a result of releases and transfers to other countries, the number had dropped down to about 200 by June 2009. The Department of Defense has sought to prosecute some of these detainees before military commissions, but for a variety of reasons (including the *Hamdan* decision described below) only one military commission trial had been completed as of June 2009 (although one detainee was convicted in a commission process pursuant to a plea bargain in 2007).[a]

3. *Johnson v. Eisentrager.* Both the majority opinion and Justice Scalia's dissent in *Boumediene* discuss Johnson v. Eisentrager, 339 U.S. 763 (1950). In that case, the U.S. military had captured 21 German nationals in China near the end of World War II and prosecuted them in a military tribunal for providing assistance to the Japanese after Germany had surrendered. After the German nationals were convicted, they were moved to a prison in occupied Germany, and they subsequently filed petitions for habeas corpus in a federal court.

In an opinion by Justice Jackson, the Supreme Court held that the detainees were not entitled to petition for habeas corpus relief in a U.S. court. The Court noted early in its opinion that: "We are cited to no instance where a court, in this or any other country where the writ is known, has issued it on behalf of an alien enemy who, at no relevant time

---

a. Military commissions are courts created by the Executive Branch and composed of military officers. They have historically been used in three situations: to administer justice in territory occupied by the United States; to replace civilian courts in parts of the United States where martial law has been declared; and to try enemy belligerents during wartime for violations of the laws of war. Military commissions were used extensively during the Civil War and during the post-Civil War Reconstruction period. In 1942, the Supreme Court upheld the use of a military commission created by President Roosevelt to try a group of Nazi agents who had surreptitiously entered the United States with plans of committing sabotage. See Ex parte Quirin, 317 U.S. 1 (1942).

and in no stage of his captivity, has been within its territorial jurisdiction. Nothing in the text of the Constitution extends such a right, nor does anything in our statutes." The Court subsequently observed that each petitioner in this case:

> (a) is an enemy alien; (b) has never been or resided in the United States; (c) was captured outside of our territory and there held in military custody as a prisoner of war; (d) was tried and convicted by a Military Commission sitting outside the United States; (e) for offenses against laws of war committed outside the United States; (f) and is at all times imprisoned outside the United States.

While acknowledging that aliens within the United States are entitled to the "privilege of litigation," the Court noted this was because "permitting their presence in the country implied protection," whereas "no such basis can be invoked here, for these prisoners at no relevant time were within any territory over which the United States is sovereign, and the scenes of their offense, their capture, their trial and their punishment were all beyond the territorial jurisdiction of any court of the United States."

The Court in *Eisentrager* further noted that habeas corpus litigation typically requires that the prisoner be produced before the Court, which in this case "might mean that our army must transport them across the seas for hearing," which "would require allocation of shipping space, guarding personnel, billeting and rations," and "might also require transportation for whatever witnesses the prisoner desired to call as well as transportation for those necessary to defend legality of the sentence." The Court also expressed concern that, if the writ of habeas corpus were available to enemy aliens held abroad, it "would be equally available to enemies during active hostilities as in the present twilight between war and peace," and "[s]uch trials would hamper the war effort and bring aid and comfort to the enemy." "It would be difficult to devise more effective fettering of a field commander," the Court observed, "than to allow the very enemies he is ordered to reduce to submission to call him to account in his own civil courts and divert his efforts and attention from the military offensive abroad to the legal defensive at home."

Justice Black dissented, joined by Justices Douglas and Burton.

4. *Rasul v. Bush.* In Rasul v. Bush, 542 U.S. 466 (2004), various detainees at Guantanamo filed petitions for habeas relief in the U.S. District Court for the District of Columbia. In an opinion by Justice Stevens, the Court held that there was jurisdiction under the federal habeas statute, 28 U.S.C. § 2241, to hear these petitions. The Court noted that the petitioners had alleged that they were being held in federal custody in violation of the laws of the United States, and that it was undisputed that the district court had jurisdiction over the petitioners' custodians. "Section 2241, by its terms, requires nothing more," said the Court.

The Court distinguished *Eisentrager* in two ways. First, the Court noted that the petitioners in this case

> differ from the *Eisentrager* detainees in critical respects: They are not nationals of countries at war with the United States, and they deny that they have engaged in or plotted acts of aggression against the United States; they have never been afforded access to any tribunal, must less charged with and convicted of wrongdoing; and for more than two years they have been imprisoned in territory over which the United States exercises exclusive jurisdiction and control.

Second, the Court noted that the Court in *Eisentrager* had focused primarily on whether the detainees there had a *constitutional* right of habeas corpus because it was assumed at the time that the federal habeas statute applied only to detainees within the territorial jurisdiction of a federal district court. See Ahrens v. Clark, 335 U.S. 188, 192 (1948). After *Eisentrager*, however, the habeas statute was construed in Braden v. 30th Judicial Circuit Court of Kentucky, 410 U.S. 484 (1973), as requiring only that the custodian, not the detainee, be within the federal court's jurisdiction. Thus, said the Court, the basis for the Court's assumption in *Eisentrager* that there was no statutory habeas jurisdiction had been effectively overruled, and as a result "*Eisentrager* plainly does not preclude the exercise of § 2241 jurisdiction over petitioners' claims."

Justice Kennedy concurred, reasoning that, although *Eisentrager* "indicates that there is a realm of political authority over military affairs where the judicial power may not enter," this case was distinguishable. Whereas in *Eisentrager* the detainees "were proven enemy aliens found and detained outside the United States, and ... the existence of jurisdiction would have had a clear harmful effect on the Nation's military affairs," Guantanamo Bay "is in every practical respect a United States territory, and it is far removed from any hostilities," and "the detainees at Guantanamo Bay are being held indefinitely, and without benefit of any legal proceeding to determine their status."

Justice Scalia dissented, joined by Chief Justice Rehnquist and Justice Thomas. Justice Scalia argued that, although it was not the principal focus of the Court's decision, *Eisentrager* did effectively hold that there was no statutory habeas jurisdiction in that case and that this statutory holding had not been overturned by *Braden*, which did not concern a detention outside the United States. Justice Scalia also argued that:

> The consequence of [the Court's] holding, as applied to aliens outside the country, is breathtaking. It permits an alien captured in a foreign theater of active combat to bring a § 2241 petition against the Secretary of Defense. Over the course of the last century, the United States has held millions of alien prisoners abroad. ... A great many of these prisoners would no doubt have

complained about the circumstances of their capture and the terms of their confinement.

5. *Hamdi v. Rumsfeld* and the CSRTs. Another important war on terror decision issued by the Supreme Court in 2004 was Hamdi v. Rumsfeld, 542 U.S. 507 (2004). In that case, a U.S. citizen, Yaser Hamdi, was captured while allegedly serving with Taliban military forces in Afghanistan. He was deemed an enemy combatant by the Department of Defense and was ultimately transferred to military custody in South Carolina. There was no dispute that he had the right to file a habeas corpus petition challenging his detention, since he was a U.S. citizen being held in the United States and there had not been any suspension of the writ of habeas corpus. The issue was whether he could lawfully be subjected to military detention.

A plurality of the Supreme Court, speaking through Justice O'Connor, and Justice Thomas in dissent, concluded that, assuming the facts were as the government alleged, Hamdi was properly subject to military detention. The plurality reasoned that the AUMF, in granting the President the authority to use "all necessary and appropriate force" against "nations, organizations, or persons" associated with the September 11, 2001, terrorist attacks, implicitly authorized him to detain individuals who are determined to have been part of or supporting forces hostile to the United States in Afghanistan and to have engaged in an armed conflict against the United States. The plurality noted, among other things, that the detention of enemy combatants during wartime "is a fundamental incident of waging war." The mere fact that Hamdi was a U.S. citizen did not alter this conclusion, reasoned the plurality, because "such a citizen, if released, would pose the same threat of returning to the front during the ongoing conflict."

The plurality also concluded, however, that due process required that, as a precondition to holding a U.S. citizen in the United States as an enemy combatant, the government must give the detainee "notice of the factual basis for his classification, and a fair opportunity to rebut the Government's factual assertions before a neutral decisionmaker." The Court observed that it was possible that these requirements "could be met by an appropriately authorized and properly constituted military tribunal." But "[i]n the absence of such process," said the plurality, "a court that receives a petition for a writ of habeas corpus from an alleged enemy combatant must itself ensure that the minimum requirements of due process are achieved." In a partial concurrence, Justice Souter, joined by Justice Ginsburg, joined in the plurality's due process requirements "to produce a judgment."

Although the due process holding in *Hamdi* technically applied only to U.S. citizens held in the United States, the Department of Defense subsequently adopted procedures at Guantanamo designed to satisfy the *Hamdi* due process requirements there. In particular, the Department of Defense established Combatant Status Review Tribunals (CSRTs), which review challenges by detainees at Guantanamo to their designation as enemy combatants. Under this process, each detainee at Guantanamo is given notice of the factual basis for his detention and an opportunity, with the assistance of a "personal representative" (a military officer who will not act as a lawyer or advocate), to challenge his designation as an enemy combatant. The challenges are heard at the naval base by panels of three commissioned military officers not involved in the detainee's apprehension, detention, interrogation, or screening. The detainees have the right to call witnesses if reasonably available, question other witnesses, testify, and introduce relevant documentary evidence. Additional aspects of the CSRT procedures are discussed in *Boumediene*.

    6. The Detainee Treatment Act. In late 2005, Congress enacted the Detainee Treatment Act (DTA). Among other things, the Act amended the federal habeas statute to provide that:

> Except as [otherwise provided in this Act], no court, justice, or judge shall have jurisdiction to hear or consider—
>
> > (1) an application for a writ of habeas corpus filed by or on behalf of an alien detained by the Department of Defense at Guantanamo Bay, Cuba; or
> >
> > (2) any other action against the United States or its agents relating to any aspect of the detention by the Department of Defense of an alien at Guantanamo Bay, Cuba, who—
> >
> > > (A) is currently in military custody; or
> > >
> > > (B) has been determined by the United States Court of Appeals for the District of Columbia Circuit in accordance with the procedures set forth in [this Act] to have been properly detained as an enemy combatant.

The DTA also provided that the U.S. Court of Appeals for the D.C. Circuit would have "exclusive jurisdiction to determine the validity of any final decision of a Combatant Status Review Tribunal that an alien is properly detained as an enemy combatant," and that the D.C. Circuit's jurisdiction:

> shall be limited to the consideration of—
>
> > (i) whether the status determination of the Combatant Status Review Tribunal with regard to such alien was consistent with the standards and procedures specified by the Secretary of Defense for Combatant Status Review Tribunals (including the requirement that the conclusion of the Tribunal be supported by a preponderance of the evidence and allowing a rebuttable presumption in favor of the Government's evidence); and
> >
> > (ii) to the extent the Constitution and laws of the United States are applicable, whether the use of such standards and

procedures to make the determination is consistent with the Constitution and laws of the United States.

The DTA contained a similar provision for D.C. Circuit review of the decisions of any military commission trials held at Guantanamo. Finally, the DTA contained an "effective date" section, the first part of which stated that "[t]his section shall take effect on the date of the enactment of this Act," and the second part of which stated that the D.C. Circuit review provisions "shall apply with respect to any claim ... that is pending on or after the date of the enactment of this Act."

7. *Hamdan v. Rumsfeld*. In Hamdan v. Rumsfeld, 548 U.S. 557 (2006), the Court considered a habeas corpus challenge to the military commission trial system that the Department of Defense had established at Guantanamo pursuant to President Bush's November 2001 Military Order. Before addressing the merits of that challenge, the Court had to decide whether there was habeas corpus jurisdiction in light of the DTA. In an opinion by Justice Stevens, the Court concluded that there was jurisdiction because the petitioner's case was pending in the lower courts when the DTA was enacted, and the Court construed the DTA's habeas restriction as inapplicable to pending cases. The Court reasoned that, unlike for the D.C. Circuit review provisions, there was nothing in the DTA stating that the habeas restriction would apply to pending cases. On the merits, the Court concluded that the military commission system was invalid because it violated statutory requirements imposed by Congress in the Uniform Code of Military Justice (a statute that, among other things, regulates the use of courts-martial to try U.S. service personnel). Justice Scalia dissented, joined by Justice Thomas and Justice Alito. Chief Justice Roberts abstained from participating in the case because he had participated as a judge in the lower court proceedings in the case.

8. Section 7 of the Military Commissions Act of 2006. Several months after *Hamdan*, Congress enacted the Military Commissions Act of 2006. It specifically authorized a military commission system at Guantanamo and prescribed the procedures for such commissions and the crimes that could be tried before them. In addition, in Section 7(a), it amended the federal habeas corpus statute, 28 U.S.C. § 2241(e), to include the following new provisions:

(1) No court, justice, or judge shall have jurisdiction to hear or consider an application for a writ of habeas corpus filed by or on behalf of an alien detained by the United States who has been determined by the United States to have been properly detained as an enemy combatant or is awaiting such determination.

(2) Except as provided in [the Detainee Treatment Act], no court, justice, or judge shall have jurisdiction to hear or consider any other action against the United States or its agents relating to any aspect of the detention, transfer, treatment, trial, or conditions of confinement of an alien who is or was detained by the

United States and has been determined by the United States to have been properly detained as an enemy combatant or is awaiting such determination.

Section 7(b) of the Act further provided that this habeas amendment "shall take effect on the date of the enactment of this Act, and shall apply to all cases, without exception, pending on or after the date of the enactment of this Act which relate to any aspect of the detention, transfer, treatment, trial, or conditions of detention of an alien detained by the United States since September 11, 2001." The effect and constitutionality of Section 7 are considered above in *Boumediene*. Note that Congress did not purport in the Military Commissions Act to be exercising its authority under Article I, Section 9 of the Constitution to suspend the privilege of the writ of habeas corpus "when in cases of rebellion or invasion the public safety may require it," and the government did not argue in *Boumediene* that a suspension had occurred.

Although Congress revised the Military Commissions Act in 2009, it did not eliminate the habeas restriction contained in Section 7 of the 2006 Act. That restriction therefore still applies to the extent that it is not unconstitutional.

9. Questions and Comments on *Boumediene v. Bush*. Consider first the Court's treatment of precedent in *Boumediene*. The majority purports to distinguish *Eisentrager* rather than overturn it. Are the majority's distinctions persuasive? After *Rasul* and *Boumediene*, what is left of *Eisentrager*? Another precedent that is the subject of debate in *Boumediene* is *Hamdi*. As noted above, five Justices in *Hamdi* held that a U.S. citizen being detained as an enemy combatant in the United States was entitled only to a fairly minimal process. Is the majority in *Boumediene* in effect giving more process to non-U.S. citizens being held outside the United States than *Hamdi* held was necessary for a U.S. citizen being held within the United States?

Now consider the Court's test in *Boumediene* for the geographic scope of the right of habeas corpus. The Court adopts a functional approach that involves at least three factors: "(1) the citizenship and status of the detainee and the adequacy of the process through which that status determination was made; (2) the nature of the sites where apprehension and then detention took place; and (3) the practical obstacles inherent in resolving the prisoner's entitlement to the writ." In general, a functional approach tends to be most useful in the law when each situation has potentially material differences, because such an approach gives courts the flexibility of tailoring the law on a case-by-case basis. A more formal or rule-like approach, however, can provide greater predictability and can reduce the need for judicial supervision. Which considerations are more important in this context?

Boumediene also presents an interesting case study on constitutional avoidance. The Supreme Court has often said that it will construe statutes to avoid holding them unconstitutional, if it is "fairly possible" to do so. In

Boumediene, should the Court have tried harder to interpret the DTA provisions to confer what it believed was necessary to provide an acceptable alternative to habeas corpus, as Chief Justice Roberts argues in dissent? The majority appears to have been concerned that if it went too far in that direction it would have been acting contrary to the overall thrust of Congress's intent in enacting the DTA. But wouldn't Congress prefer to have its provisions interpreted broadly rather than have them invalidated as unconstitutional?

At its most general level, the debate between the majority and the dissents (especially Justice Scalia's dissent) is over the proper role of the federal courts in the U.S. constitutional system of separation of powers. The majority is concerned that, if the government were able to avoid habeas corpus review by placing detainees at Guantanamo, it could "switch the Constitution on or off at will," thereby "leading to a regime in which Congress and the President, not this Court, say 'what the law is.' " Does this concern beg the relevant questions, as Justice Scalia argues? Are there situations in which, notwithstanding *Marbury v. Madison*, the decisions of the political branches are properly immune from judicial review? Is this one of them?

10. ***Munaf v. Geren.*** The Court decided *Boumediene* and Munaf v. Geren, 553 U.S. 674 (2008), on the same day. *Munaf* involved the detention of two U.S. citizens in Iraq by the U.S. military operating as part of a UN-authorized multinational force. The detainees sought to file habeas corpus petitions, and they also sought to enjoin the U.S. military from transferring them to Iraqi authorities for criminal prosecution.

In a unanimous opinion, the Court held that the detainees had a statutory right to file habeas corpus petitions in a U.S. federal court. The Court reasoned that even if the detentions were not viewed as under U.S. authority, the U.S. military had the unilateral power to produce or release the detainees and thus the detainees were being held "in custody . . . of the United States" for purposes of the federal habeas statute, 28 U.S.C. § 2241(c)(1). The Court distinguished Hirota v. MacArthur, 338 U.S. 197 (1949), a short per curiam opinion that had disallowed habeas corpus petitions filed by Japanese citizens detained in Japan after World War II pursuant to the judgments of an international military tribunal. The Court stated in *Munaf* that "we decline to extend our holding in *Hirota* to preclude American citizens held overseas by American soldiers subject to a United States chain of command from filing habeas petitions."

The Court also held, however, that U.S. courts exercising their habeas jurisdiction did not have the authority to enjoin the U.S. military from transferring the petitioners to Iraqi custody. The Court explained that "[h]abeas is at its core a remedy for unlawful detention," and "[t]he typical remedy for such detention is, of course, release." The petitioners here, however, were not seeking unconditional release from U.S. custody, which would expose them to arrest by Iraqi authorities, but rather "a court order requiring the United States to shelter them from the sovereign government seeking to have them answer for alleged crimes committed within that sovereign's borders." The Court further noted that the petitioners did not dispute that they had voluntarily traveled to Iraq and were alleged to have committed crimes there. "Given these facts," reasoned the Court, "our cases make clear that Iraq has a sovereign right to prosecute [the petitioners] for crimes committed on its soil." The Court also observed that "habeas is not a means of compelling the United States to harbor fugitives from the criminal justice system of a sovereign with undoubted authority to prosecute them." Finally, the Court explained that its conclusion was not altered by the petitioners' allegations that they might be tortured by Iraqi authorities. While such allegations "are of course a matter of serious concern," said the Court, "in the present context that concern is to be addressed by the political branches, not the judiciary." The Court noted, among other things, that "[p]etitioners here allege only the possibility of mistreatment in a prison facility; this is not a more extreme case in which the Executive has determined that a detainee is likely to be tortured but decides to transfer him anyway."

11. Military Detention in the Obama Administration. After taking office in January 2009, President Obama issued an executive order directing that the Guantanamo detention facility be closed within a year. Although the Obama Administration subsequently managed to repatriate a number of the Guantanamo detainees to other countries, it did not meet the one-year timetable for closing the detention facility, and it was unclear as of June 2010 when the closure would occur. President Obama also established a Justice Department task force to review the status of each of the Guantanamo detainees, and this task force issued a report in January 2010 that concluded, among other things, that nearly 50 detainees should be held in long-term detention without trial. The Obama Administration has asked Congress to appropriate money to purchase and renovate a prison in Thomson, Illinois, to hold the detainees who are not sent to other countries, but this proposal has generated significant controversy.

Despite its efforts to close the Guantanamo detention facility, the Obama Administration has maintained that it has the legal authority to hold terrorist detainees in military custody. In particular, the Administration has (in briefs filed in various cases) claimed the following detention authority:

> The President has the authority to detain persons that the President determines planned, authorized, committed, or aided the terrorist attacks that occurred on September 11, 2001, and persons who harbored those responsible for those attacks. The president also has the authority to detain persons who were part of, or substantially supported, Taliban or al-Qaida forces or associated forces that are engaged in hostilities against the United States or

its coalition partners, including any person who has committed a belligerent act, or has directly supported hostilities, in aid of such enemy armed forces.

This standard is similar to the one advocated by the Bush Administration (for example, in the Combatant Status Review Tribunals), except that it requires that individuals who are detained based on their support of, rather than affiliation with, the Taliban or Al Qaeda must have provided "substantial" support. Also, unlike the Bush Administration, the Obama Administration has grounded its detention authority solely in the AUMF and has not invoked an independent authority to detain alleged terrorists based on the Commander in Chief power.

12. Habeas Corpus Litigation After *Boumediene*. Since *Boumediene*, the federal district court in Washington, D.C. has been adjudicating a variety of habeas corpus actions brought on behalf of Guantanamo detainees. In these cases, the judges on the district court have considered whether the evidence against each detainee is sufficient to establish, by a preponderance of the evidence, that the detainee falls within the government's detention authority. The judges have also had to resolve a variety of procedural and evidentiary questions, including the nature and placement of the burden of proof, the admissibility and weight to be given to hearsay evidence, and how to handle evidence allegedly obtained by coercion. For a detailed study of these cases, see Benjamin Wittes, Robert Chesney & Rabea Benhalim, The Emerging Law of Detention: The Guantanamo Habeas Cases as Lawmaking (Jan. 22, 2010), at www.brookings.edu/?/media/ Files/rc/papers/2010/0122_guantanamo_wittes_chesney/0122 _10guantanamo_wittes_chesney.pdf.

In a series of decisions, the district court judges accepted the Obama Administration's claim that the military can detain individuals shown to be "part of" the Taliban, Al Qaeda, or associated forces, but some of the judges rejected the claim that the military could detain individuals who merely provided substantial support to the Taliban or Al Qaeda forces or directly supported hostilities. In Al–Bihani v. Obama, 590 F.3d 866 (D.C. Cir. 2010), however, the D.C. Circuit upheld the government's support-based detention authority. Although the petitioner in that case had not been directly involved in combat, he had worked as the cook for a paramilitary brigade in Afghanistan and had carried a brigade-issued weapon. In concluding that he was properly subject to detention at Guantanamo, the court reasoned that "wherever the outer bounds [of detention based on support] may lie, they clearly include traditional food operations essential to a fighting force and the carrying of arms." The court in *Al-Bihani* also rejected the petitioner's argument that, in discerning the scope of the detention authority implicitly granted by the AUMF, courts should take account of the limitations imposed by the international laws of war. "[W]hile the international laws of war are helpful to courts when identifying the general set of war powers to which the AUMF speaks," reasoned the court, "their lack of controlling legal force and firm definition render their use both inapposite and inadvisable when courts seek to determine the limits of the President's war powers."

The author of the lead opinion in *Al-Bihani*, Judge Judith Rogers Brown, also wrote a separate concurrence, in which she expressed the view that the common law process was not well suited for this war on terror context:

> The Supreme Court in *Boumediene* and *Hamdi* charged this court and others with the unprecedented task of developing rules to review the propriety of military actions during a time of war, relying on common law tools. We are fortunate this case does not require us to demarcate the law's full substantive and procedural dimensions. But as other more difficult cases arise, it is important to ask whether a court-driven process is best suited to protecting both the rights of petitioners and the safety of our nation. The common law process depends on incrementalism and eventual correction, and it is most effective where there are a significant number of cases brought before a large set of courts, which in turn enjoy the luxury of time to work the doctrine supple. None of those factors exist in the Guantanamo context. The number of Guantanamo detainees is limited and the circumstances of their confinement are unique. The petitions they file, as the *Boumediene* Court counseled, are funneled through one federal district court and one appellate court. And, in the midst of an ongoing war, time to entertain a process of literal trial and error is not a luxury we have.

Is her argument persuasive? Why has Congress not provided more guidance to the courts on issues relating to detention?

13. Habeas Rights Outside of Guantanamo. A central question after *Boumediene* and *Munaf* is whether the right of habeas corpus extends to non-U.S. citizens in places outside the United States other than Guantanamo, such as in Iraq or Afghanistan. The D.C. Circuit addressed this question in Al Maqaleh v. Gates, 605 F.3d 84 (D.C. Cir. 2010). In that case, the court held that the habeas restriction in Section 7(a) of the Military Commissions Act of 2006 (i.e., the provision at issue in *Boumediene*) validly precluded habeas review of the detention of three individuals being held at the Bagram Airfield Military Base in Afghanistan, at least two of whom were initially captured outside of Afghanistan. In reaching this conclusion, the court considered the three factors articulated by the Supreme Court in *Boumediene* and also relied heavily on *Eisentrager*.

The court found that the first *Boumediene* factor ("the citizenship and status of the detainee and the adequacy of the process through which that status determination was made") weighed against the validity of the habeas restriction, because the detainees here had received less process than the detainees in either *Boumediene* or *Eisentrager*. However, the court found that the second factor ("the nature of the sites where apprehension and then detention took place") heavily supported the preclusion of habeas review. Unlike in *Boumediene*, where "[t]he United States has maintained its total control of Guantanamo Bay for over a century, even in the face of a hostile government maintaining de jure sovereignty over the property," the court noted that at Bagram "there is no indication of any intent to occupy the base with permanence, nor is there hostility on the part of the 'host' country." Finally, the court found that the third factor ("the practical obstacles inherent in resolving the prisoner's entitlement to the writ"), especially when considered along with the second factor, "weighs overwhelmingly in favor of" upholding Congress's denial of habeas review. The court noted that Bagram and all of Afghanistan remain a "theater of war," making the government's arguments against habeas relief more powerful than in either *Eisentrager* (which concerned detention in a place where active hostilities had ceased but security threats remained) or *Boumediene* (which involved detention in a place where there were no active hostilities and few security threats from the enemy). Finally, the court said that it was not ignoring the petitioners' concern that the government might transfer detainees into an active conflict zone in order to evade judicial review but insisted that "that is not what happened here" and stated that it did not need to make any "determination on the importance of this possibility, given that it remains only a possibility; its resolution can await a case in which the claim is a reality rather than a speculation."

Why should the ongoing military conflict in Afghanistan justify the denial of habeas rights to detainees picked up outside of Afghanistan and brought to Bagram? How can the court be so certain that the government did not send these detainees to Afghanistan in part to avoid judicial review?

14. Suspending the Writ. Article I, Section 9, clause 2 of the Constitution states that "[t]he privilege of the Writ of Habeas Corpus shall not be suspended, unless when in Cases of Rebellion or Invasion the public Safety may require it." Because of the placement of this clause in Article I, which is focused on Congress, most commentators assume that only Congress has the power to suspend the writ. At the outset of the Civil War, however, President Lincoln controversially suspended the writ on his own authority. In subsequently explaining his action to Congress, Lincoln famously asked, "are all the laws but one to go unexecuted and the Government itself go to pieces lest that one be violated?" In *Hamdi,* all of the Supreme Court Justices appeared to agree that only Congress could suspend the writ, and that its authorization of force in the AUMF did not constitute a suspension. In *Boumediene,* the Court assumed that Congress was not relying on its suspension authority in enacting the Military Commissions Act.

There has been substantial debate among commentators over whether a suspension of the writ broadens the government's substantive authority to arrest and detain during an invasion or rebellion or whether it merely precludes the particular remedy of a judicial order of discharge. For the view that the suspension power does not provide legal authority for any arrest or detention that could not be made in the absence of the suspension, see Trevor W. Morrison, Suspension and the Extrajudicial Constitution, 107 Colum. L. Rev. 1533 (2007). Under that view, executive officers may be vulnerable to subsequent civil suits for unlawful arrests and detentions that occur during a suspension unless Congress separately confers immunity for such conduct. For the view that a congressional suspension of the writ overrides substantive rights that would otherwise restrict arrest and detention, and that subsequent civil suits relating to such conduct are thereby also precluded, see Amanda L. Tyler, Suspension as an Emergency Power, 118 Yale L.J. 600 (2009). See also David L. Shapiro, Habeas Corpus, Suspension, and Detention: Another View, 82 Notre Dame L. Rev. 59, 89 (2006) (arguing that a suspension of the writ "frees the Executive from the legal restraints on detention that would otherwise apply").

15. Bibliography. There is an extensive literature on issues relating to habeas corpus and the war on terror. Relevant scholarship includes Janet Cooper Alexander, Jurisdiction–Stripping in a Time of Terror, 95 Cal. L. Rev. 1193 (2007); David J. Bederman, The Classical Constitution: Roman Republican Origins of the Habeas Suspension Clause, 17 S. Cal. Interdisc. L.J. 405 (2008); Patrick J. Borchers, The Conflict of Laws and *Boumediene v. Bush*, 42 Creighton L. Rev. 1 (2008); Curtis A. Bradley, The Military Commissions Act, Habeas Corpus, and the Geneva Conventions, 101 Am. J. Int'l L. 322 (2007); Christina Duffy Burnett, A Convenient Constitution? Extraterritoriality After Boumediene, 109 Colum. L. Rev. 973 (2009); Emily Calhoun, The Accounting: Habeas Corpus and Enemy Combatants, 79 U. Colo. L. Rev. 77 (2008); Jesse Choper & John Yoo, Wartime Process: A Dialogue on Congressional Power to Remove Issues from the Federal Courts, 95 Cal. L. Rev. 1243 (2007); Laurence Claus, The One Court that Congress Cannot Take Away: Singularity, Supremacy, and Article III, 96 Geo. L.J. 59 (2007); Richard H. Fallon, Jr. & Daniel J. Meltzer, Habeas Corpus Jurisdiction, Substantive Rights, and the War on Terror, 120 Harv. L. Rev. 2029 (2007); Richard H. Fallon, Jr., The Supreme Court, Habeas Corpus, and the War on Terror: An Essay on Law and Political Science, 110 Colum. L. Rev. 352 (2010); Daniel A. Farber, Justice Stevens, Habeas Jurisdiction, and the War on Terror, 43 U.C. Davis L. Rev. 945 (2010); Paul D. Halliday & G. Edward White, The Suspension Clause: English Text, Imperial Contexts, and American Implications, 94 Va. L. Rev. 575 (2008); Martin J. Katz, Guantanamo, *Boumediene*, and Jurisdiction–Stripping: The Imperial Presidency Meets the Imperial Court, 25 Const. Comm. 377 (2009); David A. Martin, Judicial Review and the Military Commissions Act: Striking the Right Balance, 101 Am. J. Int'l L. 344 (2007); Daniel J. Meltzer, Habeas Corpus, Suspension, and Guantanamo: The *Boumediene* Decision, 2008 Sup. Ct. Rev. 1; Trevor W. Morrison, The Middle Ground in Judicial Review of Enemy Combatant Detentions, 45 Willamette L. Rev. 453 (2009); Gerald L. Neuman, The Extraterritorial Constitution After *Boumediene v. Bush*, 82 S. Cal. L. Rev. 259 (2009); Gerald L. Neuman, The Habeas Corpus Suspension Clause After *Boume-*

diene v. Bush, 110 Colum. L. Rev. 537 (2010); James E. Pfander, The Limits of Habeas Jurisdiction and the Global War on Terror, 91 Cornell L. Rev. 497 (2006); Judith Resnik, Detention, the War on Terror, and the Federal Courts: An Essay in Honor of Henry Monaghan, 110 Colum. L. Rev. 579 (2010); Carlos Manuel Vazquez, The Military Commissions Act, the Geneva Conventions, and the Courts: A Critical Guide, 101 Am. J. Int'l L. 73 (2007); Stephen I. Vladeck, Deconstructing *Hirota*: Habeas Corpus, Citizenship, and Article III, 95 Geo. L.J. 1497 (2007); Stephen I. Vladeck, *Boumediene*'s Quiet Theory: Access to Courts and the Separation of Powers, 84 Notre Dame L. Rev. 2107 (2009).

CHAPTER VIII

STATE SOVEREIGN IMMUNITY AND THE ELEVENTH AMENDMENT

Page 1020, add a footnote at the end of *Ex parte Young*:

a. A recent symposium on *Ex parte Young* included the following articles: Rochelle Bobroff, *Ex parte Young* as a Tool to Enforce Safety–Net and Civil–Rights Statutes, 40 U. Tol. L. Rev. 819 (2009); Charlton C. Copeland, *Ex parte Young*: Sovereignty, Immunity, and the Constitutional Structure of American Federalism, 40 U. Tol. L. Rev. 843 (2009); James Leonard, *Ex parte Young* and Hard Times, 40 U. Tol. L. Rev. 889 (2009); Marcia L. McCormick, Solving the Mystery of How *Ex parte Young* Escaped the Federalism Revolution, 40 U. Tol. L. Rev. 909 (2009); Edward A. Purcell, Jr., *Ex parte Young* and the Transformation of the Federal Courts, 1890–1917, 40 U. Tol. L. Rev. 931 (2009); Michael E. Solimine, *Ex parte Young*: An Interbranch Perspective, 40 U. Tol. L. Rev. 999 (2009).—[Footnote by eds.]

Page 1021, add a footnote at the end of Note 1:

a. The questions raised in the text reflect the widely accepted account of *Ex parte Young* as a circumlocutory exception to sovereign immunity. This understanding is challenged in John Harrison, *Ex Parte Young*, 60 Stan. L. Rev. 989 (2008). Harrison's claims are summarized in the editorial introduction to the article as follows: "*Ex parte Young* does not represent an exception to ordinary principles of sovereign immunity, it does not employ a legal fiction, it does not imply a novel cause of action under the Constitution or other federal law, and it does not create a paradox by treating officers as state actors for one purpose and private persons for another." Instead, Harrison sees *Ex parte Young* as a traditional use of equity power to restrain proceedings at law and argues that a proper understanding curtails many of the modern inferences drawn from that decision.

Page 1027, add at the end of the carry-over paragraph at the top of the page:

For a contrary view of the historical validity of *Hans*, see Kurt T. Lash, Leaving the *Chisholm* Trail: The Eleventh Amendment and the Background Principle of Strict Construction, 50 Wm & Mary L. Rev. 1577 (2009). Lash argues that the modern emphasis on *Chisholm* as the "generative source of the Eleventh Amendment is historically incorrect" and that it was in fact only one of a number of suits dramatizing the "*concept* of an individual compelling a state to answer in federal court." If hostility to this concept drove the Eleventh Amendment, the notion that *Hans* departed from that provision is a "modern myth."

Page 1028, add at the end of footnote a:

Michael E. Solimine, Congress, *Ex Parte Young*, and the Fate of the Three-Judge District Court, 70 U. Pitt. L. Rev. 101 (2008).

Page 1051, add a footnote at the end of Note 3:

d. Perhaps because *Fitzpatrick* was unanimously decided, its correctness has been widely assumed. This assumption is questioned in John Harrison, State Sovereign Immunity and Congress's Enforcement Powers, 2006 Sup. Ct. Rev. 353. Harrison argues from history that the people who framed and ratified the Fourteenth and Fifteenth Amendments "probably did not believe that the amendments gave Congress power to create private causes of action against states." He also examines the question from the perspective of modern decisions and concludes that, if the doctrine of *Seminole Tribe* (excerpted as the next main case) is correct, *Fitzpatrick* is not.

Page 1089, add a footnote at the end of Note 5:

g. For extensive commentary on *Katz* from a variety of perspectives, see Richard Lieb, Federal Supremacy and State Sovereignty: The Supreme Court's Early Jurisprudence, 15 Am. Bankruptcy Inst. L. Rev. 3 (2007); Martin H. Redish and Daniel M. Greenfield, Bankruptcy, Sovereign Immunity and the Dilemma of Principled Decision Making: The Curious Case of *Central Virginia Community College v. Katz*, id. at 13; Thomas E. Plank, State Sovereignty in Bankruptcy After *Katz*, id. at 59; Ralph Brubaker, Explaining *Katz*'s New Bankruptcy Exception to State Sovereign Immunity: The Bankruptcy Power as a Federal Forum Power, id. at 95; Randolph J. Haines, Federalism Principles in Bankruptcy After *Katz*, id. at 135; Susan M. Freeman and Marvin C. Ruth, The Scope of Bankruptcy Ancillary Jurisdiction After *Katz* as Informed by Pre-*Katz* Ancillary Jurisdiction Cases, id. at 155.

Page 1121, add to the citations in the carryover paragraph from page 1120:

Rebecca Goldberg, The "How" of Enforcing the Fourteenth Amendment: Why the Rehnquist Court's Treatment of Implementation, Not Interpretation, Is the True Post-*Boerne* Failing, 47 Washburn L.J. 47 (2007) (focusing debate on the difference between Congressional interpretation and implementation).

CHAPTER IX

42 U.S.C. § 1983

Page 1165, add a citation after the reference to Neuborne in the first full paragraph:

Gil Seinfeld, The Federal Courts as a Franchise: Rethinking the Justifications for Federal Question Jurisdiction, 97 Cal. L. Rev. 95 (2009).

Page 1173, add a new paragraph before the last paragraph of Note 3:

In Van de Kamp v. Goldstein, 555 U.S. ___ (2009), the Supreme Court ruled that at least some prosecutorial administrative responsibilities triggered absolute immunity. After securing his release from prison under federal habeas corpus, Goldstein sued a former Los Angeles county District Attorney and his chief deputy, asserting that they were liable for failure to train and supervise subordinates, who had failed to disclose impeachment material to the accused, as required by Giglio v. United States, 405 U.S. 150 (1972). The trial court ruled that the defendants were not entitled to absolute immunity, as their alleged failings were "administrative," not "prosecutorial," in nature. The Ninth Circuit affirmed. Although the Supreme Court agreed that the wrongs complained of involved administrative procedures, the Court unanimously upheld absolute immunity. Speaking through Justice Breyer, the Court said:

> [W]e conclude that prosecutors involved in such supervision or training or information-system management enjoy absolute immunity from the kind of legal claims at issue here. Those claims focus upon a certain kind of administrative obligation—a kind that itself is directly connected with the conduct of a trial. Here, unlike with other claims related to administrative decisions, an individual prosecutor's error in the plaintiff's specific criminal trial constitutes an essential element of the plaintiff's claim. The administrative obligations at issue here are thus unlike administrative duties concerning, for example, workplace hiring, payroll administration, the maintenance of physical facilities, and the like. Moreover, the types of activities on which Goldstein's claims focus necessarily require legal knowledge and the exercise of related discretion, e.g., in determining what information should be included in the training or the supervision or the information-system management. And in that sense also Goldstein's claims are unlike claims of, say, unlawful discrimination in hiring employees. [We therefore] believe absolute immunity must follow.

As *Van de Kamp* makes plain, even within the broad category of "administrative" responsibilities, some prosecutorial failings will be subject to absolute immunity. In every circumstance, one must ask how closely associated with the "judicial phase" of criminal prosecution, the alleged misconduct was.

Page 1195, delete Note 2 and substitute the following:

2. *Pearson v. Callahan* and the Sequence of Decision. Note that in *Brosseau*, three Justices expressed concern at *Saucier*'s mandate that courts determine the constitutionality of the defendant's conduct before addressing qualified immunity. In Pearson v. Callahan, 555 U.S. ___ (2009), the Supreme Court reconsidered and overruled this requirement.

The underlying dispute in *Pearson* was an interesting question of search-and-seizure law. Having learned from a confidential informant of Callahan's sale of methamphetamines, a Utah drug task force arranged for the informant to purchase drugs while wired. The informant did so and, after the drugs had been produced, signaled to the police, who entered Callahan's trailer, arrested him, and seized the drugs. His subsequent conviction was set aside by the Utah Supreme Court on the ground that the warrantless search violated the Fourth Amendment. Callahan then sued several officers, including Pearson, for damages under § 1983. The District Court upheld the officers' defense of qualified immunity on grounds that they could reasonably have believed the search authorized by the doctrine of "consent once removed." In the words of the Supreme Court, this doctrine authorizes "warrantless entry by police officers into a home when consent to enter has already been granted to an undercover agent or informant who has observed contraband in plain view." Consensual entry by the undercover agent is valid despite the pretense of wanting to purchase drugs, and "once-removed" kicks in when the agent calls on outside officers to enter and make the arrest. Although several circuits had endorsed this theory and none had squarely denied it, the Tenth Circuit concluded not only that the search was unlawful, but also that it violated "clearly established" constitutional law.[a]

If the Supreme Court had followed *Saucier*, it would have had to endorse or reject this interpretation of the Fourth Amendment before invoking qualified immunity. Instead, the Court skipped the merits and ruled unanimously that the officers were entitled to qualified immunity. Most of Justice Alito's opinion for the Court detailed the defects of *Saucier*. Most obvious was the "substantial expenditure of scarce judicial resources on difficult questions that have no effect on the outcome of the case." Moreover, in some cases (unlike *Pearson* itself), the merits are so factbound that a decision resolving them would have little precedential effect.

---

a. Specifically, the Tenth Circuit ruled that consent-once-removed suffices when outside officers are called by an undercover officer who was invited into the premises and sees the contraband but does not extend to similar actions by a confidential *informant*.

Similarly, the factual basis for adjudicating the merits may be obscure at the pleading stage, when qualified immunity claims are ideally resolved. The Court also worried that the briefing on the law might be inadequate and that judges who had already mentally decided on qualified immunity might not give the merits full consideration.

The most dramatic (though surely unusual) problem arose in Bunting v. Mellen, 541 U.S. 1019 (2004). There two cadets at the Virginia Military Institute, a state institution of higher education, challenged the school's practice of conducting a prayer before the evening meal. They sued Bunting, the Superintendent of VMI, seeking declaratory and injunctive relief, as well as nominal damages. The District Court entered summary judgment in favor of the plaintiffs, awarding them declaratory relief and enjoining Bunting from continuing to sponsor the prayer, but found that Bunting was entitled to qualified immunity from damages because his arguments were not "so obviously incorrect that a reasonable government official in [his] place should have known that his actions violated ... the Establishment Clause." Both sides appealed—the superintendent challenging the District Court's decision on the merits, and the cadets challenging the ruling on qualified immunity, but while the appeal was pending, Bunting retired, and the cadets graduated. The Court of Appeals therefore vacated as moot the judgment for declaratory and injunctive relief but affirmed the ruling on the damages claim, agreeing with the District Court that the supper prayer violated the Establishment Clause but that Bunting was nevertheless entitled to qualified immunity.

Bunting and Peay, the new Superintendent of VMI, petitioned for certiorari, seeking review of the determination that the supper prayer was unconstitutional. The Court denied the petition, but several Justices commented on odd interaction of the *Saucier* sequencing principle and appellate review. In dissenting from the denial of certiorari, Justice Scalia, joined by Chief Justice Rehnquist, noted the decision created the kind of conflict with decisions of other circuits that would normally make the case a strong candidate for certiorari, but that it would violate the settled practice against entertaining an appeal by a party who won a favorable judgment below.

The *Pearson* Court found the potential difficulty in obtaining an appellate review an additional reason to overrule *Saucier*'s sequencing requirement. The Court, however, did not forbid merits-first adjudication but concluded that the lower courts "should have the discretion to decide whether that procedure is worthwhile in particular cases."[b] The continued

---

b. This conclusion was supported by an influential article by Judge Pierre Leval, Judging Under the Constitution: Dicta About Dicta, 81 N.Y.U.L. Rev. 1249, 1275–81 (2006), and by an influential opinion by Judge Jeffrey Sutton, Lyons v. City of Xenia, 417 F.3d 565, 581 (6th Cir. 2005) (Sutton, J., concurring), as well as by academic commentary. Thomas Healy, The Rise of Unnecessary Constitutional Rulings, 83 N.C. L. Rev. 847 (2005). For pre-*Pearson* argument to the contrary, see Sam Kamin, An Article III Defense

viability of *Saucier* as a permissive procedure was illustrated later in the same term in Safford Unified School District v. Redding, 557 U.S. __ (2009), where the Court ruled against the constitutionality of a (partial) strip search of a thirteen-year-old student suspected of bringing prescription and over-the-counter drugs to school. Although eight Justices, speaking through Justice Souter, agreed that the search was too intrusive to be reasonable, they also found that the lower court decisions "viewing school strip searches differently from the way we see them" were sufficiently numerous and well reasoned to raise doubt whether the law had been sufficiently clear. Accordingly, qualified immunity was warranted.

Page 1330, add at the beginning of footnote c:

For trenchant criticism of "implied" congressional preclusion of § 1983 remedies for constitutional rights, see Rosalie Berger Levinson, Misinterpreting "Sounds of Silence": Why Courts Should Not "Imply" Congressional Preclusion of § 1983 Constitutional Claims, 77 Fordham L. Rev. 775 (2008).

Page 1372, insert a new note as follows:

NOTE ON ENHANCEMENT FOR SUPERIOR PERFORMANCE

The question in Perdue v. Kenny A., 559 U.S. __ (2010), was whether the lodestar fee award could be enhanced for superior performance leading to exceptional results. Plaintiffs' lawyers brought a class action to reform Georgia's system of foster child care. After extensive litigation, the parties entered into a consent decree, which resolved all issues other than fees. The district court came to a lodestar calculation of approximately $6 million, then enhanced that award by 75 percent on the grounds that the lodestar failed to account for "(1) the fact that class counsel were required to advance case expenses of $1.7 million over a three-year period with no on[-]going reimbursement, (2) the fact that class counsel were not paid on an on-going basis as the work was being performed, and (3) the fact that class counsel's ability to recover a fee and expense reimbursement were completely contingent on the outcome of the case." The judge also found that lawyers had exhibited "a higher degree of skill, commitment, dedication, and professionalism ... than the Court has seen displayed by the attorneys in any other case during its 27 years on the bench" and that the results obtained were "extraordinary." The court further commented that, "[a]fter 58 years as a practicing attorney and federal judge, the Court is unaware of any other case in which a plaintiff class has achieved such a favorable result on such a comprehensive scale." The court therefore added $4.5 million to the lodestar for a total fee award of approximately $10.5 million.

of Merits–First Decisionmaking in Civil Rights Litigation: The Continued Viability of *Saucier v. Katz*, 16 Geo. Mason L. Rev. 53 (2008).

Speaking for the Court, Justice Alito distilled six rules from prior decisions on attorney's fees:

First, a "reasonable" fee is a fee that is sufficient to induce a capable attorney to undertake the representation of a meritorious civil rights case. Section 1988's aim is to enforce the covered civil rights statutes, not to provide "a form of economic relief to improve the financial lot of attorneys."

Second, the lodestar method yields a fee that is presumptively sufficient to achieve this objective. . . .

Third, although we have never sustained an enhancement of a lodestar amount for performance, we have repeatedly said that enhancements may be awarded in " 'rare' " and " 'exceptional' " circumstances.

Fourth, we have noted that "the lodestar figure includes most, if not all, of the relevant factors constituting a 'reasonable' attorney's fee," and have held that an enhancement may not be awarded based on a factor that is subsumed in the lodestar calculation. We have thus held that the novelty and complexity of a case generally may not be used as a ground for an enhancement because these factors "presumably [are] fully reflected in the number of billable hours recorded by counsel." We have also held that the quality of an attorney's performance generally should not be used to adjust the lodestar "[b]ecause considerations concerning the quality of a prevailing party's counsel's representation normally are reflected in the reasonable hourly rate."

Fifth, the burden of proving that an enhancement is necessary must be borne by the fee applicant.

Finally, a fee applicant seeking an enhancement must produce "specific evidence" that supports the award. This requirement is essential if the lodestar method is to realize one of its chief virtues, i.e., providing a calculation that is objective and capable of being reviewed on appeal.

Analyzing this case, the Court concluded that the trial court had not provided sufficient justification for the large enhancement of fees. The Court seemed to contemplate that extraordinary outlays for expenses and unusual delay in reimbursement might justify enhancement, but the district court had not specified the amount attributable to such factors. The results obtained were relevant only insofar as they flowed from the lawyers' superior performance (as distinct from poor performance by the defense counsel, unexpectedly favorable judicial rulings, or an especially sympathetic jury), and superior performance did not ordinarily warrant enhancement, as it should be reflected in the hourly rate and hours worked and therefore incorporated in the lodestar. Finally, the trial court's reliance on contingency contravened City of Burlington v. Dague, 505 U.S. 557 (1992). In applying these factors, the Court emphasized the need for specific findings that facilitated effective appellate review:

> [I]nsofar as the District Court relied on a comparison of the performance of counsel in this case with the performance of counsel in unnamed prior cases, the District Court did not employ a methodology that permitted meaningful appellate review. Needless to say, we do not question the sincerity of the District Court's observations, and we are in no position to assess their accuracy. But when a trial judge awards an enhancement on an impressionistic basis, a major purpose of the lodestar method—providing an objective and reviewable basis for fees—is undermined.
>
> Determining a "reasonable attorney's fee" is a matter that is committed to the sound discretion of a trial judge, but the judge's discretion is not unlimited. It is essential that the judge provide a reasonably specific explanation for all aspects of a fee determination, including any award of an enhancement. Unless such an explanation is given, adequate appellate review is not feasible, and without such review, widely disparate awards may be made, and awards may be influenced (or at least, may appear to be influenced) by a judge's subjective opinion regarding particular attorneys or the importance of the case.

The discretion of the trial judge and the difficulty of second-guessing his or her decision figured largely in the dissent of Justice Breyer, with whom Justices Stevens, Ginsburg, and Sotomayor joined. The dissent emphasized the effectiveness of the lawyers, the fact that the foster-care litigation was "lengthy and arduous," and that the results obtained "appear to have been exceptional." Breyer concluded that these circumstances likely made this an appropriate case for fee enhancement and that in any event "it was neither unreasonable nor an abuse of discretion" for the trial court to have reached that conclusion.

After *Perdue*, the question is whether the "rare and exceptional" circumstances that justify fee enhancement will ever be realized. For the majority, at least, superior performance and excellent results were, like contingency, not enough to support enhancement. In identifying circumstances that might justify such enhancement, the majority said the following:

> First, an enhancement may be appropriate where the method used in determining the hourly rate employed in the lodestar calculation does not adequately measure the attorney' true market value, as demonstrated in part during the litigation. This may occur if the hourly rate is determined by a formula that takes into account only a single factor (such as years since admission to the bar) or perhaps only a few similar factors. In such a case, an enhancement may be appropriate so that an attorney is compensated at the rate that the attorney would receive in cases not

governed by the federal fee-shifting statutes. But in order to provide a calculation that is objective and reviewable, the trial judge should adjust the attorney's hourly rate in accordance with specific proof linking the attorney's ability to a prevailing market rate.

Second, an enhancement may be appropriate if the attorney's performance includes an extraordinary outlay of expenses and the litigation is exceptionally protracted. . . . [W]hen an attorney agrees to represent a civil rights plaintiff who cannot afford to pay the attorney, the attorney presumably understands that no reimbursement is likely to be received until the successful resolution of the case, and therefore enhancements to compensate for delay in reimbursement for expenses must be reserved for unusual cases. In such exceptional cases, however, an enhancement may be allowed, but the amount of the enhancement must be calculated using a method that is reasonable, objective, and capable of being reviewed on appeal, such as by applying a standard rate of interest to the qualifying outlays of expenses.

Third, there may be extraordinary circumstances in which an attorney's performance involves exceptional delay in the payment of fees. An attorney who expects to be compensated under § 1988 presumably understands that payment of fees will generally not come until the end of the case, if at all. . . . But we do not rule out the possibility that an enhancement may be appropriate where an attorney assumes these costs in the face of unanticipated delay, particularly where the delay is unjustifiably caused by the defense. In such a case, however, the enhancement should be calculated by applying a method similar to that described above in connection with exceptional delay in obtaining reimbursement for expenses.

The common themes here seem to be two. First, the circumstances justifying enhancement need to be "extraordinary" and not simply the usual attributes of civil rights litigation, such as contingency, the need to advance expenses, and the usual delay in payment. Second, those extraordinary circumstances need to be specifically documented and explained by the court that awards enhancement. Any global approach to enhancement—such as that used by the trial court in *Perdue*—is likely to be disapproved.

APPENDIX B

SELECTED FEDERAL STATUTES

Page B–48, replace the text of § 1988(b) with the following:

(b) Attorney's fees

In any action or proceeding to enforce a provision of sections 1981, 1981a, 1982, 1983, 1985, and 1986 of this title, title IX of Public Law 92–318, the Religious Freedom Restoration Act of 1993, the Religious Land Use and Institutionalized Persons Act of 2000, title VI of the Civil Rights Act of 1964, or section 13981 of this title, the court, in its discretion, may allow the prevailing party, other than the United States, a reasonable attorney's fee as part of the costs, except that in any action brought against a judicial officer for an act or omission taken in such officer's judicial capacity such officer shall not be held liable for any costs, including attorney's fees, unless such action was clearly in excess of such officer's jurisdiction.

†